RIIS

STAGES OF LIGHT AND DARK

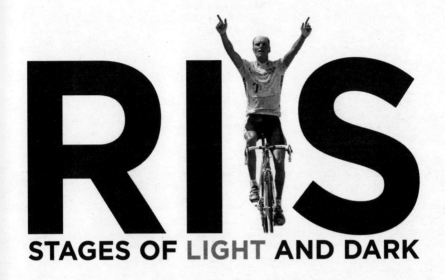

RIIS
STAGES OF LIGHT AND DARK

BJARNE RIIS
with Lars Steen Pedersen

Translated by Ellis Bacon

VSP

Published by Vision Sports Publishing in 2012

Vision Sports Publishing
19-23 High Street
Kingston upon Thames
Surrey
KT1 1LL

www.visionsp.co.uk

ISBN: 978-1907637-51-3

First published as *Riis* in 2010 by People's Press, Copenhagen.
© 2010 Bjarne Riis and Lars Steen Pedersen
© 2010 People's Press, Copenhagen

English language translation © 2012 Ellis Bacon

Translated by Ellis Bacon
Copy editing: Alex Morton
Cover design: Neal Cobourne

Typeset by Palimpsest Book Production Limited,
Falkirk, Stirlingshire

Printed and bound by CPI Group (UK) Ltd, Croydon, CR0 4YY

A CIP Catalogue record for this book is available from the British Library

CONTENTS

ABOUT THE
AUTHOR AND
TRANSLATOR

Lars Steen Pedersen is a Danish journalist and author, whose books include boxer Johnny Bredahl's autobiography, *Kampen*, and footballer Stig Tøfting's autobiography, *No Regrets*, which became the best-selling sports book in Denmark, and was also named the world's best sports biography by international magazine *World Soccer*. As a reporter, Lars has covered the Tour de France, the Olympics and the football World Cup and European Championships, as well as working on television documentaries about professional sport. He helped to start TV2's magazine programme *Lige på og Sport*, and has been chief editor at newspaper *BT* and television channel DR's sports and news desks. He is now editor on DR's investigative news show *21 SØNDAG*.

Ellis Bacon is a writer and journalist covering professional cycling. Fluent in Danish and French, having lived in both Copenhagen and Avignon, he has translated a number of books and articles, and has written about the sport for a variety of magazines and newspapers. He is also a regular contributor to *Cycle Sport* and *Cycling Weekly* magazines, and the former deputy editor of *Procycling*. Following the pro peloton has taken him all over the world, interviewing riders and attending races in Australia, North America and the Middle East, and he has covered nine Tours de France, as well as the Beijing Olympics. He lives in London with his wife, Lucy, and their dog, Sooty, and doesn't ride his bike quite as often as he should.

ACKNOWLEDGEMENTS

Bjarne Riis would like to thank:

My lovely wife and best friend, Anne Dorthe, and my children, Jesper, Thomas, Cristian, Matias and Andreas, for always being there for me. A special thanks to Mette, and to everyone I have met in my life. Thanks to Dad, who is always in my thoughts.

A huge thanks to Lars Steen. Your commitment to this project has been second to none. Thank you for pushing me and helping me through what has been a fantastic process.

Lars Steen Pedersen would like to thank:

My wife, Trine Panum Kjeldsen, and my children, Nikoline, Oskar and Alma Josefine, for their support, patience and time, which has allowed this project to be realised. My brother, journalist Flemming Steen Pedersen, for his input, criticism and good advice. My editor at People's Press, Thomas Rasmussen, for his informed and very useful suggestions. Lea and Anders for their proofreading and suggestions along the way.

To everyone else who has been there ready to help – and especially to Anne Dorthe Tanderup and Mette Nybo. And, lastly, a huge thank you to Bjarne for the confidence and trust you showed me, every step of the way.

FOREWORD

The whole of Denmark celebrated when, in July 1996, Bjarne Riis won the Tour de France. Poul Nyrup Rasmussen, the prime minister at the time, called the victory, "The most amazing individual performance in Danish sports history."

Millions sat glued to their television screens as Riis fought his way through the mountains on his way to his win in France. Back in Denmark, he received a hero's welcome, driven through the streets of Copenhagen in an open-topped car as thousands of Danes lined the route to a huge celebration in the capital's Tivoli gardens.

Bjarne Riis epitomised the Danish dream: a quiet and shy man from Jutland with big ambitions and the ability to beat the world's best riders. Magazines, newspapers and television stations flocked around "Mr and Mrs Denmark" – Bjarne and Mette – and their two small children. The name Riis meant an increase in sales and extra viewers, and the nation couldn't get enough of it. As Bjarne's team-mate and friend, Brian Holm, pointed out during my research for this book: "At one point, Bjarne was second only to the royal family in popularity in Denmark."

But then came the fall from grace. Riis had to play second fiddle to his young Telekom team-mate, the German Jan Ullrich, at the 1997 Tour de France – a race Riis drew a line under by throwing his time trial bike to the side of the road when it all got too much. Then came his divorce from Mette, and later accusations that he'd doped. His cycling career was ended after a crash in 1999, and Riis went to live abroad with his new girlfriend, handball player Anne Dorthe Tanderup, hoping to be left in peace.

But that wasn't the end of the story by any means. The press were not prepared to leave the famous couple alone, and then Riis came back into the public eye as owner of Denmark's top professional cycling team. "We want to be the world's best cycling team," said Riis, and set about doing things his way. Riis the cyclist became Riis the businessman, introducing a set of values under which the team was to be run, with a former special forces soldier employed to help inspire the riders.

The team did become the best in the world, but there was still something missing: the truth as to whether Riis had doped to win his 1996 Tour de France title. The truth came out at a live TV press conference, although it was a far cry from the tear-strewn revelations from some of Riis's former Telekom team-mates on German television.

A combination of admitting to doping and his father, Preben's, death shortly afterwards led the former Tour winner to a process of self-introspection – a process which helped lead to this book.

RIIS is Bjarne Riis's story, told in his own words – the story of a man, a bike rider and a businessman. Riis has chosen to lay his life out before the readers, giving them the opportunity to hear the whole story in its proper context and to draw their own conclusions. The only condition he made is that he didn't want to name anyone in connection with his doping: "I'm the only one responsible for having doped during my career – no one else."

Several sources have been interviewed as part of the research for this book in order to confirm, document and relive episodes, events and how they all hung together. Among those sources are friends, team-mates, competitors, colleagues, family and various experts. An extensive archive – 15-20 boxes of clippings, photos and video tapes – collected by Riis's father has also been essential in helping to slot everything together.

It has been a tough, emotional process for Bjarne to produce this book, as it is the first time he has revealed many of his innermost secrets. It is a book that has taken courage and more than a few tears to make – and it is told from the heart.

Lars Steen Pedersen, Bagsværd, Denmark

1 THE BREAKDOWN

I t is the middle of the night, and I'm wandering around in the dark, alone on a mountain. It's freezing, but I'm enjoying the silence and the solitude. It is late November 2007. Together with the riders and staff from the cycling team, I'm on a team-building trip in Norway, which has been arranged by BS Christensen – a former soldier with the Danish Special Forces. As he's done for us in the past, he has put together a programme made up of the kinds of tasks that require the participants to work together. And while I'm stomping around in knee-deep snow on the mountain, the others are out on a night mission.

The trip has definitely been good for building camaraderie, morale and motivation within the team, but something is missing: me – as both a person and a leader. Physically, I am there, but mentally it is as though I am somewhere else entirely. I feel lethargic and don't seem to be able to concentrate on anything. When giving the riders my team talks, I feel as though I have plenty to say, but I just can't get the message across. Spending time out on the mountain is giving me the opportunity to try to get my head together and to work out how on earth it has all come to this.

As a rider, I used to spend hours in the saddle on training rides going through any problems I had in my head, coming up with solutions and forming plans to deal with it all. It's that same kind of isolation that I am craving now. The previous few months haven't gone quite as I'd expected them to. It is as though I don't know myself any more. All the happiness and energy seems to have disappeared.

It's only been six months since I stood up and admitted to having doped as a rider. The world had got its admission from me, while I was able to lay to rest the ghost that had haunted me for so long. Or so I thought. The truth is that it still hasn't given me peace of mind. And with every day that has passed since, I've felt more and more drained of energy.

There have been days at home in Switzerland when I have been so tired that all I have wanted to do is sleep, and have only managed to get out of bed once the kids have gone to school. Some days I'd even lie in bed all day, staring up at the ceiling, with the curtains drawn and the lights off. My wife, Anne Dorthe, would take care of everything that needed doing, like looking after the kids and running the house. But one day she'd had enough, and came storming into the darkened room. "Right – I think it's time you came out of here now. You've been lying in here for four days in a row. The rest of us live here with you too, you know," she said.

When I finally managed to pull myself out of bed to go into the office, I just sat in front of the computer. It didn't help at all – I just couldn't be bothered with anything. It felt like I had tunnel vision, and that the tunnel was getting narrower and narrower.

One evening in particular made me feel that I had finally lost it. I was in Denmark doing a talk for the managers at electronics company Siemens. I'd gone over my notes before starting my speech, but completely fell apart once I got up to talk. My thoughts were all over the place, and I couldn't remember anything that I'd written down. What actually came out wasn't very coherent at all. The speech was an absolute disaster. I was annoyed with myself for not being able to express myself properly, despite having prepared and written everything down beforehand. As I left, all I could think was, "What the hell is wrong with me?"

My team press officer, Brian Nygaard, could tell that something was up. He rang one day to discuss a few things, but then asked me, "How are you really feeling, Bjarne?"

"Okay," I replied.

"It just seems to me like you've been going through a hard time lately," he said.

His concern somehow pressed the right buttons, and suddenly

I couldn't hold back my feelings, or the tears, any more. "It has been hard," was all I was able to get out before I started crying. Hard to have to admit that I was wrong when I'd thought that admitting to my doping past would make everything all right. Deep down, I'd perhaps thought that coming clean would bring some sort of relief and closure, but instead I'd been left feeling as though it had just made things even worse.

Out there in the dark on that mountain in Norway, something didn't really feel right. I hoped that it was just the result of sheer exhaustion from BS's training programme. I felt a bit better the next morning, and gave Anne Dorthe a call back home.

"I'm not really feeling too great," I said, and told her about my night on the mountain.

"It sounds as though you're overly stressed. You've had a hard time lately," she said.

Maybe she was right, but if anyone wasn't going to admit to that being the case, it was me. Instead, what I needed to do was to get through to the end of this team-building trip in one piece.

On the last day, I stood up and made a farewell speech, during which I tried to appear inspirational and on top of things. Afterwards, I asked Brian how he thought it had gone.

"To be honest, although the trip has been great, your talk just then wasn't that fantastic," he replied.

That wasn't exactly what I wanted to hear, but we both knew that he was right.

"It's probably fair to say that you've never really been the sort of person who makes a big song and dance about things," he told me, "but you have always been able to motivate us all and give us the belief that we can go out there and have a fantastic season. That's what was missing this time.

"But listen," he continued. "You've always been able to bounce back from things. And there are not that many people out there who are capable of doing that. Maybe you just need to take a bit of time off, and then you'll come back feeling much better."

And with that, I headed back home to Switzerland, to where Anne Dorthe and the children were waiting for me.

In the days that followed, I tried to get hold of my dad, Preben.

He was looking after our other house back in Vejle, in Denmark, and was living in the house's annex, taking care of our dog, Oscar. Dad had always been the one constant in my life. It was with him that I had lived growing up, and it was him that I took after. He had lived a hard life, and it had taken its toll. But now, at 68, he could live a nice, peaceful life in Vejle. He'd look after our house and take care of the gardening for us, and just generally help to keep things in order. We might not have ever really spoken that much to each other, but then we didn't really need to: we were more than comfortable in each other's company and understood each other perfectly. He had always supported me and always trusted me to make my own decisions, and never judged me on those decisions, either in my private life or in my career. We'd talk regularly on the phone, although they weren't exactly deep and meaningful conversations. They were more chats that just showed that we were thinking of each other, and supported each other, keeping up with what each of us was up to. But this time, after finding that his phone was turned off for three days in a row while trying to call him, I was worried.

Anne Dorthe's dad, Peder, needed to go by the house to do something, so we asked him to make sure that my dad was all right. It felt like a long day, waiting for Peder to call us. He rang that evening, just as he was arriving at the house. He got out of his car, had a walk around the house, and looked in through the windows, but could see no sign of my dad, even though his car was there in the driveway.

"There's no one here," Peder told us.

"You'd better have another look," I said.

I stayed on the phone as he went and had a look through the windows of the annex.

"Oscar's here," he said.

I could immediately tell that something was wrong.

"You'll have to break in through the door," I told him.

The phone went silent while Peder tried to open the door.

And then he spoke again: "Your dad's lying on the floor."

He was dead.

"This can't be happening," I just about managed to say before breaking down in tears.

Dad had died from either a blood clot or a heart attack, and had collapsed in the kitchen. He had probably been there for a number of days while poor Oscar had wandered around wondering what the matter was.

Despite being more than 40 years old, I had never lost anyone close to me. I had never even been to a funeral, and yet suddenly there I was having lost the person who had had the biggest influence on my life. It's only when you lose someone so close to you that you truly realise just how much they meant to you. All of a sudden, I missed my dad so much that I could hardly bear it. It was just too much. I couldn't believe that I was never going to be able to speak to him again. There were just so many things that we hadn't finished talking about, things that we needed to still clear up. I just wasn't ready for this to happen.

Early the next morning, Anne Dorthe and I went back to Denmark. I hoped that, somehow, it was all just a bad dream, and that I'd soon wake up. On our way there, I realised that my dad may well have died on the same night that I was out on that mountain during the team-building trip in Norway. When we arrived at the house in Vejle, I couldn't bring myself to go to the annex. Oscar was being looked after by some friends as he wasn't in great shape after having gone so many days without food.

The thought of Oscar caused me to conjure up images of the last few minutes of my dad's life, and how poor Oscar must have felt, trapped inside for days without anything to eat or drink, with the body of someone he loved so much lying there on the floor. It was too much to bear thinking about, and I had to force myself not to.

My brother, Flemming, who lived in Jutland, in the west of Denmark, arrived at the house, and together we tried to help each other come to terms with what had happened. He had seen my dad's body, but I wasn't sure whether I wanted to, to say goodbye before the funeral. "If you're not sure that you want to, then don't," Flemming told me. "That way, you'll remember him as he was, not as he is now."

The sheer pain and sorrow of it all affected me physically. I felt tense, exhausted and my stomach was in knots at the thought of all the things that had never really been resolved between us.

When you've lived the life of a professional sportsman, with people watching your every move, looking for any little sign that you've pushed yourself too hard, then you know yourself how it feels to be so close to completely breaking down. That's how it felt for me while I was still at the house in Vejle. I was close to breaking point. It felt like I was barely functioning, and as though I'd been like that for a number of months. It was a constant battle to hold back the tears. I really wanted to say a few words at the funeral, but really wasn't sure whether I'd be able to do it without breaking down and crying. I decided to call my physiotherapist friend, Ole Kåre Føli. After talking for less than a minute, he could hear how bad things were. "I'm on my way," was all he said.

When he arrived at the house a couple of hours later, he set up his treatment table in the living room. We didn't say much to each other, but that was because we knew each other so well; we simply didn't need to say anything. After so many years of treatment, Ole knew everything about me and how I functioned, and after just a few prods and pushes, my body started to react. All those feelings I thought were hidden away, all of life's frustrations, all the pain I'd felt as a result of my dad's death – it all started to come out and, lying there on that treatment table, I cried and cried. But neither Ole, nor I, was finished. He put his hand on one of my knees, and gently held on.

"I'm freezing," I said, but his hand glowed with warmth.

As Ole continued to hold on, I broke down. "Let it out," he whispered, seemingly knowing what was to come.

My whole body cramped up, and I was completely out of control for almost a quarter of an hour, just sobbing. All my worries, pain and stress, which had built up and hidden itself away inside me, came out. My 15-year-old son, Thomas, was there with us in the living room. He sat completely still, but was clearly shocked at the sight of seeing me in that state.

"It's all been too much," said Ole. "You were on the brink of a nervous breakdown."

He and Thomas left me alone to recover and, while lying there on the treatment table, it suddenly seemed very clear what I wanted to say in the church at my dad's funeral – a way I could properly say goodbye to him.

In the few hours following Ole's treatment, I realised that I had just been living my life without ever confronting those things that needed to be confronted. For what felt like the first time in a long time, I felt calm and relaxed, and as though I was in control again. For months I had felt as though I wasn't in command of what was going on in my life – that other people were steering things, and at a pace I couldn't keep up with. It had felt like being a guest in my own life. But Ole's treatment was like flicking a switch. He'd switched off the immense pressure I'd been feeling, both in body and mind.

The day after Ole's visit, I was back to feeling on top of things, and felt that I could cope better with having to say goodbye to Dad. I needed to clear his things out of the annex and clean it. Up until then, I hadn't felt strong enough to go and see where he had died but, together with my sons, Jesper and Thomas, we went to the annex and let ourselves in. Every step inside was difficult to take, but having my sons there with me was a great help.

One of the first things we saw was a dried pool of blood on the floor in the kitchen, where Dad had collapsed. The sight of the blood was painful, reminding me that he had died in such lonely and undignified circumstances. No one deserves that. Thomas and Jesper could tell that this was hard for me, and that I might not be able to cope with clearing up. "We need to do this, Dad," they assured me.

Despite my sadness, I was very proud of them at that moment – that at such a young age they could stick with their decision to help their dad when he needed them most.

Silently, we got on with boxing up Dad's things, but every time we took a box outside, we had to go past the pool of blood. It was unbearable to think about how he had spent the last few minutes of his life. When I found his scrapbooks full of newspaper and magazine articles about my career as both a rider and a team manager that he'd cut out, it really hit me hard. He'd painstakingly cut them all out and glued them into the books in chronological order. He had been my biggest fan, following everything I did in cycling. He videoed everything I was involved in on television, too – the proud father, all the way to the end. He'd always defended me, always stood up for me, whenever people criticised me or judged me – again, all the way to the end.

Clearing up the annex got me thinking even more about all the complicated feelings we'd had for each other. He had always done everything for me, always been there for me and looked after me, but the big question I asked myself was whether I had looked after him enough. He had lived a hard life, and that was mostly because he'd spent most of it trying to help others rather than himself.

When I married my ex-wife Mette in October 1989, my dad had struggled to get up and make a speech. That kind of thing really wasn't easy for him. The next day, Mette and I sat with her parents watching the wedding video, which included the speeches. Watching my dad's speech again, it was pretty clear that it was difficult for him to get the words out. But, showing off, I decided to commentate as we watched. "Come on, Dad – you can do it," I said as he struggled through it.

Mette's dad, Jørgen, however, wasn't impressed by my sarcasm.

"Don't make fun of your father, Bjarne," he told me. "It wasn't easy for him to do that, yet he did it for your sake. Think of everything he's gone through in life. Just because you've had it easy, it doesn't mean you can make fun of other people."

He'd certainly told me, and I felt highly ashamed. I'd only meant what I said for a bit of fun, but maybe there was something in what Jørgen had said. Maybe I'd not shown my dad enough respect, especially not to a man who had always done everything for me. It had been embarrassing for me that Mette's dad had felt he needed to say what he thought to his new son-in-law, but it had also served to remind me that I needed to show a lot more respect, thanks and care towards my own father.

"I think we're almost there," I heard Jesper and Thomas say to me, waking me from my thoughts.

We'd managed to clear up the annex, but it was mostly thanks to the boys, as I really hadn't been a great deal of help.

At my dad's funeral, I stood next to his coffin with his old stopwatch in my hand. That stopwatch had served him well during all the hours he'd spent training with me as a boy and a teenager.

"My dad always thought of others before himself," I said during my speech. "I have a huge amount of respect for that, and think that it's something the rest of us can all learn from."

Everything went as my dad would have wanted it. Everyone whose lives he had touched, and who had appreciated the part he'd played in their lives, was there.

Later that evening, I went up to the annex alone to say my own goodbye. I imagined myself lifting his body up off the floor and taking him out into the garden – a place where he'd spent so much of his time, pottering about, getting stuff done. With its view out to the fjord – a place where you would catch glimpses of wild deer who, like Dad, would come to enjoy the quiet and stillness of the place – it was here that his soul would be buried.

And now, I decided, it was time for me to grab hold of life with both hands, and live it with the same values that my father had taught me. From now on, it was going to be easier for me to really be myself than it had been so far.

2 CHILDHOOD

Out in the countryside, the only sound to be heard was the noise of the engine of my dad's old Saab, while I had my head down, riding hard, waiting for the signal. A beep from the car horn meant I had to sprint, until the next beep. This was my interval training. My dad's training philosophy was that no matter how old you were – even if you were only 10 years old – you needed to get out there and get some kilometres in your legs.

I enjoyed every single moment of that time alone with my dad on those training runs: him the encouraging coach in the car, and me the young rider who would show him that all the time he spent helping me would be worth it. The old two-stroke Saab was somewhat on its last legs, but Dad was happy to squeeze every last kilometre out of it. One day, there was suddenly a loud noise – not unlike a helicopter's rotor blades – and I saw something come whirling through the air past me and land with a thud. Somewhat startled by this, I stopped cycling. Dad came to a halt, too, and got out of the car and, about 50m away in the field where this object had landed, was a big piece of metal. We looked back at the old Saab and realised that it was missing its bonnet. Clearly, the old car had been even rustier than it looked, and at high speed the bonnet had come loose and flipped off into the field. I was pretty lucky that it hadn't taken my head off.

Our training sessions out on the open road were our chance to spend some quality time with each other. In our clear roles as rider and trainer there was a comfortable and mutual understanding, and it brought us closer together. Cycling was something for just us to share – something that gave us both the enjoyable feeling of being in control.

My dad was an old-fashioned, working-class man. He was a trained typographer, which was a job that gave him the chance to roll up his sleeves, work hard and not ask too many questions. My mum, Bodil, was a teacher, but lived in Århus with my older brother, Flemming, after my parents had divorced when I was a year old. My dad married again relatively quickly, and had three more children, but it was a messy and turbulent marriage, and he and his wife split up, got back together again, and then went their separate ways for good.

After that, I lived a nomadic existence with Dad, often moving for work and new girlfriends, living in different places like Randers and Herning. At one point, Dad got a job that put him in more of a management role, which he was good at, even if he wasn't really a natural leader. He was perhaps more the kind of man who could get others to work together as a team, preferring to avoid any kind of confrontation. But the new job also gave him a little more free time, during which he became a coach for a number of young riders after he helped start up Holstebro Cycling Club. As a rider himself, he'd won the "B"-class – or second-category – version of the Fyn Rundt time trial, catching all 18 of the riders who had started ahead of him.

I was only eight when I rode my first race, in 1972. "If you win this race, I'll get you a proper racing bike," my dad had promised me. A promise like that was all I needed.

There were six of us in my age category, and the race was a time trial. After the names were picked out of a hat, I happened to be starting last. I was annoyed at going off last, as I didn't understand what a time trial was really about: that it didn't matter whether you started first or last, and only that you got the fastest time. But with the promise of a new racing bike swinging in front of me like a carrot, I eventually decided that I didn't care when I started.

When I got sent on my way that day in Herning, I gave it everything, stamping on the pedals, with the thought of winning the only thing on my mind. One by one, I caught the riders who had started ahead of me. They looked back at me, shocked, as I flew past them like a chugging locomotive. I could ignore the pain in my legs or my screaming lungs simply by thinking about the new bike that was waiting for me if I could only win. I roared across the finish line in first place, having overtaken everyone. It was the first race win of my career, and I'd made my dad proud by having set myself a goal and achieving it.

Dad started a training log for me after that, and for the rest of the year my training schedule looked like this:

August: 229km
September: 278km
October: 176km
November: 118km
December: 95km

Now I was a proper bike rider. Later, my dad told me, I'd have to take care of the training diary myself, logging all my training miles. The log needed to contain how many kilometres I'd done each day, my resting pulse rate morning and evening, and my changes in weight. I needed to do it in order to learn discipline and to take responsibility for myself. Dad was good at judging just how much he could push me, where my strengths and weaknesses were, and at understanding how seriously I was taking my riding.

In those first few seasons, I won loads of races, and was both Jutland and Fyn champion. The cups and trophies began to mount up, soon filling up the shelves in my room.

At one point we moved into my grandma's house in Herning to give me a bit of stability, both at school and in my home life. Dad and I shared a large room in the house, but had it divided in two so we each had our own space. In Grandma's house there was a photograph of a boy I didn't recognise, and one day I took it upon myself to ask who he was.

"That's your big brother Michael," my grandma said, then added: "The one that drowned."

I wasn't told any more than that, and didn't really feel like I could ask any more questions, either. It was a subject that clearly no one wanted to talk about. And that worried me. Despite Dad doing everything he could to help me with my cycling, I still felt like there was something missing in my life. There were just so many questions that were still unanswered.

For as long as I could remember, my parents had been divorced, and it was as though Dad had always had trouble staying on top of things. He was restless and unable to commit to things emotionally for very long at a time, living a nomadic existence. Since the divorce, my mum and my brother had lived in Århus and Ry, and contact with them was minimal. For a while, my mum lived in a commune, and I didn't like visiting her there. Whenever I did, I just wanted to have her and Flemming to myself, and not share them with the other people living at the house. So, by way of protest, I refused to visit very often. Also, her job as a teacher took her around to various different schools, meaning I saw even less of her, and we didn't establish a very close relationship. Perhaps subconsciously I saw her choice to live in the commune as a sign that she didn't really want to spend time with me.

Dad was my anchor, but because he worked a lot, and spent a lot of time at his girlfriend's house, I spent a lot of time with my grandma – my dad's mum, Anne – at the house in Herning. She was the one who really brought me up. Dad tried to compensate for the lack of real quality time at home with me by being there for me as my cycling coach. Even if it was just a training session in the local park, he was there, timing me and encouraging me. But I needed more from him than that – not just a dad who helped me train. I wanted him to be there for me on a daily basis, and it annoyed me that I didn't know when I was going to see him next. Sometimes it felt like I only ever saw him at the cycling club. And when training was over, he'd be off again, back to work and to stay over at his girlfriend's house. I never felt like I had him to myself – that I was always sharing him with other people. On more than one occasion I'd ride home from training with tears streaming down my face because I'd had to say goodbye to him at the club and missed him already. The next training session would always seem so far away, and I felt as though we never got the chance to talk about the other things that were going on in my life – just normal stuff, like how I was getting on at school.

Back home, I'd sometimes sit for hours, staring out of the kitchen window looking to see if Dad was coming, after he'd mentioned that he "might come by". More often than not, I'd wait in vain, with Grandma delivering the crushing message: "He's not coming home today, Bjarne."

After he divorced my mum, my dad had quite a few girlfriends, many of whom seemed really nice, and who tried to do the right thing. Dad would move in with them, with me in tow, of course. But whenever the relationships began to get more serious, Dad would end them, and we'd be off again.

I remember once that we had to make our escape on Christmas morning. We'd spent Christmas Eve with Dad's then-girlfriend and her parents, and were staying the night, and then the plan was for Dad, his girlfriend and me to go to Grandma's for Christmas dinner.

But early that morning, Dad woke me up. "We've got to go," he whispered.

"What, just the two of us?" I asked.

Dad nodded his head and, as his girlfriend and her parents slept, we crept down to the car and drove home to Grandma's house in Herning. It turned out that Dad and his girlfriend had spent all night arguing.

I drifted through school doing just about enough to get by. Homework, for example, usually played second fiddle to training or my part-time jobs, and I didn't pay much attention to many subjects other than those that really interested me. Geography, history and particularly maths appealed – the useful subjects. And PE, of course. Because I was fit from cycling, I was pretty good at most sports. I was good at running and high jump in particular, and I was definitely one of the better footballers, too. I liked winning, and enjoyed ignoring the pain and effort when I was competing. I'd be the one still running when the rest were tired and ready to give up, and I think having the right frame of mind for training helped me, too.

At Herning Cycling Club we trained no matter what the weather. As our trainer, Dad had his own particular methods and ideas.

Sometimes it felt like he was perhaps a little harder on me than some of the others, but then that was only because he couldn't be seen to be favouring me. There was one particularly hard day's training in the depths of winter, with snow covering the roads. There were six or seven of us from the club out battling the elements, which, after about 20km, ended up freezing our chains, making it difficult to change gear. So we had to get off and piss on the chains so that our gears worked again and we could carry on. Those hard sessions were certainly character building, and made me appreciate the need to be disciplined when it came to training.

As a junior rider, I was selected to ride for the Danish national team by coach John Struve. I'd been riding at senior level in category two races, and after doing pretty well I'd moved up to first-category racing. Struve wanted me to be even more disciplined, and expected 100 per cent commitment to the sport, but moving up to the national team meant things wouldn't ever be the same again between me and my dad. Getting selected gave me the self-confidence and belief that I could stand on my own two feet and, slowly but surely, I relied on Dad less and less, building up the courage to give my own opinions when it came to the two of us discussing strategy, tactics or evaluating how a race had gone. Until that point, Dad's thoughts on such things had been more or less gospel. There had been plenty of times when I hadn't agreed with him, but it was rare that I had actually said anything. He was often critical of my performances, and would be furious if I didn't win the races he thought I should have won. On more than one occasion we'd drive home from a race in complete silence because he was so angry at me for not having stuck to his race plan.

At one race, when I was 17, my dad was giving me my pre-race talking-to about tactics – except this time I was having none of it.

"Dad, I'm the one riding," I told him.

"Okay," was all he said, and that was the end of the conversation.

It must have hurt to have had me say what I said. Cycling simply was our father-son relationship. Speaking up for myself for the first time must have seemed like I was saying that I didn't agree with what that relationship had become. Of course, the reality was that he meant everything to me. He was the one whose opinion I valued most. He accepted that he would have to take a step back when it came to my cycling, even though he would continue to support me. He still came to every race, within reason, and would happily save his money in order to be able to afford to drive me to races that were a bit further away. We established a new kind of relationship, whereby he wouldn't give his opinion on how a race had gone. He'd still gladly give his advice, but only if I asked for it. He still had big plans on my behalf when it came to turning professional. It was a dream that he encouraged me to pursue, and he wasn't afraid to tell anyone who'd listen that he expected great things of me.

There were about 15 or 16 of us at the cycling club who hung out together, including Per Pedersen and Alex Pedersen, who I both trained with and partied with. Up until the age of 12, I'd won loads of bike races, and that was down to pure talent and the fact that I took it a lot more seriously than the others. But as a 13- and 14-year-old, I didn't develop physically as quickly as the others, and suddenly talent alone wasn't enough to keep my winning streak going. The bigger boys I was racing against were giving me a good hiding, and the gap between wins got longer and longer. That frustrated me enormously, as I was just as serious and ambitious, and training as much, as I always had been.

At one point, I took a bit of a break from cycling to have a go at some other sports while I tried to decide whether I wanted to keep racing, and whether it was all worth it. But my love of cycling won through and, after a couple of good training sessions, I knew that I couldn't live without it. From that point on, I was even more focused on getting faster, and just accepted that the competition had got tougher.

When I finished school, I worked in a local factory that made elastic. I'd rather have been on the dole and cycling full time, but the council were having none of it, and threatened to send me off to a job working alongside a bunch of former criminals. So the job at the factory was a much better option. It was shift work, and I'd work a week of nights, followed by a week of afternoons and evenings. It meant that I just had to structure my training sessions the best I could around my working hours. My dream was still to turn professional, but two of my contemporaries – my friend Per Pedersen and another rider called Kim Eriksen – were both considered bigger talents than me. But in July 1982 I received a letter from the Danish cycling federation informing me that I was eligible for a Team Denmark grant because the federation had faith in my abilities as a rider. The grant was for 1,750 kroner (£120) a year to help me pay for equipment. The idea was that the money would help my chances of getting selected for the junior world championships. It was a bit of a long shot, but to give myself every chance, I took part in as many selection races as possible.

My chances were given an extra boost when I won one of the main selection races in Hillerød. It was the Danish junior team time trial championships, and my dad was our trainer. That win was enough to convince national coach Struve to select me for the junior world championships in Italy, together with Kim and Per. And it turned out to be an experience we'd never forget, although not in a good way. We'd gone there believing that we could be up there with the best, but the Russian riders ensured that it was a brutal race. They were big bruisers of riders, far more physically developed than the rest of us, and they made sure we knew it. They would lean on us, elbow us and push us out of their way whenever they wanted. And there were no official motorbikes riding with us to see what was going on. We were woefully under-prepared to be shoved about like we were, and we all crashed at least once. Per came off worst and ended up going to hospital, where they gave him 18 stitches. I crashed, and my forks were so bent that I needed a spare bike, except that it took so long to get a replacement that I was left far behind and had to quit the race.

It was around this time that I met Mette. We were the same age, and went to the same school, although we weren't in the same class. We met for the first time at the end-of-term party in year nine, and finished the evening with a kiss. However, rather than that being the start of it all, nothing really happened after that, and she didn't show any more interest in me. It wasn't until about a year later that her sister caught up with me one day and asked me: "Why don't you give Mette a call?"

"I didn't think she was interested," I told her.

"Why not give it a try?" she replied.

So I did, and we arranged to go out to the cinema. We were back on.

Mette went to college, and her father, Jørgen, was a businessman who owned a chain of grocery stores. Mette was sensible and down-to-earth, and natural and cheerful. We were perfect for each other. She also knew what she wanted in life, and that was to go to work as an au pair in France so that she could learn the language properly, and then get a good education at university. We spent a lot of our time at her house, and it was there that I found what I'd been looking for: a normal family life.

At dinner time, we'd sit around the table for ages, just talking. At Jørgen and Edith's house, there was always time to have a chat about anything and everything – and that included education and careers.

"So then, Bjarne – what are you planning to do in the future?" Mette's dad asked me one day.

"I'm going to be a bike rider," I told him.

"Aren't you going to get a job?" he said.

Experiencing this kind of normality, and the way other families lived, made me even more critical of my dad and the way he lived his life. I couldn't really understand why things just never seemed to go his way. The explanation, it turned out, had been on the wall in Grandma's house all along: that photograph of my big brother, Michael – "the one that drowned".

In February 1964 my mum was pregnant with me, and my parents lived in a little house in Herning with one-year-old Flemming and two-year-old Michael. They were the perfect family, with a regular income, and a third little one on the way. "The perfect couple", people used to call them. But one day, Michael squeezed through a hole in the fence into the neighbour's garden, managed to lift the cover on their pond and fell through the thin ice into the freezing water. The pond was so deep that he drowned. My mum found Michael in the pond, dragged him out and tried to resuscitate him. He was taken to hospital and put into a coma to try to save his life. He remained like that for nine months, and during that time I was born.

My parents were beside themselves with worry, not knowing whether Michael would survive, and had a newborn baby to look after at the same time. Eventually, the doctors told them that Michael was so brain damaged that he couldn't be saved. The tragic news hit my parents hard. Michael had survived long enough that they'd begun to hope that he might pull through. Now they had to face every parent's worst nightmare: they were going to have to bury their own child. Even though my grandma tried everything she could to help us as a family, nothing could stop my mum and dad eventually going their separate ways. The story of Michael – and the tragedy of my mum and dad – was never one I was ever told properly. The details only slowly came out, piece by piece: the unspoken reason why my family ended up the way it did.

Dad and I would much rather talk about cycling than anything else and, even though we were always pretty short of money, he always supported me and encouraged me to take the opportunities that presented themselves to me. An example was the time I had the chance to ride a junior race in Bremen, Germany – and a chance to get some international experience. Despite our lack of money, off we went in Dad's rubbish old car, with my bike attached to the roof. We drove slowly in the hope that the car would make it, which didn't make us too popular with the other road users. We arrived the day before the race, and checked in to a youth hostel, but when we woke up the next day we found that we had been locked in, and by the time we managed to get out the race had already started.

Dad drove me to a point on the route, and I jumped on my bike and joined the peloton. We'd driven all the way to Bremen for that race, so what else could we do? Sure enough, a couple of kilometres later, I was pulled out of the race – disqualified for not having been there from the start. However, they told me I could race in the second-category senior race instead, which was a bit later that day.

I was just about to start that race when they disqualified me again; apparently as a foreign rider I wasn't allowed to race in that category. But I could race in the first-category senior event, I was told, although there seemed to be no rhyme or reason what difference it made me being a foreigner. Finally, I was on my way, racing. But unfortunately it had been such a chaotic, eventful day that

I was pretty drained by the time I began the race and my result was nothing worth writing home about. At least I had a good story to tell my mates back home at the club, though: I would be one of the few riders ever to have taken part in three different races in one day.

Herning Cycling Club was more than just a club to me. I had an emotional attachment to it, not least because my dad had been one of its driving forces for as long as I could remember. "Your dad's always here," as Alex Pedersen had once said to me. And so when I decided to leave the club, in 1983, some of the members took it quite badly. A new, ambitious team – Team Esbjerg – had offered me a contract, which gave me the chance to live as a semi-professional. The national junior coach, John Struve, had been brought in as the manager, and my mates Kim Eriksen, Lars Jensen and Hans Thomsen were also joining the team. The deal was that they'd find me a part-time job where I'd work in the morning, and then I'd train in the afternoon and race for the team at weekends.

"But I don't understand it, Bjarne," said Alex. "We win everything with Herning. Why change teams?"

My decision had nothing to do with anything other than wanting to try something new in order to improve as both a rider and as a person. But it was hard on my dad, who found himself caught between the club and my ambition.

Three of the new Team Esbjerg boys lived in the same apartment, but I had my own place in the town of Esbjerg. We had all our cycling equipment paid for, and there were training camps to Club La Santa in Lanzarote. It was the kind of stuff that the other amateur teams could only dream of, and I loved it. We all knew that this team was the stepping stone to a possible future contract with a pro team, and so everyone was determined to make a name for themselves. We raced abroad a lot, and in one race in Norway, I got in a breakaway with Denmark's biggest name at the time, Kim Andersen, who was off to ride in the Tour de France just a few days later. In another senior world championship selection race, I took a surprise stage win ahead of big names like Jørgen V Pedersen, John Carlsen, Jens Veggerby and Jesper Skibby.

While riding for the team, my role seemed to develop into being a domestique – a helper – for the other riders, who I'd try to set up for the win at the finish. The chances to ride for myself were few and far between, and this really annoyed my dad. "They're just using you. They're making you do all the hard work, yet they don't appreciate it," he would say.

It was true that I was being held back and wasn't fulfilling my potential, and towards the end of the season there was no denying that that was the case. So I quit the team, and went home to Herning, and Herning Cycling Club. My deal with them was pretty similar to the one with Esbjerg: I'd work part-time, and train and race the rest of the time, living as a semi-pro. The job was at Jydekompagniet, who made bikes for countries like China, among others. I was employed as a sort of product developer, and helped to design new models. It was exciting, as jobs go, as I was of course working in something that I was interested in, which I appreciated. It wasn't the future career that I'd been dreaming of, though. I still hoped to be able to earn a living by racing for a foreign team, and I still had ambitions to go to the Los Angeles Olympics in 1984, and was taking part in a lot of races in the hope of getting selected. I was back with Dad as our trainer at Herning, and he had a good relationship with Struve, who was in charge of the selection committee. And Struve knew me well, although there were plenty of others in the committee who didn't. I rode quite a few races abroad in the hope of convincing them that I should go to the Games. I felt like I was going well, and managed to win a couple of stages at a race in Luxembourg, and got some good results in some races in Germany. I also took part in the Swedish Postgirot stage race, but halfway through I got a throat infection, and by the last stage I wasn't going well at all. It prompted the national coach, Otto Olsen, to make a beeline for me after the race, and he pulled me to one side. "Bjarne Riis, I think you should go home, hang your bike on a hook and give up riding," he told me, and then left me standing there, gob-smacked, in the car park. I couldn't believe it. It really was a smack in the face when I thought I was on course for Olympic selection, and still dreamed of turning pro. If I was to accept what Olsen had said, it would have been accepting that I simply didn't have the ability to turn professional. It hurt to think like that, and at that moment I suddenly missed Mette very much, and I really wished that she was there with me. She had moved to Nice to learn French, and we hadn't seen each other for a long time. But perhaps the national coach was right. Perhaps I didn't have it in me. And perhaps no one had ever dared to say it to my face before then.

3 ROUGHING IT

The damp, 200-year-old house looked about ready to fall down. This was home for me and a number of other riders, but at least we each had our own room. What we shared was the same dream to become pro riders. In February 1985, Per Pedersen, my mate from Herning, had grabbed the bull by the horns, and off we went to live in Luxembourg. After having been told that I should give up trying to make a career out of cycling by the national coach, I'd been left with two options: do what he suggested, and stop – or head off abroad and start all over again. A friend of mine in Denmark, Per Sandal, had some contacts in Luxembourg, and invited Per and I to go with him. The plan was that Mette would follow me if I got a contract with a pro team. In the meantime, Per Sandal introduced me to Marcel Gilles, the sports director of a semi-pro team called ACC Concern. "You won't regret giving me a chance," I promised him.

"In that case, you're in!" said Gilles.

The team was a long way from the pro teams I'd seen on TV taking part in the Tour de France. There was no wage, but the team paid for all our equipment and covered everything we needed to race and train. The directeur sportif, Gilles, was one of the good guys, with his heart in the right place. He'd put his hand in his own pocket to help cover our rent whenever our own pockets were empty. The truth, though, was that, rather than pay rent, we should have been paid to stay in that crappy old house, which really wasn't habitable, but as young riders we couldn't expect to live in luxury. On a good day, we could come away from a race with

1,000 kroner (£55) each, splitting any prize money we won between us. And by keeping my living costs and outgoings down, the prize money we earned was just enough to get by on.

I'd survive on spaghetti with tomato ketchup, or tinned tomatoes, or even some meat if I was feeling flush.

Gilles understood how hard things were for us, financially. "You boys hungry?" he'd occasionally ask us, and either invite us to eat with him at his house, or take us out to a local restaurant. He felt an element of responsibility towards us, I think, and didn't want us to go hungry. Still, it never seemed that bad, either, as with no real responsibilities – no girlfriend, wife or kids – I only had to look after myself. But our poor existence served as a good reminder that we had to make every kilometre of every training ride count if we wanted to get a pro contract out of it.

That way of life wasn't for everyone, though. A number of riders tried their luck in Luxembourg, including Jesper Skibby, who would later turn pro. A couple of months in Luxembourg as part of Gilles's team, however, didn't live up to Jesper's expectations. "I can't be doing with this shit," he decided, and went off to seek his fortune elsewhere.

Per and I had both had a pretty promising start to our time in Luxembourg, and won a good number of races between us. We raced a lot in Belgium, Holland and France – it was those races that we had to do well in if we wanted any chance of becoming better riders. You could almost feel the desperation among the riders in these races. Everyone wanted to get noticed in order to keep their dreams of being spotted by the professional teams alive. And that meant that no one was scared to race all out – taking risks, making good use of their elbows and using all sorts of dirty tricks. The other riders were hungry, ambitious, and some were just plain idiotic in the way that they rode. It made for some very tough racing, but I learned a lot. Some riders were scared of how dangerous it was, but I felt like I thrived on it. I tried to use each race as a stepping stone to something better.

During the races, I began to get a good idea of what my strengths were, and found that I was particularly good on the climbs, which gave me one over on most of the others. Climbing fascinated me, as it provided a kind of natural selection. Each time I managed to drop the others, it gave me a much-needed confidence boost. During our first season in Luxembourg, Per won 11 races, while I did even better by winning 16. This must have looked pretty good from the outside, but I still felt like I needed more control over where my career was headed.

I'd often use Gilles's office phone to ring Dad for a chat, which always helped cheer me up, and he always reassured me that I was doing the right thing. He'd ask what the races were like, and whether I could keep up. Every time I won something, I'd give him a call, too. "That's brilliant, Bjarne," he'd say each time, proudly. It was great to have such good support, and it was the same with Mette, too, who I'd ring from the office, or sometimes from a phone box if I had a bit of money.

I'd fill in my training diary every day, as I always had, but none of what was in there was structured training. I had no one to tell me how to train or to give me advice, so I just stayed at the same level. The training methods in Belgium and Luxembourg at that time were rudimentary and old-fashioned: ride a load of kilometres in training, and you'll eventually reach some kind of good form. Day after day, hour after hour, I'd be out on my road bike, in every kind of weather and with varying degrees of intensity and enthusiasm. Five hours' training, with no goal, structure or system, was miserable and demotivating in the long run. But the sheer number of kilometres in my legs, the hard racing and the training in the hills all appeared to have added up when I went back to Denmark to race. It was a good gauge of where I was compared to the riders I'd grown up racing against. Especially noticeable was how much better I'd become at climbing, and that gave me real satisfaction – the kind of satisfaction you can only get from having done something yourself to improve your performance. Racing in Denmark also gave me an extra little push in that it felt like it was me against the world. In front of those who hadn't believed in me, those who had stopped me from going to the Olympics and those who had said I should have packed it in a long time ago, I would show them all that they were wrong.

Even though I had made a good name for myself in Luxembourg cycling circles, I had no idea what would happen next. I just hoped that my results would be good enough for the bigger teams to take notice of me. I'd won 16 races, after all, including small stage races in Belgium and France, but there didn't seem to be any professional teams falling over themselves to sign me.

Gilles did what he could to get Per's name and my name out there. He wrote several letters to the bigger teams recommending us, but nothing came of it, and a lot of them didn't even bother to answer. Time was running out, and it didn't look too likely that I would get a pro contract with anyone.

But then, suddenly, there was some unexpected interest. One of Gilles's contacts was starting a new pro team called RMO, and had been on the lookout for decent, ambitious riders. Gilles put both Per and I forward, but was told that the team actually only needed one more rider. Just like that, Per had switched from being a friend to being the competition. It was pretty awkward, as both of us knew that whoever wasn't picked was likely to have to give up and go home. Eventually, the manager of the new team chose Per. "He's the one I want," he told Gilles. It was tough to have to put on a brave face and congratulate Per. He thanked me, but hid his happiness well. He knew that the chances of me getting any kind of contract at this late stage were pretty slim.

Everyone was gearing up for the new season, and the possibility of a contract had all but disappeared. Gilles was disappointed for me, and told me that all the teams worth joining had filled their rosters.

"What's left?" I asked him.

"Only crap teams," he told me.

"One of those will do me," I said.

The teams that were left were the small ones – the pro teams that were badly organised, Gilles warned me. He said that they weren't really places to progress as a rider, and that they might actually damage my career. "I'm happy to try anything," I told him. I didn't have any choice.

He knew some people in Belgium who were setting up a new team called Roland Van de Ven. Florent Van Vaerenbergh was the directeur sportif, while Guillaume Driessens was team manager.

They looked at my results and listened to what Gilles had to say about me, and it apparently convinced them that "the Dane" had some potential, and they offered me a contract. I signed it immediately without so much as a second thought, and finally I could call myself a professional bike rider. The salary was a modest 6,000 kroner (£500) a month, plus prize money. Signing the contract meant that we would have enough money for Mette to move in with me. She'd finished her qualification as a chiropodist that year – 1986 – and was willing to give living together abroad a go.

Mette got herself a job as a chiropodist and, together with my salary from the Roland team, we were soon able to get a new flat, which we were happy with and which we could afford – and where it was just the two of us, too. No more mould on the walls, no more washing up piled up in the sink, and no more sweaty cyclists stinking out the whole house.

Cycling in Belgium in 1986 was exactly what Gilles had warned me it would be like: a school of hard knocks, where it was a daily battle for survival as part of a small team like ours. Joining the Roland Van de Ven team was like stepping back in time. The main sponsor, Roland, was a Belgian organ – and these days keyboard – manufacturer, and most of the team was made up mainly of neo-professionals. The team owner, Guillaume Driessens, was a charismatic, older man, and a big name in Belgian cycling circles, who still dined out on the fact that he had once been one of cycling legend Eddy Merckx's directeurs sportifs. Driessens ran the Roland team as though it was still the 1960s, and that meant that it had the same values as a team from "the good old days", too.

During the Tour of Belgium, where there was a split stage, meaning that we had to ride two stages in one day, he ordered us to eat steak for breakfast, and then again in between the two stages, and once more in the evening. "That's a real cyclist's diet," he told us. As dietary advice went, it was a new one on me, but if that's what we were told to do, then that's what we had to do, and we tucked into our steaks. Driessens loved telling old stories about heroes, villains and how to win bike races. I took it all in, but knew that there were only a few things that I could learn from him that were genuinely useful.

Belgium is a traditional cycling nation, and the Belgians like nothing better than a home-grown hero. Every town with any self respect has its own race, too. Belgians are also used to fighting for things. As a young rider, you have to show your worth before you can expect to be shown any respect, and so it was for me. My job was to uncomplainingly work for the others on the team. Whenever a decision had to be made about tactics or strategy, no one ever asked for my opinion. I'd just listen, nod, and get on with doing what I was told to do, accepting my place at the bottom of the pile.

Racing and training on those rain-drenched Belgian roads was tough. Finding myself feeling alone in this strange bubble reminded me what an odd career choice it was. It was certainly character-building – no doubt about that. But on the other hand, I could also just have considered it a waste of my time and talent when the possibility of career progression was made up of a couple of pieces of really quite average advice at the dinner table occasionally. Perhaps my preference for good advice and some proper coaching was stronger than for some of the other team members. It didn't make it any easier that I couldn't count 100 per cent on my team-mates. Everyone just rode for themselves, and plans were not usually stuck to.

The team's star rider was 29-year-old Belgian Ludwig Wijnants, a past winner of a stage at the Tour de France. Winning something like that earned you both respect and status. But, for the rest of us, getting the backing of your team-mates all depended on how much of a chance you had going into a race. If they thought they had a chance of winning, they'd be desperate for my support, although when a race was more suited to my strengths, they were usually nowhere to be seen. Luckily for me, I had two Danish team-mates – Brian Holm and Jan Østergaard – to hang out with. I got on especially well with Brian, who knew what he wanted from his career, and was prepared to start from the bottom and work his way up. Brian's riding in the peloton was quite reckless and, unlike me, he didn't think before he acted. He took risks, used his elbows when necessary, and was cheeky enough to take chances. In comparison, I was too nice, too analytical, and would think too much about things. During a race, I'd try to think through how I could win. Except that, by the time I'd made up my mind what to do, the winning breakaway would have disappeared up the road. Driessens had noticed that I needed to believe in myself a bit more. "Don't think so much about things, Bjarne," he told me once when we were talking about why I wasn't in the mix at the end of races too often. "Just ride."

My biggest hope for success was in stage races, where I could plan several days ahead, scout out stages beforehand, and get stronger and stronger as the race went on. It was also during stage races that I'd get the chance to use my strength on the climbs, which meant not necessarily having to work for anyone else. But stage races weren't big things in Belgium. It was all about one-day races there, and it would be my task to ride for the others as I didn't have much of a sprint to speak of.

The other end of the spectrum to normal road racing was kermesse racing, which I got introduced to while riding for Roland. A Belgian phenomenon, the one-day races were cycling's equivalent of the Wild West. Virtually every Belgian town organised its own kermesse, which was a kind of carnival based around a bike race. There would be fairground rides, betting stands, loud music and food carts selling chips and waffles. Spectators drank and ate while they watched the racing. The races themselves tended to be around 150-170km long, and were made up of spectator-friendly circuits, which were perhaps 10 or 14km long, often on narrow, dangerous roads. Many of the smaller Belgian teams existed for kermesse racing alone; prize money was good, and there were plenty of races.

Brian was somewhat of a kermesse specialist, and helped teach me how to ride them – and win some money in them. He referred to the races as "paid training". He lived in Belgium and knew most of the riders and team managers, which meant that he knew who we needed to stick close to in order to earn some money. He'd study the start list before the race, picking out the local teams who would be desperate to win the race on their own turf. We'd do some work for the local hero, he'd win, and his team would pay us for having contributed to their victory. Sometimes we were the ones who were desperate for the victory – such as the time when we took part in a kermesse in Ludwig Wijnants's home race in Putte. "The King of Putte" they called him, and it was imperative that he stood on the top step of the podium.

Many of the riders taking part in the kermesses were not always in good form, yet they always seemed to ride like greyhounds for the first 100km. One day, Brian explained why that was. "You're in for a shock," he told me. Kermesses rarely had doping controls, and the riders knew that. Riders would often get changed for the races in local riders' or managers' garages, and it was here that they'd prepare themselves for the races, too – with amphetamine-filled syringes. "It won't be long before they're doing hundreds of press-ups, playing football with the garbage cans and acting crazy," Brian warned me.

Sure enough, once they were ready to go, many of the riders were like different people. They were absolutely wired, with wild eyes and, once on their bikes, they stamped on the pedals like crazy. "But I'm not interested in all that," Brian told me.

"Me neither," I replied.

We both distanced ourselves from what they were doing, which was a real culture shock, and not something we were used to.

But right from the off, the racing was fast, and that meant that, on the narrow roads, you needed to make sure that you were up near the front. It was a real fight to be up there, too, and any sign of weakness often meant that you'd end up on the ground.

"If you can survive a kermesse, you can survive anything," Brian would say.

They were so fast, though – often ridden at an average of 50km/h for the first hour. But at that point, riders would suddenly tire. It was as if the amphetamines only worked for about 100km at most. The pace would drop, and a quick look around revealed that a lot of riders would be on their last legs, having ridden at such a crazy pace for most of the first part of the race.

The prize money normally went down to 30th place, so it was all about making sure you were still there at the end. And if you'd also made the right deals, you could earn enough money to cover your transport costs and even have enough left over to pay some of the household bills. The best kermesse riders knew just how to play the game, and would enter into multiple alliances so that they earned their money almost no matter who won.

The bunch sprints could be frightening. Brian hit the deck in one once and ended up in hospital having fractured his skull. Still, that didn't stop me giving it a go a couple of times. Sprinting really wasn't my strong point, and I'd end up getting squeezed out of contention, but at least I'd managed to get through it unscathed.

"What are you doing sprinting?" Brian would ask.

"How else am I going to learn?" I'd reply.

Very occasionally, anti-doping officials would turn up at the kermesses unannounced – but there were ways around them, of course. Two hundred metres before the finish line, you'd suddenly catch a glimpse of a man at the side of the road crazily waving a flag. This was to warn the riders that the anti-doping officials had turned up, and there were two options to avoid giving a positive test. The first was to stop before the finish and simply disappear. The second, similar, tactic was to sprint across the finish line and then keep sprinting for a couple of hundred metres and lose yourself in the crowds.

But despite a kermesse being a colourful, good place to learn and a way to supplement the regular wage, this Belgian style of racing wasn't really for me, and I didn't end the season with any decent results to my name.

When Roland started planning for the following year, it was without me on the team roster. The sponsor was putting more money into the team, and so was trying to attract some bigger-name riders, rather than hold on to an unknown Danish domestique. After just one year as a pro, I was left without a contract. But again, I was saved at the 11th hour by another small Belgian squad.

I'd entered into contract negotiations with the Lucas team, although "negotiations" was probably too strong a word. I didn't have any other teams interested in me, and the proposed salary was actually pretty good. Just as I'd done the year before, I signed the contract without any fuss, and the deal was done. The downside was that a number of people had warned me that the people behind the team were a bunch of gangsters. Rumour had it that they weren't exactly on top of their finances and were likely to muck me about. The salary was 9,000 kroner (£800) a month – but only when it turned up, which wasn't too often. The riders on the team frequently had to chase the management to get paid. "But we don't understand it," we'd be told. "We'll make sure we get it sorted." But nothing would happen.

After not being paid for a number of months, I'd had enough.

The main sponsor, Lucas, made furniture and, furious, I turned up at their factory one day. "I want my money," I told them.

"Well, we'd better get it all sorted, then," they told me, clearly surprised that one of the team's unknown riders had confronted them over it.

"You've said that before, and yet nothing's been done. If you can't pay, then I want furniture in lieu of what you owe me," I continued, and pointed at the pieces of furniture in their collection that I wanted.

They dutifully noted it down. "We'll sort out your money," they said.

A few days later, a removal van turned up outside our house. "What's going on?" Mette asked me, pointing out of the window at the van. We watched as the removal men unloaded a load of furniture onto the pavement. The crooks had taken what I'd said seriously and gave me furniture instead of my salary.

I resigned myself to the fact that things were as they were, but made up my mind to make the best of the situation and be a bit more selfish with the way I rode. I started to think about doing my own thing in races more often, in the hope of attracting the interest of some other teams. That chance came unexpectedly at three-week stage race the Vuelta a Espana, or Tour of Spain.

Our Lucas team rode on Spanish Orbea bikes, and we had a few Spanish riders on the squad as a result. The race started surprisingly well for us when one of the Spanish riders won a stage. It was a massive deal, and everyone was thrilled – and it showed that perhaps we could play ball with the big boys after all. It was almost too good to be true and, sure enough, a few days later our stage winner was suddenly in a hurry to pack his bags and leave our hotel. The explanation came only weeks later when we heard the results of a dope test taken on the day of his victory. After that, the team fell apart completely. One after the other, my team-mates left the race, and by the end of stage 10 I was the only rider left. I wasn't in contention for the race's overall classification, but I'd gone into the race hoping to do as well as I could, again in the hope of catching the eye of another team.

I was my own boss now, and didn't need anyone's permission to ride my own race in an event that was perfect for me. But the idea of using the Vuelta as my own shop window for my talents wasn't one my Lucas team shared – especially not the two directeurs sportifs, two mechanics and two soigneurs, who took care of things like massages, who were still left on the race with me. "Bjarne, don't you think you should quit the race so that we can all just go home?" one of the directeurs sportifs asked me.

"I'm not going anywhere," I told him. "I'm feeling in good form, and I've got no plans to quit."

Two days later, though, the team got their wish. I woke up with a nasty stomach ache, which got progressively worse as the day went on. On the bike, I felt completely drained of energy and had no choice but to retire from the race.

"I have to give up," I told the directeur sportif who had stopped next to me in the team car.

"That's a shame," he said, although I somehow doubted that he meant it.

I had no proof whatsoever, but I was convinced that the team had poisoned me in order to make me quit so that they could go home. After that, there were no two ways about it: I had to get out of that team, and quickly.

The Danish rider Kim Andersen was a big name in cycling, and with the results he'd achieved it meant something when he recommended me as a rider. He had twice worn the yellow jersey at the Tour de France, over a number of days in both 1983 and 1985, and had won stages there, too. They were the kinds of achievements I would have killed for. And Kim put my name forward when a new French squad, Toshiba, was being put together from the remnants of the La Vie Claire team.

"You've got a year to show us what you can do," the team told me as I put pen to paper on a contract worth 12,000 kroner a month (£1,000) for the 1988 season. I was 23 years old, and it was the chance of a lifetime.

The big star on the team was the Frenchman Jean-François Bernard, who had finished third at the 1987 Tour de France. Bernard, who had also worn the yellow jersey that year, and won two stage victories, including the mountain time trial on the legendary climb of Mont Ventoux, was definitely one of the big boys. My role on the team was as a domestique to Bernard and the others – their loyal helper, who would keep them sheltered from the wind and generally look after them. Bernard was a strong rider – or he was when he was in form, at least – and was at a level way above anyone I'd been on a team with before.

The Toshiba team was quite different to the small teams I'd previously been part of. The main difference was just how many riders there were, which meant that the team had more of a choice over who was selected for particular events. And that meant that you needed to make your presence felt, else risk being ignored and forgotten. We had all the big races on our programme, the riders on the team were all really good, and I was given the opportunity to prepare for the races that suited me. I'd always dreamed of taking part in the Italian grand tour, the Giro d'Italia, and with Toshiba I got my chance. It was going to be my biggest race so far as a pro cyclist.

I arrived at the start line full of ambition, as did the team, and everything was going to plan when Bernard took the pink leader's jersey. If I could help the team get the success it was after, I realised that the race could also be the chance for me to get my international breakthrough. Bernard had won three stages, and we were managing to defend the jersey, when it all went horribly wrong. He crashed, and injured his back so badly that he had to quit the race, which was a real blow for the team and left us a bit direction-less.

On one of the mountain stages, I was told to help the German rider, Andreas Kappes, who was higher up in the team's hierarchy than me. But on this particular stage, Kappes wasn't feeling great, and was dropped by the peloton. The directeur sportif drove up alongside me. "You need to help Kappes get through this stage," he ordered me. It was hard to see the reasoning behind the order, as to me the German looked to be have had enough, but I let myself drop back to him in order to help him as much as possible. And to me, he was acting as though he'd already decided to call it a day, and was just going slower and slower.

"Just ride, Bjarne," he puffed. By that, he meant that I should leave him to his fate – that there was no need for me to risk not making the time limit for the stage.

"No – I'll stay with you. Team orders," I told him.

But with 100km still left to go, he'd had enough. "I'm finished," he said, and climbed off his bike to wait for the broom wagon.

All that effort on my part had been for nothing, and now I was left far behind by the rest of the race, and by a team who couldn't care less about me. But I decided I'd show them I wasn't the sort of rider who gave up just because the going got tough and my chances of making the time limit to stay in the race didn't look good. For kilometre after kilometre I kept going through the mountains, which were made that much harder by the fact that I was on my own. Using up my last ounces of energy, I made it to the finish, and promptly collapsed off my bike. The only thing that mattered was whether I'd made the time limit, and could continue in the race.

"Did I make it?" I asked the people standing over me.

"You missed it by a minute and a half," came the reply.

I was out of the race, and felt like a laughing stock. I'd been handed an impossible task and had given it everything, only to have my own race ruined. All I could do was go back to the hotel, pack my suitcase and head home to Luxembourg.

In the weeks that followed, I waited to hear what my programme was for the rest of the season from the team. But no one contacted me. The silence from the team management was deafening, and I was left to try to work out what their lack of communication meant for me. I had no idea whether I was being punished for what had happened at the Giro, but in the meantime I just knuckled down to training and tried to keep my form in readiness for whatever my next race would be. Gradually, though, it dawned on me that they'd written me off, having given me a chance at the Giro and seen that I wasn't up to the job. Clearly they were now simply waiting for my contract to run out. It was frustrating to feel as though I was simply being ignored until I went away.

I was sitting, disillusioned, in our flat in Luxembourg when my former directeur sportif, Marcel Gilles, called. "How do you fancy riding the Tour of the European Community?" he asked me.

Again, he'd come to my rescue. He was offering me the chance to race the French stage race as part of a mixed team of riders from Denmark and Luxembourg that he'd put together. Everyone on the team had their own agenda for taking part. Some were there to get some training miles in their legs ahead of the Six Day track season, others just wanted to maintain an element of fitness, while I was there for one reason and one reason only: to try to get myself a contract with a team for the new season.

The race started in Paris, and then followed a route through Belgium, Holland and Germany, before finishing in Luxembourg. The big name competing in the race was the Frenchman Laurent Fignon, known as "The Professor", due to his round glasses and ponytail. He'd won the Tour de France twice, in 1983 and 1984, as well as the Milan-San Remo Classic earlier in the season. Fignon's team, Système U, was one of the stronger teams in the race, while our little team just got smaller and smaller as riders – especially those from Luxembourg – dropped out as the race went on.

As the race neared its conclusion, only Kim Eriksen, Pascal Carrara, Jan Østergaard and I were left from our team. The Système U stars – Fignon and another Frenchman, Gérard Rué – were having to work quite hard to stay at the head of the race by this point. However, Kim knew Rué pretty well, and without there ever being any official deal done, our team started to help them out. We rode up at the front of the race with the Système U boys, helping to cover breakaways and generally helping out when they needed us. It wasn't only in the Belgian kermesses that alliances were formed, but such alliances in the pro peloton were a little different to those established in the Belgian Wild West. They were a little more serious and clear-cut.

If the team defending the leader's jersey in a stage race needed a little extra help, for example, they might enter into a deal with a team not interested in the overall classification, but which was still looking for a stage victory. Such teams would often be the ones with the best sprinters. It would mean that there was a shared interest in keeping the bunch together: the first team in order to defend the leader's jersey by stopping anyone gaining time in a breakaway, and the second team to ensure that all break-aways were reeled in before a bunch sprint. Most deals like that would be arranged by the directeurs sportifs, but occasionally it would be the riders out on the road who would have to make such decisions.

Occasionally money would exchange hands, although that tended to be between individual riders in a breakaway. If three riders, say, were in a break together, they might agree to all give it everything they had, but then whoever won would pay the other two something like 5,000 kroner each (£420) for their efforts if the break succeeded in staying away to the finish.

At the Tour of the European Community, Système U had apparently been happy with our efforts.

Fignon nodded his appreciation in our direction on the days that we'd worked hard for them. During the race, I managed to exchange a few words with Rué, and mentioned that I didn't have a team for the following year. He told me that he'd talk to the team's manager, Cyrille Guimard, about it.

The race ended in success for Système U. Fignon won the overall classification, while Rué got second. He and Guimard thanked me for my help, and I took the opportunity to ask one more time whether they might have any room for me on the team for next season. They didn't. However, Fignon came up to Kim and I at the finish holding an envelope from which he pulled out a wad of banknotes, and handed them to us as a thank you. There was 30,000 kroner (£2,500) to share between us.

Gilles continued to try to find a team for the 1989 season that needed "a good Dane", but no one was interested. For the last few months of 1988, I rattled around in our flat in Luxembourg, readying myself to admit that my time as a professional bike rider was about to come to an end.

I was proud that I'd achieved my dream of turning pro, but was deeply disappointed not to have managed to do better in the races I'd been given the chance to ride.

Mette and I prepared ourselves to move back to Denmark in the new year, when I'd have to get out there and find myself a proper job outside cycling. Gilles had always been one of the few who had always believed in me, but even he had to admit that it was over. But even then, he didn't abandon me. "Do you fancy earning a bit of money while you think about what you're going to do next?" he asked me.

"That would be great," I answered.

Gilles also managed a travel agency, and they needed an odd-jobs man to do stuff like sort the post and run errands. "The job's yours," he smiled. It was better than nothing.

4 DOMESTIQUE

It was a cold winter's morning on 4 January 1989 and I was pacing back and forth in Mette's parents' house in Denmark when the phone rang. Mette and I had resigned ourselves to the fact that we'd have to return to our flat in Luxembourg to pack up all our stuff once the Christmas holidays were over. We'd move back to Denmark and start a new life. No teams had come to me with any contract offers, so it seemed like the right time to put a stop to my cycling career and move on. Since finishing my season, I'd been doing a bit of cyclo-cross racing and had been on a detox diet, which had combined to cause me to lose a few kilos. I suppose that there had been one small part of me that still hoped that a team might be able to use me.

But it was my accountant and good friend, Rene Thill, who called me that day. Rene told me that he'd been in touch with Laurent Fignon and his Système U manager, Cyrille Guimard. The team, which was to change its name to Super U for the 1989 season, was still missing a good domestique, and apparently Fignon had thought of me. I was soon speaking to Guimard on the phone, the upshot of which was that he told me to get myself to the team's training camp in France as quickly as I could. I'd been saved again, and this time to the tune of a contract worth 12,000 kroner (£1,000) a month.

I arrived at the camp in Rennes unsure of whether I was good enough to be on a team of this level, but also excited at the chance to ride for them. And the cyclo-cross training, and the weight loss as a result of the diet, meant that I wasn't turning up out of shape. It was a chance for me to show them that they had made the right decision in offering me a contract. I said hello to Fignon, who was very much still the star of the team, and a rider who commanded a huge amount of respect from those around him. Everyone was in awe of him, and there was absolutely no question as to who the top dog was. He was the one who would bring the team success; it was his results that were paying our wages. He was quite a shy man, and did his own thing without worrying about what anyone thought. He was an intellectual who oozed self-confidence, and this courage to be a bit different pervaded the whole team.

Our French directeur sportif, Guimard, was a hard man – but in a good way. He was competent, knowledgeable, really knew how to read a race, and had a unique ability to motivate his riders.

As a rider, he had been a star at the start of the 1970s, winning several stages of the Tour de France, even battling against the legendary Eddy Merckx for the yellow jersey in the mountains in 1972.

His own experiences as a pro made Guimard perfect for the role of directeur sportif. He knew how riders thought, how they felt and what they needed when it came to different race situations.

As a team manager, he'd discovered American talent Greg LeMond, and had also worked with Tour winners Bernard Hinault and Lucien Van Impe. He'd watch you, without making you feel like you were being watched, and then suggest things you could adjust or change to make you a better rider.

Even though Guimard was a friendly, accommodating type of person, you could tell that he was also a man used to telling people what to do. "You don't discuss things with Guimard," five-time Tour winner Hinault once said. "You do what he tells you."

The story goes that 1976 Tour winner Van Impe was once on the receiving end of Guimard's fury – that same year he won the race. Guimard was the Belgian's directeur sportif, and on one stage in the mountains told him to attack. But Van Impe ignored Guimard's command, and so the Frenchman allegedly drew up next to Van Impe in the team car and threatened to run his star rider off the road if he didn't do what he was told. The threat must have worked, as Van Impe attacked, dropped his rivals and went on to take the overall race victory in Paris. Personally, I hoped such methods wouldn't be necessary for Guimard to threaten me with.

During the training days around Rennes that followed, I was very surprised to find that I was able to follow Fignon on the climbs. When he managed to drop me, I was quickly able to catch up again on the descents. And it seemed that both Fignon and Guimard had noticed. For the first time ever, I felt as though I actually did have some potential as a pro rider: that with the right training, the right lifestyle, the right team-mates and the right management, I really could reach a high level. Certainly Guimard thought that I had what it took to be an important domestique for Fignon. "Bjarne, go home and ride 1,000km over the next five days," Guimard told me. "That should put you in really good form."

It had been a long time since anyone had taken the time to try to help me become a better bike rider, and something just clicked when I talked to Guimard. It meant that someone believed in me, had confidence in me, and was interested in helping me improve.

I went home to Denmark, and set about getting the kilometres under my belt. Dad accompanied me by car on each training session. It was hard, and I got more and more exhausted with each day that passed. But by my first race, I could tell that I was in better condition than I'd ever been in. Guimard's ideas about training proved to be spot on, which in turn gave me confidence that his interest in me and my career was genuine.

My role on the team was clearly defined: I was to help Fignon in whichever way he needed me. At first, we hardly said a word to each other. I could speak a little bit of French, having learned at school, but neither of us was particularly chatty by nature anyway. Almost immediately, though, things worked perfectly. There was this mutual understanding between us on the bike – a sort of chemistry between our personalities, as we both knew our roles. During races, I had to be alert to Fignon's needs, and take care of them quickly and effectively. After a while, it came naturally to me, and I'd know what he wanted before he even had to tell me. My main tasks were to keep him sheltered from the wind so that he could save energy, and to guide him safely up through the peloton to the front when the mountains approached. It was all about making things as effortless as possible for him. He needed to be able to trust me implicitly – to know that it was safe to sit behind me on my wheel, and that I would never let him down.

During the previous months, when it had looked like my cycling career was about to be over, I'd made a promise to myself that if I ever did get another chance, then I'd make myself indispensable to my team. Now that I had got that chance, I wanted to be the absolute best domestique possible for Fignon, which meant setting aside my own ambitions and hopes of good results for myself. I also treated it as a learning experience – an opportunity to really learn the tricks of the trade. Guimard had originally picked out a different rider to be Fignon's right-hand man, but he had been forced to change his mind when Fignon himself told him that he wanted it to be me. Him choosing me meant that Guimard quickly gave me even more attention, keen to help me be as good a bike rider as I could be. And he didn't hold back when telling me what I needed to do. My riding position wasn't right, he told me. "You're sitting all wrong on your bike. It's too small for you," he pointed out, and said that they would build a new one for me. My new bike was 2cm higher and 4cm longer than before, and gave me a much better position.

Every training ride and every race I did with Fignon helped my confidence, and taught me a lot about what it takes to be a leader. I was learning something new every day. During a race, Fignon would give instructions in a neutral and friendly tone. There was no shouting or swearing – he was always calm, and a complete gentleman. He just had so much experience; there seemed to be nothing in a race that he hadn't seen before. But it was his way or no way, and I experienced that first hand in the run up to the spring Classic, Milan-San Remo. The team had got together in Italy two weeks before the race to prepare, and I was sitting at the dinner table in our hotel opposite Fignon on the evening that Guimard announced which riders had been selected for the one-day race. When he'd finished reading the list, my name hadn't been called out. I was immensely disappointed, as Fignon and I had trained so much together in the lead-up to the race. It must have shown on my face, too.

"Did you want to ride this one, Bjarne?" he asked me.

"I'd hoped to, yeah," I told him honestly.

"Okay – you're riding," he said, as though it was the most natural thing in the world to make such a decision without running it past Guimard. And, sure enough, I did ride.

Fignon's philosophy was that, as a team captain, you use your team. "You can never win on your own," he'd say. For him, a team needed to be made up of different riders who could come together to complement each other. He'd spend a lot of his time in the peloton studying his rivals. He'd analyse them individually – how each of them was looking, what kind of form they had, whether their facial expressions and the way they were holding themselves on the bike meant that they were about to crumble. "It's about discovering their strengths, their weaknesses and their sore points," Fignon would tell me. I'd lap up his words of wisdom, filing it all away to perhaps use later.

The Frenchman always looked as though he was a step ahead of his rivals in terms of reading a race, knowing how it was going to play out before anyone else. "Always keep abreast of what's going on," he'd warn me. "Never lose your head." He was always watching. He'd see the tiniest movement or change in the bunch that might influence the race. If something looked like it was about to happen, he'd already be thinking about what that would mean. He taught me that just a moment's inattention could prove critical, but that at the same time you shouldn't react to every single wave that goes through the peloton. It was about picking and choosing the right times to use your energy.

He would train a lot. His thinking was that if you didn't have enough kilometres in your legs, it was because you didn't want it enough. I was on the receiving end of that one, too, when we were in Sicily for the Giro d'Etna.

When I came down for breakfast on the morning of the 180km race, Fignon was already sitting at the table. He'd had an idea. "I'm going to cycle to the start to get in a bit of extra training," he told me. "Do you want to come with me?"

He'd worked out that it was about 40km from our hotel.

"Sure!" I answered, proud to have been invited along for the warm-up.

We rode the 40km to the start, and then added on another 180km of racing. Slightly exhausted after my 220km, I was looking for our team car to take us back to the hotel when Fignon rolled up beside me. "Shall we cycle back to the hotel? We may as well, eh?"

It was less of a question and more of a suggestion.

"Why not?" I found myself replying.

We were quickly on our way, and we weren't hanging around, either. At such a speed, the 40km Fignon reckoned it was back to the hotel were going to fly by. But it was also beginning to get dark, and perhaps it was that that had an effect on Fignon's sense of direction. Or he had miscalculated the distance from the finish to the hotel.

We were soon riding through towns I'd definitely never seen before, and which I was pretty sure weren't on the route we should have been taking. As it got darker, I began to worry that perhaps this island, of all the islands we could have been on, was perhaps not the best one to be lost on, considering its Mafia connections. But Fignon seemed completely unperturbed. "Nearly there!" he chirped.

I had long suspected that he had absolutely no idea where we were, and he was virtually dragging me along with him. I was completely finished, and had to really fight to follow his wheel as we ploughed our way through the streets of yet another unfamiliar town. It had gone 9pm, by which time it was pitch black, when we finally found the hotel. The others had been worried about us, and had been out several times to look for us. Fignon shrugged his shoulders and smiled. "A good few extra training kilometres, eh?"

It was all I could do to drag myself up to bed, having ridden at least 300km in one day. I was learning all right.

That April, Guimard told me that I was going to ride the Giro. My role? To be Fignon's shadow and help him to win the overall classification. My selection for the race was proof that I had passed the test – that they could count on me, and believed in me as a loyal domestique.

From the very first stage, I stuck to Fignon like a limpet. Each time I turned my head just a few centimetres behind me, there he was with his ponytail and round glasses. I'd guide him through the peloton, keeping him out of harm's way and protecting him from the wind. A grateful nod or look was generally all the feedback I got, or needed, from him to let me know that I was doing a good job. But he was particularly appreciative on the occasions that I'd be dropped on a climb and then claw my way back up to him in the front group on the descent, and get back to work for him on the front. He was a rider who would fight against everyone and everything, but he thrived on it. He didn't suffer fools gladly, and was very selective with whom he would give his attention to. He also had friends and a life outside of cycling, which he was very protective of, and which meant he could distance himself from the sport when he wanted to.

Being able to see Fignon as a person as well as a sportsman was also helpful when it came to my willingness to ride for him. If he'd been an idiot, I doubt I would have been willing to sacrifice myself for him the way I did, like a good domestique should. You need to be as willing to fight for your team leader as you are to fight for yourself. And victory for your leader is good for your bank account, too. For every decent result Fignon attained, it meant a share of the prize money for me. Good results for him would also put me in a better position when it came to negotiating my contract later in the season. Most importantly, though, working for Fignon had brought me up to the sort of level that I had never even been close to, and would never have dreamed of reaching. My riding at that Giro showed just how far I'd come, and Fignon was in the perfect position in the overall classification going into the second week, just half a minute down on the race leader.

The 221km-long ninth stage of the 1989 Giro between L'Aquila and Gubbio on Monday 29 May should have been just another day, when I'd "gulp the wind" and work for Fignon. Whenever

I rode hard, I'd do it with my mouth gaping open – as though I really was gulping in the wind, protecting Fignon from it. On that stage to Gubbio, I was feeling pretty good – and Fignon had apparently noticed. I was up at the front of the bunch, helping to chase down a breakaway, when Fignon rode up next to me. "You should go for it today, Bjarne," he said.

"No – I'll stay here and work for you," I replied.

But it seemed that the boss had already made up his mind, and I wasn't going to argue.

"Get on my wheel, and I'll help you get a gap," Fignon told me.

I did as I was told, and with 7 or 8km left to go, I managed to get away from the peloton and found myself in a break with Enrico Galleschi, Dmitri Konyshev and fellow Dane Rolf Sørensen. Having established a decent enough gap back to the bunch, it was pretty clear that the stage winner was going to come from one of the four of us. But a quick look around at the others made me realise that I wouldn't have a chance in hell against them if we were going to sprint it out between us, so I needed to come up with a plan. Rolf shouted at me, as though I was his domestique and working for him. "Come on – ride, ride!" he yelled. He was hoping that I'd ride for him to help him win – that I would give it everything so that he could nick victory in the sprint. But I wasn't going to let that happen.

The last 500m were slightly uphill, and this was my chance. I decided that I was going to attack just when they least expected it, and would then have to be ready to have to do a very long sprint. But I knew that Rolf and Konyshev would do whatever it took to ruin my plans. I tried to conjure up everything that Fignon had ever taught me. The time had come to just do it and not think too much – and do it before it was too late to attack. I patiently waited until the last 500m, hanging on until just the right moment. I would prove to Fignon and Guimard that they'd made the right decision by giving me a place on the team, while showing everyone who had ever written me off what they were missing. This new version of me was better, smarter and worked harder, and was able to mix it with the best at the highest level. The moment that Rolf and Konyshev forgot about me and started to look at each other was going to be my signal to attack. And when that second came, it was all the time I needed, and I went for it. Every pedal stroke I made was with a rage and will to win that I'd never felt before in my professional career, and each new pedal stroke filled me with more self-confidence. Only Rolf could go with me, but the shock of my attack had bought me a couple of precious metres on him. However, I knew that he was just as hungry for the stage win as I was. But there was no way that I was going to let him pass me as we sprinted to the finish line.

The stage win was the highlight of my career so far, and my most important victory to date. The pride and joy I felt was overwhelming. This was more than just a win; this meant recognition and respect going forward. Fignon was thrilled for me when he crossed the line. "Congratulations, Bjarne," he said, and I could tell that he really meant it. Giving me the opportunity to ride for myself was also his way of saying thank you. It was a reward for my loyalty, and in my world it was huge that he was prepared to let me, an unknown young rider, take all the attention and glory that comes with winning for a day. But he could be sure that I'd pay my appreciation back. We both knew it. He'd now got himself an even more dedicated domestique, while I was left feeling appreciated both as a rider and as a person.

Guimard was full of praise for me when talking to the Danish journalists who were there covering the race, and who quickly needed to find out who I was for their reports. "The Dane still has a lot to give as a rider, so that's why I'm bringing him to the big stage races – so that he can learn. What he's lacking is experience, but he's got a lot more to give yet," Guimard told the Danish press.

I rode the rest of the race 100 per cent for Fignon, not letting him out of my sight, sheltering him from the wind and from his rivals, and doing my best to make sure he was exactly where he needed to be when it mattered. Fignon won that Giro overall, and in doing so gave the Super U team what they had needed and had hoped for: the successful return to form of their French star. But what I had needed to do was convince Guimard and Fignon that they should extend my contract and keep me on the team for the following year. Guimard informed us that he was looking for a new main sponsor so that the team could continue the following year. "Would you like to be part of the team again next year, too?" he asked me. He didn't need to ask twice.

My performance at the Giro had convinced Guimard that I was irreplaceable when it came to helping Fignon to try to win his third Tour de France in the summer. One of my biggest dreams was about to come true.

Fignon's main rivals for the 1989 Tour were the American 1986 winner Greg LeMond and the Spaniard, and defending champion, Pedro Delgado. As early as stage two – a 40km-long team time trial – the Tour was proving to be everything I had hoped it would be. With Gérard Rué, Thierry Marie and Fignon at the head of affairs, we hammered away from the start. We rode fast – really fast. I was flying, and was giving it absolutely everything every time I took my turn at the front of the line. Fignon and Marie were among the world's best time triallists and could ride fast for long turns at a time, and every time they took over at the front it was like trying to ride behind a rocket. Fignon was keen to show the French public that he was still capable of winning a third Tour, and for the second half of the stage he stepped it up again and rode like he was from another planet. He took kilometre-long turns on the front, and the rest of us had to absolutely kill ourselves to try to stay in contact. We won the stage and, up on the podium, I could barely believe that it was happening. I'd won a stage of the Tour de France, and yet less than a year before I was considering finishing my career.

In the Alps and the Pyrenees, where the race would be decided, it was my job to support Fignon and leave him in the best possible position once I could no longer follow the pace. On stage 10, a mountainous stage that included the climb of the Tourmalet, the specialist climbers took over. I worked hard for Fignon, and he managed to distance his biggest rival, LeMond, and take the yellow jersey. That night, back at the hotel, there was even more good news.

"We're so satisfied with the work you're doing that we'd like to offer you a two-year contract," smiled Guimard.

They were offering to more than treble my salary, from 12,000 kroner (£1,000) a month to 40,000 (£3,600). But for me it wasn't only about the money; it meant that they really valued me.

Nine days later, Fignon won the 91km-long mountain stage to Villard de Lans, and in doing so increased his advantage over LeMond to 50 seconds. The Frenchman was all smiles at the dinner table that evening. He'd got through the mountains well, despite the competition from LeMond, and was now in a very good position to win the Tour de France. "I should win if I can keep riding like I am now," he announced confidently.

It was unthinkable that LeMond would be able to overturn our captain's 50-second advantage over the final stage, the 24.5km time trial between Versailles and the Champs-Elysées in Paris. Even though LeMond was an excellent time triallist – even better than Fignon – no one thought that such a deficit could be overcome over such a short stage. It would have meant LeMond going two seconds faster per kilometre than Fignon. At the hotel, the others on the team had started to work out what Fignon winning the Tour would mean for us in terms of prize money. The win would net him 1.5 million kroner (£123,500), which would be shared out between the riders and the team staff.

Everyone was in a really upbeat mood that Sunday, while Guimard and Fignon were locked in conversation about which handlebars Fignon should use. Fignon was against using the so-called clip-on "tri bars" that LeMond was using, as he hadn't tested them himself. The position they gave you on the bike, which was much more aerodynamic and also produced more power, was borrowed from the world of triathlon. Fignon didn't want to take any chances on such an important stage of the Tour, when as a team we'd never used them.

As race leader, Fignon would be the last man to start, while LeMond would start a place ahead of him. It would give Fignon an advantage, as he'd be able to hear LeMond's time checks, and so stay that little bit more in control of how fast he was going himself. I rode that 24.5km final stage in a good time, and was proud to finish the 1989 Tour in 95th place overall. Not bad for a first attempt. Then all we had to do was sit back and wait for Fignon to make his victory official, dreaming in the meantime about all the prize money that was headed our way.

LeMond, however, had other ideas. The American took to the start ramp in his streamlined helmet and tri bars that Fignon had decided not to use. He was banking on these different aerodynamic aids buying him some valuable seconds. We stood in the sponsors' pavilion, a stone's throw away from the finish line, watching the race on the television. They'd split the screen so that we could follow the progress of both LeMond and Fignon at the same time. LeMond rode powerfully, smoothly and in control, while Fignon looked more ragged.

At the first time check, after 10.7km, a gasp went up. Fignon had already lost 21 seconds to LeMond. We looked nervously at each other, and the pavilion went silent. Everyone was there – wives, girlfriends, guests and sponsors – all ready to celebrate a Fignon victory. LeMond pushed onwards, elegant and effortless, with more and more belief that he could do the impossible and win. Fignon pushed onwards, too, but was fighting his bike, desperately trying to keep the momentum going. Hearing the time checks had forced him to give it everything. The American had started two minutes before Fignon, which meant that the crowds could watch both of them on the long Champs-Elysées. Everyone around us, though, kept their eyes glued to the TV screens and the time checks that showed the difference between them. Everyone had stopped talking long ago. We stood, our mouths wide open, staring at the screens.

LeMond crossed the finish line with easily the best time of the day – 26 minutes and 57 seconds. It meant that Fignon needed to finish inside 27 minutes and 47 seconds to win the Tour. It was unbearable to watch, especially having been so close to the person who had battled so hard for victory, as Fignon had. By now he was pedalling squares – desperate and completely having lost his rhythm. The clock was counting down, while the TV showed LeMond also watching Fignon's ride, barely believing what was happening himself. "No, no, no!" a number of the wives and girlfriends had begun crying in the pavilion. The French commentators were shouting and screaming themselves, too. Fignon hadn't made it, crossing the line 58 seconds slower than LeMond. We watched the American break down in tears. He'd won the Tour de France by a measly eight seconds. Then we saw Fignon virtually fall of his bike, collapse on the ground and break down in tears as well.

Around me, people simply couldn't believe what they'd witnessed, and some began to cry.

We had just lost the Tour by eight seconds. We'd ridden over 3,000km, yet just eight seconds had cost us victory. It had cost us about 100,000 kroner (£8,400) per rider in prize money, too. "We killed ourselves for three weeks to lose it all at the last minute like that," one of the riders lamented.

Thierry Marie was inconsolable. "If only I could have swapped my time trial with Fignon's," he mumbled, having finished second on the stage to LeMond.

Everyone felt so sorry for Fignon when he stood on the podium as runner-up, trying to hold the tears back and keep the disappointment hidden.

That night, a big party had been planned at a restaurant. The team decided that we should stick with it and have a party anyway, and it was good to see that Fignon was determined to have a good time, despite his huge disappointment. "I thought you were the strongest rider," I told him.

"Thanks, Bjarne," he said, unable to completely hide how hard it was to accept that he'd been beaten.

We drowned our sorrows with champagne and partied long into the night. At one point, someone produced a copy of the next day's *L'Equipe*. On the front page, the French sports newspaper featured a picture of Fignon just after he'd realised that he'd lost the Tour. "Put that away so that he doesn't see it," Guimard hissed. There was no need to ruin the party.

On 28 October 1989, back in Denmark, Mette and I got married. She was six months pregnant by then, but looked stunning standing there at the altar, and I thought how lucky I was that she'd stuck with me. Despite everything we'd been through, she'd always supported me, and never told me that we should just give up and go home. When we came out of the church, all my former Herning Cycling Club team-mates formed an arch of bike wheels for us to walk through.

Three months later came yet another fantastic day of my life, as our son, Jesper, was born. As I held him in my arms, I couldn't have been happier. Now we were a proper family. It was the end of selfishly doing whatever we wanted to do as a couple; now little Jesper was relying on us. And I hoped this new-found maturity would translate well into my cycling career, too.

For the 1990 season, the Super U team changed its name to Castorama, but it was still Guimard's team. Fignon, Marie and Rué were all still there, as well as big-name riders such as Luc Leblanc and Pascal Simon. At just 25 years of age, I was right-hand man to the number one rider in the world – Fignon – and that meant that I was also allowed to ride for myself in some of the smaller races. I got my chance at that year's Tour of Luxembourg. Guimard gave me free rein for the race for the first time, even though Fignon himself was riding.

Fignon showed during the race that he was only too happy to work for me. On one stage, when I had to drop back with a mechanical problem, Fignon dropped back with me before pacing me back up to the peloton. Unfortunately, I had to settle for sixth place overall, but the confidence shown to me by Guimard and Fignon only served to fill me with even more self-belief.

Next up was the Giro d'Italia, where Fignon was the favourite. However, he crashed on a descent as we went through a badly lit tunnel early in the race, and from then on in it was a real battle for him to even stay in the race. He'd injured his back quite badly, and was having to take painkillers each morning just to keep going. Halfway through stage nine, he turned and looked at me. "That's it," he said, stopped and got off his bike. The pain had been too much for him, and it was the Italian, Gianni Bugno, who went on to dominate the race and win the 1990 Giro.

Things didn't go much better at the Tour de France in July. Everyone expected Fignon to be out to avenge his second place of the year before, but he just wasn't himself during the race.

As early as stage three, he crashed, but was able to get to the finish in Nantes and play down the seriousness of his accident. But in the days that followed, he seemed disheartened and demotivated.

Stage five was a 305km-long slog through pouring rain to Rouen, and Fignon was more than 11 minutes down on the race leader and looked like he would have preferred to have been almost anywhere else. When we got to the feed zone, he declined to take a musette bag of food. It wasn't a good sign.

"Carry on," he instructed us, and looked over his shoulder.

I knew what was coming next. A following team car pulled up and Fignon stopped and jumped into the back seat. He'd lost his morale, and so I was left in the race to ride for myself.

When we hit the Alps, I felt great. On every climb, I felt really comfortable, and was encouraged further by the fact that I was able to keep up with a lot of the big names. But on the morning after the Alpe d'Huez stage, I woke up with a temperature, and felt awful. The team doctor confirmed that I had a fever and wouldn't be able to continue. I was furious. I'd got my chance to show what I could do, and it had been going so well, and yet I'd been stopped by illness. I packed my suitcase, said goodbye to the others and headed home to Mette in Luxembourg, where, after a further medical examination, the doctor told me that I'd been racing with a kidney infection.

By the time the 1991 season came around, Castorama wasn't in the best of health, either. Guimard and Fignon's relationship was on the slide. It was obvious that they couldn't work with each other any more, and were ready to go their separate ways. However, they jointly owned the company that held the licence for the team – and their disagreements apparently stemmed from the fact that they both wanted to do things their own way. Unfortunately their business disagreements affected the team and our results. What had been a fantastic working environment suddenly became less pleasant.

In the spring Classics, I was the unlucky victim of crashes on several occasions, including at Ghent-Wevelgem where I smashed into one of the officials' motorbikes at full speed. I hit my head hard on the ground, and walked away with minor concussion. In the ambulance, I met my old mate Jesper Skibby, who'd also fallen. Despite being battered and bruised, it was still pretty funny to share an ambulance together. "What the fuck are you doing here?" he laughed when he saw me.

★　★　★

At the season's first big goal for the team, the 1991 Giro d'Italia, the unrest in the team was clear to see for anyone. Fignon was our team leader, yet it seemed that he didn't have the support of all the riders. He and Guimard appeared only to be talking to each other when they absolutely had to, and it seemed unlikely that they would be able to work together much longer at all. But Fignon seemed optimistic on the morning of stage nine. "I'll be in the top 10 today," he told me. For that to happen, though, he needed the support of the whole team, and not just me.

As I feared, on the first few climbs of the day my team-mates dropped back having done very little to help. I was the only one left to help Fignon on the final category one climb, which was likely to decide the stage. I was able to help him on the first part of the climb, and then it was up to him. He finished ninth on the stage – inside the top 10, just as he'd predicted. But I was furious with my team-mates, and wasn't afraid to show it in front of the Danish journalists.

"It's got to the point on the team where I'm the only one riding wholeheartedly for Laurent," I told them. "Both Laurent and the team management know that, but no one's doing anything about it, and that's what's making me most angry."

The next day, Fignon and I rode along chatting about the situation. "What's going on between you and Guimard?" I asked him.

In his answer, Fignon showed a side of himself that I'd not seen before – a more honest, vulnerable side. Maybe he didn't have too many people he could confide in, I thought.

"It's over between Guimard and me," he told me. "We disagree too often to be able to carry on working together. Our working relationship has run its course." He went on to tell me that he was already in negotiations with a number of other teams.

Once he'd told me that, I plucked up the courage to ask the obvious question: "Might I be included in your plans?"

"Of course – if you'd like to be. It'd be great to have you in the same team next year," he answered.

That was Fignon's side of the story but, the more I thought about it, the more I thought that perhaps Guimard had also begun to think more about the future, and realised that Fignon couldn't stay at the top of his game forever, while someone younger, like

Luc Leblanc, might be ready to step up a level. I was all set to follow Fignon, but it suddenly dawned on me that if I ever wanted to break out of the role of domestique, then I'd have to do it without Fignon.

On stage 10, Fignon lost a lot of time, which meant that he was out of the running for the overall classification, and so he quit the race. Maybe it was time for me to move on.

At the 1991 Tour de France, both Guimard and Fignon seemed keen to give me a contract with their new, respective, teams. But I was in no hurry. I was still considering what my next move should be – and whether I should head to a team without either of them. On the Tour's first proper mountain stage, we stole a march on everyone. Everyone in the peloton was busy watching the favourites, including Fignon, allowing our team-mate Leblanc to slip away in a 144km-long breakaway with fellow Frenchman Charly Mottet. The attack caused havoc back in the bunch, and Leblanc finished second to Mottet, but he also took over the race lead from Greg LeMond. Back at the hotel that evening, we celebrated Leblanc's yellow jersey with champagne. But behind all the smiles, there was another conflict brewing between Fignon and Guimard: who should we now ride for in the general classification? Fignon or Leblanc?

In the following few days, many of the big names suffered, and it was a quiet, young Spaniard, Miguel Indurain, who made his breakthrough. He took the leader's jersey in the Pyrenees, while Fignon was left back in sixth place as we headed towards the Alps. One day, Fignon rode up next to me and told me that he was going to tell the press that he wasn't going to remain with Castorama for the following season, and that I should be ready for journalists to ask me what my plans were. "There are a lot of teams interested, but if you want to come with me, there'll definitely be a place for you," he promised.

On Sunday, we arrived in Paris with Leblanc taking fifth overall, while Fignon was sixth. Two of our riders in the top 10, plus a certain Danish domestique in 107th place, two hours and eight minutes behind Indurain, wasn't bad.

Following the Tour, Fignon continued to talk to a number of

teams. I just played it cool and didn't let on that in fact a number of teams had also contacted me to ask if I wanted to ride for them. I decided that I'd wait until after the world championships in Stuttgart to make my decision.

Shortly before the world championships, Fignon got in touch to tell me that talks with one of the biggest teams he was in negotiations with had fallen through. "But I'm still in touch with plenty of other teams," he reassured me. His honesty, however, gave rise to some doubt in me. If I put all my trust in him finding a team, I might end up with nothing if he wasn't able to find anything for himself that he was satisfied with. I was pretty certain that he would rather end his career than sign a contract that he wasn't happy with.

At 27 years old, I felt as though it was high time that I took advantage of the fact that I was approaching the age where most riders reach the peak of their fitness and ability. Staying with Fignon would mean missing out on that chance. I'd trained with him specifically for the Stuttgart Worlds, both of us hoping to hit form for the one-day race that took place on a 15.8km-long circuit, which we had to ride 16 laps of – 252.8km in all. Gianni Bugno, Miguel Indurain and Claudio Chiappucci were all named as favourites, as the circuit featured a climb perfect for jumping clear of the bunch. A number of riders tried exactly that during the race, but on the 13th lap there was a split in the peloton, and I found myself in the front group of 34 riders, along with my Danish national squad team-mate Bo Hamburger.

By the 14th lap, I was at the front setting the tempo, and tried several attacks. I was in superb form, and my morale was equally as good thanks to me finding myself in a group alongside the sport's star names. I tried to slip off the front with Fignon multiple times, but Indurain, Bugno and the Dutchman Steven Rooks were not going to let us go anywhere. On the last lap, though, Bugno, Indurain, Rooks and the Colombian rider, Alvaro Mejia, put the hammer down on the climb, while the rest of us could only watch them disappear up the road. They got a gap, and they kept it; Bugno won the sprint to become world champion. My group trailed in 11 seconds down. I'd normally stay well away from a sprint, but this was the world championships, so I wanted to show what I was capable of. I opened up the sprint in our group, but the German, Kai Hundertmarck, came past me in the last few metres for fifth place, while I got sixth. My immediate reaction was one of disappointment, but it soon gave way to pride over the way I'd ridden. I'd shown the teams who were interested in me just what I was capable of.

We took a family holiday after the Worlds, and I waited to hear whether my results in Stuttgart had convinced any of the interested teams enough to want to sign me. I spoke to various people in the days that followed. Rolf Sørensen talked excitedly about how ambitious Ariostea, the Italian team he was on, were. The team leader was Moreno Argentin, but Rolf had a free role on the squad. Fignon rang me, too, to tell me that he was on the brink of signing with a new Italian team, Gatorade. "Do you want to join the team with me?" he asked.

The new world champion, Bugno, was going to be the leader of the new team, which gave me a gut feeling that there could be few chances for me to ever ride for myself. It would be a case of continuing where I'd left off at Castorama – namely, riding in the service of others. The money that Gatorade were offering was good, but I was thinking more about personal growth than financial gain.

"Do you mind if I think about it?" I asked Fignon.

Whether it was Rolf or someone else who put a good word in for me, I'm not sure, but Ariostea team boss Giancarlo Ferretti was soon on the phone to me. "How would you feel about riding for us?" he asked me. We talked about my ambitions, and how my role could fit in with the Italian team's goals. "I've seen you working for Fignon," Ferretti told me, "and you're good."

He went on to say that he thought I made a good stage-race rider, which is something the Italian team was looking for. He added that, with time, I'd be able to ride for myself in the bigger races. After that, things progressed quickly. We arranged to meet at the airport in Milan to go through the details of the contract. Ferretti was known as somewhat of a hard man, but we were able to agree on my salary, which was to be 60,000 kroner per month (£5,700).

Signing the contract with Ariostea meant that my working relationship with Fignon was over, and that hurt on a personal level, too, as he had been such a good teacher and had always treated me well. But I knew that something had to give if I wanted to have a crack at a successful career of my own.

5 THE BREAKTHROUGH

Giancarlo Ferretti was already at the table when we came stumbling down the hotel stairs for breakfast. "Good morning, gentlemen," he said, bright-eyed and bushy-tailed while the rest of us plonked ourselves down on our chairs. He looked like he might already have been onto his fifth espresso. "Let's get started, shall we?" he continued, impatiently, seemingly oblivious to the fact that it had only been a couple of minutes ago that most of us had rolled out of bed. He liked to hold his team meetings at the breakfast table, and it paid to be awake, as he tended to gabble through his strategies, thoughts and team orders without so much as a pause for breath. But there was something special about him. Yes, he talked a lot, and could have quite a temper, but he was also assertive, which gave him the ability to make his riders give everything for him and for the good of the team.

He looked over at me. "Are you going to do something today, Bjarne?" he asked. We both knew that he was trying to provoke me after what I'd said about taking my own chances.

"Hmm," I growled back.

I found the way he'd taunt me extremely irritating. He was looking for some aggression from me.

"Was that a 'yes', Bjarne?" he continued. "Is today the day you're going to show us what you can do?"

"I'll have to wait and see how the race develops," I mumbled back. But it was non-committal answers like that that spurred him on even more.

"You need to be more aggressive, Bjarne. Show more of your temper, Bjarne."

Yes, he was trying to provoke a reaction all right. He was goading me to break out of my "domestique's shell", as he liked to call it. And when he saw his chance to chip away at me, he took it. But his provocation was just his way of trying to convince me that I had potential. He'd worked out that I felt safe in my role as a domestique – that I was uncomfortable when it came to trying to ride for the win myself.

"If you only see yourself as a domestique, then you'll always be a domestique. You're limiting yourself," he'd tell me, which he knew hit all the right buttons.

Joining an Italian team was a bit of a culture shock. Both the teams and the riders were a lot more professional when it came to training and diet compared to what I had been used to. The riders' roles at Ariostea were very clearly defined. It was totally hierarchical: a leader at the top, the other big-name riders below him, and then the "water carriers" at the bottom. As a nation, Italy has always been extremely serious about its cycling. Riders went to bed early, they were careful about what they ate, and their training was clearly structured. And Ariostea were considered one of the best teams of them all. It was well organised, it contained a number of really decent riders and, although Ferretti could sometimes be a bit much, he was a master at motivating his riders to work together, and knew exactly how to approach each race.

The team's star rider was former world champion Moreno Argentin, whose results and experience ensured that he commanded respect. I would need to show him what I could do, both in terms of results and my willingness to work for him, before he would accept me. My fellow Dane, Rolf Sørensen, was another rider who wasn't lacking in self-confidence. He was the team's one-day specialist, expected to get results in the Classics, and so enjoyed star-rider status, too.

As a team, we dominated the first half of the 1992 season. Argentin won the Tour of Sicily, Adriano Baffi won a stage at Paris-Nice, Giorgio Furlan took victory at the Belgian semi-Classic, Flèche Wallonne, and Rolf Sørensen took the overall win at Tirreno-Adriatico. After one of the stages at Tirreno, Argentin came up to me. "Now I understand why Fignon liked having you around," he said, and told me that he wanted me to ride Milan-San Remo with him. We almost pulled it off, too. I rode the whole race for Argentin, but he had to settle for second place on the day.

All the Italian teams had their own doctors, who would double as the teams' coaches. Ariostea had Luigi Cecchini and Michele Ferrari, who would work out our training programmes, which were very specific, and tailored to each rider's strengths. Each training session had a goal; it wasn't just about getting kilometres in your legs. "You need to know what you're trying to get out of each training session," Cecchini would say. "You either need to be concentrating on building muscle strength or working on your fitness. And you need to understand why you're doing what you're doing." This more scientific approach to training intrigued me. The doctors' approach opened up a whole new world for me to try to improve my results. I realised that it was what I'd been missing: a systematic, focused approach. The way it worked was that Ferretti would work out my race programme and then pass it on to the doctors, who would use it to plan my training programme. I soon worked out that the doctors had a huge influence on the team. Their scientific knowledge was also used to help the management choose which riders would ride which races. It took a bit longer to work out how the system worked and which riders were linked more closely to which of the two doctors – Ferrari or Cecchini. I felt that Cecchini seemed to show more of an interest in me as both a person and a rider, and so I found myself gravitating to working more with him.

At the start of May, I was picked as part of the team for the Giro, which, as an Italian team, was our main goal of the season. But with around 50km left to go of the fifth stage there was a huge crash, with a number of riders going down, including me. I hit my head pretty hard, but was quickly back on my feet, looking for my bike – before falling down again, unconscious. The next thing I knew, I was on my bike again, riding, with Ferretti alongside me in the team car. "How are you feeling?" he kept asking me. I was pretty incoherent, but insisted on finishing the stage. Back at the hotel, in bed, feeling groggy, with an icepack on my head, Ferretti told me that I probably had concussion, and that we'd have to wait until the next morning to see whether I'd be able to start the next stage.

I still had a thumping headache the next day, but felt okay to ride. The day's stage was the first in the mountains, which was where we hoped to do well as a team. Roberto Conti was second in the stage for us, while Furlan moved up in the general classification to second place, half a minute down on race leader Miguel Indurain. I battled through the stage to finish 175th, 51 minutes down on the stage winner.

A few days later, I began to feel a lot better again after my crash, which meant that Ferretti thought the time was right to again start heckling me to do something in the race. "So, Bjarne, isn't it time we saw something from you?" he smiled. "We'll soon be out of the mountains again."

What he was trying to tell me was that, if I wanted to win a stage, it was now or never. The provocation worked and, 50km into stage 19 to Verbania, I went off up the road. I was no danger to the overall classification, so no one took me seriously. Besides, with 150km left to ride, attacking alone seemed like suicide. But it showed Ferretti that I was willing to take chances. I gave it everything, flying through the mountains, giving Ariostea plenty of TV time to boot.

My advantage over the rest reached four minutes at one point, and I began to hope that the main contenders would be content to just watch each other rather than try to get me back. But with 30km to go, my time in the spotlight was over, and Indurain, Claudio Chiappucci, Franco Chioccioli and Andy Hampsten came flying past me on the day's toughest climb. I'd shown Ferretti what I was capable of, though, and he was pleased with me when we got back to the hotel that evening.

Our man for the overall, Roberto Conti, eventually finished ninth, while I was 101st, three hours and 38 minutes down on the race winner, Indurain. I hoped I'd done enough to get picked for the Tour de France, but it was during the Tour of Switzerland that Ferretti came to me with the disappointing news that they weren't taking me to the Tour that year.

While my team-mates rode the Tour de France, I concentrated

on training for the world championships, which were to take place in Spain later that year. I also used my free summer to spend more time with a heavily pregnant Mette and two-year-old Jesper.

Mette had been fantastic support during the first half of my season with Ariostea. As a pro, I'd spend two thirds of the year away from home, but even when I was home, I was either out training or had cycling on my mind. I'd train between three and seven hours a day, which meant I was normally quite exhausted once I came back. It was tough trying to be a normal dad. Being a professional sportsman took its toll on my family. Mette accepted what I did for a career, but it was hard for her when I was lost in thought about my next race and wasn't giving her and Jesper enough attention. When I came home from races, I wanted to be able to rest and recover, but Mette wanted me to take part in normal family life to make up for the fact that I'd been away. I felt guilty that I was always away, but equally as guilty that it was so hard to take part in family life when I was home.

Despite how difficult it was, I think we did a good job as Jesper's parents and, while I was away racing in Italy, on 31 August, Mette gave birth to our 3.6kg bundle of joy, Thomas.

"Bjarne, you have two goals for 1993," Ferretti told me. "We want good results from you at both the Giro and the Tour." My whole season was structured around hitting form for those two races, so I sat down with Cecchini and worked out my training programme. But ahead of the Giro, Ferretti had some bad news: Ariostea had decided to stop sponsoring the team at the end of the season. Seeing as my contract also ran out at the end of the season, there was an added incentive to do well at the Giro and the Tour.

Moreno Argentin, who'd ridden for us the year before and was now with the Mecair-Ballan squad, won the first stage of the Giro, and took the pink leader's jersey as a result. The veteran rider certainly showed us that he still had it in him. When we saw each other, he greeted me with a smile. We chatted a bit about the previous year and how things were going now, and that's when he asked me whether I might be interested in riding for a new team that was being set up for the following season.

"That certainly sounds exciting," I replied.

"It's going to be a strong team," he assured me.

"I'm definitely interested," I told him. "Let me know if you want to talk more about it."

We arranged that he'd be in touch once there was something a little more concrete in place.

I spent the first half of the race trying to ride on the offensive and show off the Danish champion's jersey, which I'd won a few months earlier, but Miguel Indurain and his team were particularly strong. I noticed, though, that I was a lot more consistent than I had been before, and was able to follow the lead group when the Spaniard put the hammer down.

At 29 years old, I knew that the next team I rode for needed to be one where I could earn a bit of money in order to set myself up for life after my riding career was over. And so I needed to show what I was capable of at this Giro if I wanted to earn more money.

On stage seven, in Sicily, a 242km stage between Capo d'Orlando and Agrigento, I got away with two Italians, Perini and Coppollilo. We worked well together and quickly built up a good gap. At one point, we were told that we had 10 minutes on the peloton, which meant that, if we could maintain it to the finish, I'd take the pink jersey. I tried to rid myself of my two breakaway companions twice in the last 30km, but they stuck close to me and weren't prepared to let me go anywhere. The gap back to the peloton had been brought right down thanks to Argentin's team working hard to ensure that he held on to his leader's jersey, but we still had enough of a gap to ensure that one of the three of us would take the stage win.

Coming towards the finish, Pirini opened the sprint, but was dying as we neared the line. I nudged ahead of him, and managed to keep Coppollilo behind me, and it was enough to win the stage. I was thrilled, although it did little to lift me up the general classification, as the peloton came across the line just a minute behind us. Ferretti, too, was ecstatic. The team hadn't had too many wins of late, so it came at a very welcome time.

I was also encouraged by the fact that the big Italian newspaper, *La Gazzetta dello Sport*, picked me as one of their riders of the race so far. But rather than being able to impress yet further, a severe stomach ache one night had me struggling for the next couple of stages. Not even a course of antibiotics seemed to help. I also had a fever, but tried to continue regardless. But all the power was gone, and I slipped down the general classification, unable to follow the leaders when the road went upwards. I decided to quit the race after stage 18. I was hopelessly off the pace, and just didn't have any energy left, which was a major disappointment.

In the days leading up to the Tour de France, I came to an agreement on a two-year contract with Mecair-Ballan, which would change its name to Gewiss-Ballan for the following season. The manager, Emmanuele Bombini, promised me that the team was going to be strong, and that he was in a position to pick and choose the riders he wanted. My Ariostea team-mate, Giorgio Furlan, was also going to join the squad, which was continuing with Argentin as its team leader.

At the Tour, the other Danish riders taking part congratulated me on my new deal, and as early as the first stage to Lucon we were flying the flag for Denmark. Brian Holm was the first to try his luck and, when he was caught, my old friend from Herning, Per Pedersen, had a go and stayed away for 120km as part of a breakaway group. When they were pulled back in, with 5km to go, Rolf Sørensen attacked, but he, too, was caught. With just 2km left, I saw my opportunity, and with a good tailwind I quickly got a 100m gap. This was no time to be looking over my shoulder; I just gave it everything I had. I was convinced that I'd done enough to win the stage, and perhaps even take the yellow jersey, but the bunch was absolutely flying, and the sprinters barrelled past me with just 700m to go. It was perhaps a waste of energy on my part, but it at least showed that I had good form. And on a flat stage like that, the sprinters' teams were always going to be aggressive – this was their time to get noticed and win some precious prize money.

In 1993, the overall winner of the Tour de France won 2.3 million kroner (£240,000), second place got 1.1 million (£114,000), while third had to settle for 460,000 kroner (£48,000). Within each team, the money would be divided up in different ways. Some teams put all the prize money together for the whole season, and then divided it up depending on how many days of racing you'd done. At Ariostea, we took each race separately, and prize money was only given to those riders who'd ridden the race. For example, just before the start of the Tour, one of my team-mates, Marco Saligari, had won the 10-day Tour of Switzerland, with its prize money of around half a million kroner (£50,000). Fifteen per cent went to the team staff, which left the rest to be shared out between the riders on the team who had ridden to help Saligari win. A share of the prize money was a good driving force for domestiques – especially on teams like Miguel Indurain's, where some of the less well-known and less well-paid riders could virtually double their salaries if they could guide him to the top step of the podium in Paris.

On the morning of the team time trial, we had a meeting. "We'll just do it as if it was a training ride," someone suggested. Most of my team-mates were only interested in stage wins, and none of them had any ambitions for the general classification. Most of them agreed that it would be good to have an easy day, but not me. Just because the team was stopping at the end of the year didn't mean that we didn't need to be ambitious.

"Let's give it a proper go," I said. "There's no point losing a load of time and slipping down the general classification if it means missing out on publicity and prize money."

A few more riders agreed with me, so we decided to vote on it. The result was that we would race the team time trial at full bore. If there was ever a time for me to show some leadership, it was now. I took much longer turns at the front of the line than the others, and we ended up ninth on the stage, which meant we didn't lose too much time. I was still within striking distance of the big names.

Stage seven took us to Chalons sur Marne – champagne country. There was a special extra prize for the winner of the stage: 100 bottles of expensive champagne. There were more than a few riders who fancied their chances, but after 80km I saw my chance to try and slip away alone. However, I was joined by six other riders, including Max Sciandri, Johan Museeuw and my team-mate Bruno

Cenghialta. We all worked well together, and the signs were good that we'd be able to stay away all the way to the finish. I had also won four of the five "King of the Mountains" climbs along the way, and I could feel that that had taken quite a bit out of me, so I slipped to the back of the small group to try to recover a little.

Heading into the final kilometre, I pretended that I was even more tired than I really was, and made the others think that I wasn't interested in trying to win the stage so that they didn't think they needed to keep an eye on me. With a Tour de France stage at stake, everyone gave it absolutely everything. Unfortunately for him, my team-mate Cenghialta crashed, which actually opened up a bit more space for me in the last few metres. It was close, but I just pipped Sciandri and Museeuw on the line. My stage victory meant that I moved up from fourth overall to third, and even took the polka-dot "King of the Mountains" jersey, becoming the first Dane ever to wear it.

Per Pedersen's team was staying at the same hotel as us, so that evening I met him in the reception.

He cooed over the polka-dot jersey, and was about as impressed with it as I was. "Well, it doesn't look like things have worked out too well for you, eh?" he said with a smile.

"No – it's been awful," I smiled back.

This moment – the stage win, the jersey – was the culmination of the journey we'd started together in 1985, when we set off from Herning in a rusty old dump of a car to begin our adventure in Luxembourg.

The next day I met Fignon in the start village. He seemed pleased for me, and gave me a warm handshake. A few Danish journalists saw us say hello to each other, and asked Fignon what he thought about my stage win and my progress as a rider. "I'm really happy for him," Fignon told them. "He's the most loyal rider I've ever come across. He's never tried to 'steal' anything from anyone, and never tried to trick anyone. Guys like Bjarne are hard to find in this game."

I ended up losing my "King of the Mountains" jersey on the stage, due to having to change a wheel just before one of the summits where there were points on offer. None of my team-mates helped me back into the race, which felt like they were all just looking after themselves, perhaps because the team would be stopping at the end of the year. The plan was also for my team-mates to lead me out for the sprint at the finish, but that never happened, either, and I lost my third place overall, which I wasn't too happy about.

For the time trial the following day, I'd decided to give it everything, and just try to ignore the lactic acid that would come later. Sure enough, the last 10km were hellish, and I was deep into the red, on the brink of blowing up completely. I was frothing at the mouth, trying to use what little energy I had left on keeping the pedals turning. This was the moment to demonstrate that I was capable of turning myself inside out. Right as I crossed the line, my battery was completely empty. I managed to climb off my bike, but needed to use it to support myself and stop myself from collapsing. Exhausted, I slumped over my bike, trying to get my breath back. "How far behind Indurain was I?" was the first thing I managed to ask the throng of journalists.

"Four minutes and 40 seconds," one of them told me, amazed that I was measuring myself against one of the world's best time triallists.

"Okay," I said, still coughing and spitting. Inside I was proud – really proud.

"You finished 12th on the stage, which puts you fifth overall," another of the journalists told me.

I was still up there with the big boys – the superstars – while riders like Pedro Delgado, Claudio Chiappucci and Fignon were further behind me in the general classification.

But the Tour is decided in the mountains, and on stage 10 we hit the Alps. On the road to Serre Chevalier, we had to tackle two big climbs, the worst of which was the "beyond categorisation" Col du Galibier – a mountain considered amongst the toughest there are to climb by bike. After the Galibier, though, it was downhill all the way for almost 30km to the finish. It was a fearsome stage. The favourites soon established themselves at the head of affairs on the first climb, and I was able to hang on to them without any great problem. But at the foot of the Galibier, the Swiss rider Tony Rominger forced the pace, which blew the race apart. Indurain was alert to the danger and gave chase with three other riders, while I just had to stay at my own tempo to ensure I didn't explode.

I finished the stage in 19th place – over seven minutes down on Rominger, who won the stage just ahead of Indurain. In the general classification I dropped down to eighth place, almost 10 minutes behind race leader Indurain. Despite that, doing as well as I did on such a hard mountain stage was a massive victory for me. Ferretti was particularly proud of my effort, but we didn't agree on how we should tackle the following stages in the mountains. "I'm not convinced that you should use up so much energy trying to stay up at the front again," he said. "It's still more important that you try to win another stage rather than finish in the top 20." I, on the other hand, wanted to show I had what it took to ride consistently in the mountains and finish in a good position overall.

Back in Denmark, there had been a lot of interest in the race thanks to a Dane doing well there.

I rang my dad, and he told me that the newspaper *BT* had been to visit him to interview him about his son, who had become "the nation's pet". "They called the article 'The Pre-School Terror'," he laughed down the phone. Dad had told them how Flemming and I were quite strong-willed at nursery school.

"Don't tell them too many bad stories," I laughed back.

"You were frothing at the mouth during the time trial the other day," he reminded me.

"I was giving it everything I had," I replied.

"You always tried that hard when you were a boy, but I haven't seen so much of it since," he laughed, proudly. It was good to speak to Dad and, after the call, I was left in a really good mood.

Stage 11 finished at the Isola 2000 ski resort in the Alps after a 180km-long stage that took in two "category one" climbs followed by two "beyond classification" mountains. It was set to be a frightening day – especially the final climb up all the hairpin bends to Isola 2000. Once again, I felt like I was riding exceptionally well, and I tried to keep something back on the earlier climbs so that I still had something left for the final ascent.

On the penultimate climb – the Bonette Restefond, which is Europe's highest mountain pass at just over 2,800m high – I just climbed at my own pace to stop myself going into the red. With Chiappucci for company, I'd reckoned on taking the descent at the kind of speed I'd never dared to ride at before in the hope of catching the others again. A combination of self-confidence and trust in my own abilities allowed me to push it to the limit, and with our daring descent we managed to rejoin the Rominger and Indurain group, which had crossed the summit two minutes ahead of us.

We rode the first part of the climb up to Isola 2000 as a group, but I couldn't help thinking the whole time how crazy it was that I was able to sit on Rominger and Indurain's wheel. I couldn't get my head around it – it was like a dream. It was the first time that I'd been in the "final" with the big guns, and I was still even in a position to try to beat them. I tried a couple of surprise attacks, but each time I'd get away, they'd bring me back, having decided that I was a threat after all. Into the last kilometre, the others ramped up the pace, and I struggled to match it thanks to cramp in one of my legs. Rominger won the stage ahead of Indurain for the second day in a row, while I trailed in in sixth place, 31 seconds down. It actually still moved me up in the general classification – to fifth place, ten-and-a-half minutes behind Indurain.

As I recovered from my efforts in the finish area, a sad bit of news filtered through from the race: Fignon had quit the race, and I worried that it might signal the end of his impressive career. My thoughts about my former teacher were interrupted by a flock of Danish journalists, eager for an explanation of why I was going so well. Mogens Jacobsen, from the newspaper *Politiken*, was especially pleased for me, having followed my career for many years. "This must feel like a dream, mustn't it?" he asked me.

"It does, but when I'm struggling up another climb, it feels extremely real, believe me," I told him. That evening, Ferretti promised me that everyone would now be riding for me.

Back in Denmark, people were going crazy. The media had even given me a nickname: "The Eagle of Herning". A photographer from one of the Danish weekly magazines asked if he could take a couple of pictures of me in my hotel room, which I agreed to. I shared the room with my team-mate, Andrea Ferrigato, who was thrilled to have a photographer wanting to take some pictures of us. Later that evening I began to have terrible stomach pains, which kept me awake most of the night, and so did Andrea, who was also ill with the same thing.

The lack of sleep caused me to turn up to the first mountain stage in the Pyrenees on Monday 19 July feeling exhausted. I spent most of the 231km-long stage to Andorra struggling. It was like I was "pedalling squares", as cyclists say; I didn't feel good at all. But rather than let panic take over, I tried to stay calm and to ride myself back into the stage. I was still with all the big favourites as we approached the last couple of climbs. I even still had a couple of team-mates with me to help – or so I thought. On one of the climbs, where I was in a bit of trouble, I told them that I was "struggling a little". But a few kilometres later, one of them decided to attack. Luckily none of my closest rivals – Hampsten or Chiappucci – were in any mood to chase my team-mate.

The Colombian Oliverio Rincon was in his element in the mountains and also attacked, but the favourites were again happy to just watch each other. With just 6 or 7km left to go, I knew then that I could probably stay with them all the way to the finish. But Indurain soon forced the pace, and I had to use my last reserves to hold on. "Just hang on," I told myself through gritted teeth, determined not to let the Spaniard get away from me. And in the last couple of kilometres, I actually felt so good that I attacked. This time, Indurain didn't chase me, but Tony Rominger did. No one else came with us, though, so the pair of us rode up the road to duke it out for second place, as Rincon was already assured of the stage win. Rominger took second, but I was happy enough with third on the stage, plus I'd done enough to hold on to my fifth place overall. If I could defend my position all the way to Paris, I'd be writing Danish history, as no other Dane had ever finished in the top five at the Tour before. There had been plenty of interest from the Danish press, but now the foreign media were taking an interest in me, too. "Why is it that you are suddenly so good in the mountains?" one of the journalists asked me.

"I've lost three kilos, and my doctor has been more involved with my training programme," I told him. "I feel like a whole new rider, and am now just lacking a little bit of raw power, which I need for time trialling."

It was partly true.

On the rest day, I signed a contract for the following season with Gewiss-Ballan manager Emanuele Bombini – which had the perfect amount of zeros on it. He called me, and after I went for a gentle ride we met in a side street where I signed the contract. When the Danish journalists heard that I'd signed a contract, they asked if the deal had made me a millionaire. "I wouldn't tell you if it had," I smiled. "But I'm trying to earn money while I can, yes, both to build my house in Luxembourg, and to pay for insurance that will cover me and my family if I have a bad crash." The truth was that Gewiss had offered to pay me over 100,000 kroner (£10,000) a month.

Stage 16 was certainly no picnic. There were five big climbs on the menu in the 230km between Andorra and Saint Lary Soulon. It was freezing, and I shivered in a group of 30 or so riders fighting my own battle with the cold. I'd had to let Rominger and Indurain go, and we were only on the third climb of the day. But my legs were stiff with the cold, and there was nothing I could do. Somehow, we managed to catch the favourites again on the descent, but the only riders I was really watching were Chiappucci and Hampsten, as they were my closest rivals for stealing fifth place away from me. I was particularly concerned about the Italian. He looked like he was ready to attack.

On the final climb, the Pla d'Adet, I was struggling. It had been the hardest stage of the Tour so far. The climbs were particularly tough that day, and I was truly outside my comfort zone and very much on the limit.

Indurain, Rominger and the Polish rider Zenon Jaskula upped the pace, and there was no way I could hold on. More worrying, though, was what Hampsten and Chiappucci were capable of. If I was going to keep that fifth place overall, I couldn't let them get too far ahead of me. The situation was critical. Up ahead, I could see my team-mate, Roberto Conti. "Hey!" I yelled at him, hoping to get some help from him. No reaction. I could feel the anger building in me. The Italian was only thinking of himself. "Hey! Hey!" I shouted again, even louder. Roberto looked behind and saw me. He seemed to be thinking about it – considering whether he should drop back and help me out, or just ride his own race. Slowly, he let himself fall back to me, and looked at me. The Italian had decided to lend a hand. I had a friend in my suffering.

For the last 6 or 7km to the top, I sat tight on Roberto's back wheel, and it saved me. I was only two minutes behind the stage winner, Jaskula, but, most importantly of all, only 44 seconds down on Hampsten, so it was very much a case of damage limitation. "Thank you for your help," I told Conti gratefully.

On stage 17, though, I needed everybody's help. Another two big climbs – the Tourmalet and the Col d'Aubisque – needed to be tackled before the long, flat run-in to the finish in Pau. Chiappucci had decided that he fancied a crack at my fifth place, and on the Aubisque, with 120km still to go, the Italian attacked. On the climb, he and his breakaway companions built up a four-minute lead, which was enough to leapfrog me in the overall classification. None of the other favourites had any interest in chasing Chiappucci, so it was all up to me. On the descent, I looked around me and was pleased to see a number of my team-mates still with me. "We need to catch him!" I shouted to them. My team-mates – Elli, Cassani, Cenghialta, Conti and Järgmann – went to the front and buried themselves over the next 60km to try to pull Chiappucci back. We ate into his advantage, and back in the team car, each time a new time check came in, they were busy working out how much time we could still afford to lose.

With 4km to go, my team-mates had done everything they could, and now it was my turn to take over and try to reduce the gap as much as possible to defend my position. Chiappucci stayed away and won the stage, while I gave it everything all the way to the line, finishing one minute and 17 seconds down on the Italian. It still gave me an almost two-minute buffer to him overall.

The penultimate stage was a time trial over 48km. During a warm-up ride that morning, when I rode some of the route, I felt fast and powerful, and even overtook Indurain at one point. During the stage proper, however, it was a different story. My legs felt heavy, and wouldn't do what I wanted them to. The passion and morale was there, but I had almost no energy left. In the team car following behind me, Ferretti could see that I was in trouble. "Come on, Bjarne!" he yelled at me. The other news was that Chiappucci had set off like lightning, and was eating into my advantage.

I tried to stay relaxed, to find a rhythm and concentrate on my own race. But, suddenly, Rominger came tearing past me. He was a specialist against the clock, and was riding to beat Indurain, but I wasn't sure whether it was him who was riding so well or me that was riding so badly. It would have been pretty bad to lose fifth place overall on the second-to-last day of the Tour. I felt like it was mine, as I'd fought so hard to keep it over the previous two weeks. Ferretti screamed as loud as he could from the car: "Come on, Bjarne! Come on! You can do it!" Those last 10km were a nightmare. I had to just try to block out the pain. My pulse was going crazy and my legs were screaming. Exhausted, I crossed the line and promptly fell off my bike.

"You did it!" I heard someone say. "You're still ahead of Chiappucci by 52 seconds." For some time, I sat on the ground, trying to recover.

"What's it like to have beaten Leif Mortensen's record?" a journalist asked me. Leif Mortensen had been the best-placed Danish rider at the Tour de France with his sixth place overall in 1971.

"I'd never dreamt that I could have done this three weeks ago," I said. "For me, the difference between fifth and sixth place is the same as between first and second."

But I still needed to make doubly sure that I had got my fifth place. As an unwritten rule, the final stage into Paris doesn't change anything in the overall classification, but there are a number of riders who still want to try their luck to get something out of that stage. Even I was hoping I could nab another stage win. It was unthinkable, though, that Chiappucci could make up 52 seconds on a stage like this.

A few riders got away off the front, but at that point I didn't really care who they were or how many of them there were. A little later, though, I told one of my team-mates to go to the front to help bring the breakaway back. When they were caught, I noticed that Rolf Sørensen was among them. When he saw me, he was furious, and made some less-than-nice gestures in my direction. He wasn't pleased that I'd been complicit in bringing him back, albeit unwittingly on my part.

In the sprint for the stage victory on the Champs-Elysées, it was Djamolidine Abdoujaparov – "The Tashkent Terror" from Uzbekistan – who won, while I came across the line in 12th. Miguel Indurain had won his third Tour in a row, with Tony Rominger second, while I held on to that fifth place. The two commentators from Danish television channel TV2, Jørn Mader and Jørgen Leth, stood waiting for me with a bottle of champagne. There was an impatient taxi driver, too, who was going to take me to the airport. TV2 was determined that my performance should be celebrated properly, so they had chartered a private jet to fly me back to Denmark so that I could appear on their sports programme that same evening. I barely had a moment to enjoy the festive atmosphere on the Champs-Elysées – and the feeling of it all being over – before I was being bundled into the taxi and heading to the airport.

On board the plane there was champagne, wine and sandwiches, and, as we headed for Denmark, I tried to take in everything that had happened to me in the past three weeks – and especially the transformation from an unknown domestique to a famous sportsman in Denmark.

Just three hours since getting off my bike in Paris, I was back in Denmark. At the airport, I was greeted by cycling fans, friends from Herning Cycling Club and my dad.

"I'm so proud of you," he told me, with a big grin.

When we arrived at the TV studio, the man who was putting on my microphone congratulated me. "Thanks, but I didn't win," I said, although I was already dreaming about getting onto the podium the following year.

In the weeks that followed, journalists were keen to know what had made my breakthrough possible. "Hard, systematic training combined with weight loss," was my standard reply. But it was only half the truth.

6 EPO IN THE FRIDGE

The boys were playing on the floor in the living room, their toys everywhere. I sat in the middle of the chaos and watched them play. It was spring 1994, and just another day at home in Luxembourg.

I'd already been out training, Mette was busy doing the housework, and I was able to just relax with the boys. It was the moments like these that I enjoyed most. But I knew that at some point I'd need to find somewhere quiet to take care of what I needed to do.

Leaving the boys to their game, I wandered out to the kitchen, opened the fridge and took out a couple of syringes from a plastic bag. Unnoticed, but with the syringes hidden in my hand anyway, I walked back through to the bedroom to be alone. I sat on the bed and opened the packaging of one of the disposable syringes, attached a needle and pulled up the plunger. This one was an insulin injection, like diabetics use. The needle only needs to go in just under the skin – typically in either the stomach or the shoulder. You only feel a small prick, and it's all over in just a matter of seconds.

Suddenly, the door flew open, and in the few hundredths of a second that went by before I could see who was standing in the doorway, I had already gone through all the different explanations and excuses I could think of using if it was the kids. Luckily, it was Mette, who hadn't noticed that I'd come through to the bedroom. Closing the door behind her, she looked at me accusingly. "Is that really necessary?" she asked. It was a discussion we'd had plenty of times before.

"You know it is," I said, finishing off what I needed to do.

Back in the living room with the boys, who were still playing on the carpet, I tried to remember how it was that I'd got to this point – doping in order to win bike races. I was first plunged into a world of syringes and injections in my first year as a professional rider in 1986, and more specifically at the Belgian one-day Classic, Flèche Wallonne. On the morning of the race, I was lying on my bed in the hotel, just relaxing, when one of the team's masseurs threw open the door and was barely inside the room before he was waving a syringe about. "Bjarne, you just need this injection," he said, as though it was the most natural thing in the world, holding up the syringe, which was already ready to go. The masseur's name was Jef D'Hont – a well-known figure who had been in the sport for years. He was a man who knew the game, the routines and all the tricks, and so was a person who commanded a certain amount of respect. It hadn't taken long for me to realise that I had a lot to learn before I'd find my own place and own identity in the cycling world. But what I did already know was that I didn't want to turn over and let a stranger stick a needle in my backside and inject me with goodness-knows-what. It was the first time anyone had ever offered to inject me with anything.

"Sorry – what is it you want me to do?" I asked him, sitting up in bed.

Jef was clearly annoyed – he was busy – and my questions were messing up his schedule.

"What's in the syringe? Tell me," I said.

Clearly insulted, he refused to answer, and made it pretty clear that I should just shut up, turn over, and do as he said. "Don't you trust me?" he asked, coldly.

"I'm not injecting anything without knowing what it is," I replied.

Jef could tell that I'd made up my mind, but he didn't want to lose face – especially not in front of a first-year pro who was giving him attitude. He went mad, storming into the bathroom and pressing down the plunger so that the contents of the syringe went down the sink, before leaving the room without a word. I could be pretty certain that I wouldn't be getting much help or support from him again in a hurry after that. He didn't look like the kind of person who would let getting snubbed like that be forgotten any time soon, either. But it was my body, my health and my career, and if I was going to take any medicines, it was going to be through my own choice, and on my own terms, and something that was properly tried and tested. I certainly wasn't going to let a Belgian masseur force me into it.

But syringes were a normal part of professional cycling life back then, I was to find out. The doctors and soigneurs would often inject us with vitamins to ensure we got everything we needed. During tough stage races, it didn't take long to be severely lacking in all the vitamins and minerals that our bodies required. At that time, those injections were legal and, to a degree, necessary. But I still wasn't comfortable the day that I was told that I needed to learn how to inject myself with vitamins. "It's easy," I was told when I raised my concerns. But in my world it was only doctors or nurses who gave injections, and only then when someone was ill.

"You can do it, Bjarne," I told myself, the first time I was due to do it. I'd been sitting on my hotel bed for ages trying to pluck up the courage to inject the syringe full of vitamins. The syringe felt odd whichever hand I held it in, weighing up which angle of approach to use. I was thinking too much, but it was hard to actually stick a needle into your own backside, and so I gave up. After a bit of a break, I pulled myself together, stuck the needle in my buttock and pressed down the plunger. People say that the first time is the hardest. With the drama over, I was left thinking that it was nothing more than an innocent vitamin injection after all.

There were plenty of stories doing the rounds in the peloton about which riders doped, although it tended to be just whispers, hearsay and rumours. No one would admit what they were up to. There was no need to be obvious about that kind of thing. But in the first few years of my professional career, I had no idea about doping in the peloton and to what extent it went on. You heard people talking about riders who would experiment with different products, but no one seemed to have any concrete knowledge of who these riders were exactly or how they were doing it. After a while, though, I started to pay more attention to the conversations about doping that were going on – about which products people were using, how they were being administered, and who it was that could get hold of them.

The main suppliers appeared to be the teams' soigneurs, as well as the "hangers-on", who always seemed to be connected to different teams, and who had been on the cycling scene forever. A whole new world was about to open itself up to me, showing me a side of cycling that I maybe knew existed, but which I had perhaps subconsciously chosen to ignore. I could immediately tell that it appeared to be an accepted and integral part of the sport. My curiosity was such that I was actually tempted to find out for myself whether any of these medicines could make me a faster rider.

Pretty soon it wasn't a question any more of whether I should try it myself, but when and how. I was still not convinced that doping could make as big a difference as some people were saying it did. But then I decided that just a small improvement would be all you needed to be in the mix at the finish, meaning better results, and in turn making you indispensable to your team. As usual, it was a drawn-out and thoroughly thought-through decision, as all important decisions were for me. In my head, I went through the arguments for and against doping. I reached the decision that I needed to try it before I could either accept or dismiss that it could make me a better rider. "I need to try it," I told myself, already trying to justify my decision, even though deep down I knew perfectly well that it was morally wrong.

A few days later, I approached someone who was known for being able to get hold of doping products. "No problem, Bjarne," he told me, when I told him what I was after. While I was anxious, he was the picture of calm. For him, my request was nothing out of the ordinary.

"These are what you need," he told me, and pulled out a blister pack of 15 tablets. They looked completely harmless. "They're easy to use," he said, matter-of-factly. "You can just keep them in your pocket during a race. Just pop one out and swallow it with some water."

With the pills in my trouser pocket, I hurried back to my hotel. I'd taken the first step, and it was nowhere near as bad I'd worried it would be. Back in my room, I had a proper look at the pills. It was hard to imagine that these small, unexciting-looking tablets could make me a better bike rider. They were cortisone, which relieves pain and makes you stronger.

For my next race, I put a couple of the pills in my jersey pocket. I had a chance of a good result at this particular race, and it was only for races like this that I wanted to use the pills. I let the race develop, and in the meantime reminded myself of the more specific instructions I'd received as to how and when to take the tablets: "If you're there in the mix near the end, take two cortisone pills and a caffeine tablet – it'll give you the power you need to do well at the finish." My first impressions were that, sure enough, the pills did give the desired effect. I definitely felt more powerful, but it wasn't like I was unstoppable or anything.

I was keen to test them out over a longer period to be absolutely sure that it wasn't just some kind of psychological effect at work, thinking that I was faster just because I'd taken something. I tried a number of different types of cortisone: different pills, but also a liquid form, which I injected into a buttock, and drops, which I put under my tongue. But I remained unconvinced. It really didn't seem to make a great deal of difference, and I began to wonder whether I simply wasn't reacting to it. The caffeine pills that I took it with gave me cramp in my legs in one race, too. But my use of cortisone meant that the limit of what I thought was morally okay had moved forward.

At one point, I lived in a hotel room with one of the other riders from my team, who doped. One day, he brought out a big plastic tub full of all sorts of products. There were colourful ampoules, steroids, cortisone and whatever else he was able to get his hands on. He'd sit on his bed and sift through the tub like a little boy with a bowl of sweets, trying to decide which one to tuck into next. "Shall I use this one? No, that's not right for this race. Maybe this one . . ." he'd say to himself, weighing up which product he should choose. I found it hard to believe that it was happening there in front of me. I quietly watched him as he studied each ampoule. It wasn't like he was even offering me anything; he wanted it all for himself. The experience triggered a number of thoughts and questions in me, which I was having more and more frequently: Was this happening in all the other riders' hotel rooms, too? Did all of my competitors have their own tub of doping products that they'd sit and sift through before every race? If that was the case, then it was pretty obvious why there were so many riders riding so much better than me all the time.

While my team-mate arranged his selection from his tub ready for the race, I was lost in my own thoughts. Perhaps the time had come to make a decision as to whether I was going to continue using what I saw as relatively harmless products, or whether I was going to graduate to the kind of stuff that was said to really make you move. Maybe the latter was what I needed if I wanted to commit to being one of the best. As things stood, it was pointless training like a madman if the others were simply getting better results than me thanks to systematic doping. But I needed to be absolutely certain that that was what I wanted. I knew myself well enough to know that when I began a new project, it had to be done properly. I was more convinced than ever of that when I watched what happened to my room-mate in the race. His own carefully put-together combination of doping products made him neither faster nor better than the rest of us.

Before anything else, though, I decided to try a stronger form of cortisone. It appeared to have a more desirable effect on me. Kenacort, as it was called, became my cortisone of choice. I lost a lot of weight and got better power in my legs, all without any side effects. It was in the run-up to the bigger races like the Giro and the Tour that I took it, and at that time it still wasn't on the list of banned substances. Most of the time I'd just buy the ampoules myself at the chemist without a prescription, and sometimes I'd get a soigneur to get hold of it for me. But one day in autumn 1992, a rider I knew took me to one side. "Have you heard of this new stuff called EPO?" he asked me. "It works well. Perhaps you should give it a try." The rumours were that EPO was the new wonder drug, and its use was beginning to be widespread. There was a lot of talk praising its amazing and immediate effect on performance.

I'd always been of the opinion that it was the rider who had trained the most effectively, was best prepared and who was tactic- ally the smartest on the day who won races or did well. But it seemed as though none of that was necessary any more. Now I understood that it was those who had found the right drug who were winning races. It made me suspicious of riders who suddenly seemed to be a lot better than they were before. After a while, it became impossible to tell the difference between a rider who was doped and a rider who had trained hard and hit good form. It wasn't so black and white any more, and I decided that it was okay for me to try EPO too, to see if it worked for me.

Mette, on the other hand, was not happy. She'd got used to me injecting myself with vitamins and minerals, but she was worried about me trying EPO. "That's going too far," she told me.

"But it's something you need to do if you want to do things properly," I said, trying to defend my decision.

"You should be careful. You don't know what's in all this stuff," she warned me.

"I will be," I promised her.

From that point on, Mette only got told what she needed to know about my doping. I protected her from it as best I could by not giving her too many details and by not letting her know to what degree I took it. But I made sure to educate myself about what EPO actually was.

EPO is an abbreviation for the hormone erythropoietin, which is produced by the kidneys and allows the body to form red blood cells. Red blood cells transport oxygen to the muscles, and the more red blood cells you have, the more oxygen the muscles get. Artificial EPO, or synthetic EPO as it's often called, is manufactured to help patients with kidney disease, but when it's used by athletes it helps with their endurance, allowing cyclists, for example, to ride faster for longer before they get tired. More red blood cells for a cyclist, created by the use of synthetic EPO, means that their muscles will get more oxygen – up to 10 per cent more than normal. And if that was the case, then using EPO could take me to the next level.

I bought my first ampoules of EPO from people I knew within cycling. The ampoules were small, and contained just a few millilitres of a clear liquid. I used a small insulin syringe to inject myself with it. But I was extremely careful each time I used it. If you take too much of it, your blood becomes too thick, flows slower around the body, and can give you high blood pressure or even blood clots. My first time experimenting with EPO didn't meet with much success. In fact, it had no effect on me whatsoever.

When I looked closer at what had gone wrong, I realised that I had probably been over-cautious with how much I used, and had not used it regularly enough for it to have enough of an effect on me. More systematic, intelligent, goal-oriented training was needed if I wanted EPO to have more of an effect, so I began to note down when and how much of it I took. If I took it depending on the race calendar and organised my training around when I took it, I could make it work more effectively for me. I saw EPO as simply a tool for helping me to reach my sporting goals – a tool just like my bike, my training or my dieting. At that time, EPO still wasn't illegal because it was so new that it wasn't on the banned list. And there was zero risk of being caught in a doping control as there was no test for it.

During the 1993 Tour de France, the EPO I was taking had begun to take effect, and started to give me the results that people had told me it would. And that was without really even taking that much of it. It was the combination of my weight loss, serious training and systematic EPO use that made all the difference. In other words, it wasn't the EPO alone. Losing weight meant that I simply had less mass to drag up the climbs, and I'd been able to train harder and more specifically to my goals. I was able to ride hard day after day, which had a hugely positive effect on my self-confidence, as did my improved results, and the fact that I was able to follow the world's best riders. My results in that Tour de France demonstrated that I had moved up a level. I felt physically stronger, which meant that I believed in both myself and my strategic decisions during the race. My experiences at that 1993 Tour caused me to decide that I had no reason to stop using EPO, and any thoughts of it being morally wrong got pushed even further from my mind.

EPO use spread through the peloton, and some riders were exploring the possibility of combining its use with other doping products in an effort to improve their performance and steal a march on their rivals. From the outside, it must have looked like an unhealthy development, but for me, right in the middle of it all, it was a development that was difficult not to just run with, especially if I wanted to be able to compete with the best. It was quite extraordinary just how quickly and easily it had become the norm in the world I was working in. It wasn't very long before the rumour was that everyone in the peloton was using EPO.

At one race I was staying at a hotel where someone had a centrifuge, which was used to measure your haematocrit level. Your haematocrit level is the measure of the amount of your blood that is made up of red blood cells. The higher your haematocrit level, the more oxygen can be delivered to your muscles. People's haematocrit levels can vary quite a bit, but for men it would normally be between 40 and 46 per cent. Take EPO, however, and your haematocrit level will rise.

One of my team-mates was there in the room, too. We chatted while I had my haematocrit level measured, which was 47 per cent. That was an okay figure: not too high, but not too low, either. I stuck around to talk some more while he had his measured. It was 60 per cent. I couldn't believe my eyes, but he didn't even blink and carried on chatting as though it was nothing out of the ordinary. I didn't show it, but I was shocked. "What on earth is going on here?" I thought to myself as I left the room.

The figure had given me something to think about. I took EPO in moderation, which would amount to taking two to three courses of it during the season, normally in the run-up to the bigger races. But here was a colleague with a markedly higher haematocrit level compared to me, and I wondered whether that meant that he took much more EPO than I did, or bigger doses, or more courses. And I wondered whether there were many other riders in the peloton who were also riding around with haematocrit levels of 60 per cent. But such speculation was pointless, as you couldn't exactly go around the peloton asking all your colleagues what their haematocrit levels were that day. While many riders assumed that everyone was taking EPO, it wasn't something you talked much about. It was all simply rumour, gut feeling and conjecture. "A thief thinks every man steals," as the Danish proverb goes. That pretty much summed up how I felt.

With Gewiss-Ballan in 1994, my whole season was geared towards the Tour de France. It gave me time to gradually build my form up, lose weight, train properly and try out other doping products that might be able to be used together with EPO. Growth hormone had become popular. It was a product that stimulated muscle growth and improved the body's ability to burn fat. A contact of mine got hold of some for me to try, but I didn't like it. I felt as though it somehow blocked me – that my body and legs weren't functioning properly. Maybe it worked better for other people, but it wasn't right for me.

Still a couple of kilos overweight, but ready to go thanks to a combination of EPO and cortisone, I went to the 1994 Tour as joint team leader with Piotr Ugromov. I tried to deflect expectations of me in the lead-up to the race by playing down my chances, saying that I'd be happy to finish in the top 10.

On stage one, I was already involved in a crash when a load of riders came down with just 25km of the stage left to go. It made for a tough last part of the stage, battling not to lose too much time. By stage five, I was still suffering the after-effects of the accident, and was struggling to breathe properly. The team doctor said that I was suffering from a sinus infection, which I wasn't able to shake off, and I struggled through the next few stages. At one point, I seriously considered quitting the race, which prompted the doctor to give me a course of penicillin in an effort to get me back to health before the race really came alive.

Stage nine was a time trial over 64km, and arguably the most important stage so far. I'd begun to feel quite a bit better by this point, with the infection on the way out of my body, and I took sixth place on the stage. I'd still lost five-and-a-half minutes to the stage winner, Miguel Indurain, however, who had massacred his closest rivals even before we'd got to the mountains. The first mountain stage, to Hautacam in the Pyrenees, was the first real test for me to find out what my form was like. No one was able to follow Indurain and my old team-mate Luc Leblanc on the final climb but, despite a late puncture, I made it to the finish in 15th place.

Following the rest day, the next stage in the Pyrenees almost sent me home. On the Col du Tourmalet – one of the toughest climbs in the Pyrenees – I feared that I was going to blow up completely. The heat had put me in difficulty: I had a stomach ache and couldn't find my rhythm. The spectators at the roadside could tell that I was suffering, and poured water over me, which helped considerably. On the final climb, I hung on to Indurain for as long as I could, but when he upped the pace, I decided to stick to my own tempo to avoid putting myself in any more trouble. By the finish, I'd lost vital minutes, and dropped down the general classification to 18th place.

The next day was a long but flat stage to Albi, and I got into the day's breakaway group which included Johan Museeuw, Erik Breukink and Edwig Van Hooydonck. We had a good gap back to the peloton, but there were still a number of good sprinters in the group, so I really didn't fancy my chances if it came down to a sprint. With about 20km to go, I went on the attack. I wanted to win the stage alone. It was crazy, and perhaps downright foolhardy, but it was the only option to stop myself from being caught by the chasing bunch. A lot of the riders in our group weren't riding strongly enough for us to keep the chasers at bay so, as I felt strong, I decided to take matters into my own hands.

Being away on my own gave me the feeling of being strong and unbeatable. The feelings that I'd had at the previous year's Tour were coming back, and it was what I'd been looking for up until that point in the race. What wasn't there for most of the spring had now come at the right moment. I kept the chasing group behind me, and they were eventually caught by the bunch, while I crossed the finish line pleased as punch as the winner of stage 13. Danish riders dominated the Tour that year. Bo Hamburger had already won a stage, while Rolf Sørensen won the stage the day after I did.

Bad stomach pains were cause for concern on the morning of stage 15 to Carpentras, which would take us over the fearsome Mont Ventoux. I'd actually had stomach problems since my stage win in Albi a couple of days before, and I wasn't the only one. Other riders were suffering the same thing, which made me wonder whether there was some kind of virus going around. As we approached the climb of the Ventoux, I was beginning to feel weaker and weaker. My legs felt empty, and as a result I didn't feel good mentally, either. I felt nauseous and, by the time we started the climb, I was locked in my own battle for survival, all dreams of a good result having gone out of the window. My team-mate, Enrico Zaina, tried his best to help me up the mountain, but I was empty. More than 15 minutes behind the stage winner, Eros Poli, I crossed the finish line in Carpentras absolutely shattered. I dropped further down the general classification as a result, and I was deeply disappointed. I finished the Tour in 14th place overall, more than 33 minutes behind the race winner, Miguel Indurain. It really wasn't the result I'd been hoping for.

★　　★　　★

Around this time, Mette and I were on a plane travelling to Denmark. It should have been a nice, relaxed flight, during which I could have a little nap, or catch up on reading the Danish papers, but instead I sat there tense and irritable, shifting about in my seat, paranoid that all the other passengers were watching my every move. There was no doubt that I was recognised more often since doing so well at the Tour, although that's not what was bothering me. What was bothering me was the contents of my suitcase. I couldn't relax because my luggage contained a course of EPO packed into a miniature cool bag filled with ice and a number of syringes. The ampoules needed to be kept cold so that they didn't go off. The thought of the customs officers going through my things and finding my secret made it impossible to relax. If I got caught with the medicines by customs, both my career and my reputation would be in tatters and the story all over the front pages of the newspapers. As I went through customs after we'd landed, I felt like I was giving off all the signs of someone with a guilty conscience. Instead, all I got was a few nods of recognition, but it was only once we were safely out at the car with our luggage that I felt that I could relax again, albeit with the feeling that this trip had put several years on me.

During the periods that I took courses of EPO, the stuff became part of our everyday life. I'd store the ampoules in the fridge, right next to the mustard, ketchup and gherkins. They were packed securely away so that curious little children's fingers couldn't get hold of Daddy's things. When we had guests round, I'd take the ampoules out of the fridge and hide them in a cooler bag well out of sight.

A course of EPO normally lasted around 20 days, but you could change how much you had per day to suit you. You might take a thousand units each day, or perhaps 4,000 units every third day. How much you needed depended mainly on your weight, and you would start the course well over a month before the race you were targeting. At races, it became quite easy to spot which riders took EPO thanks to the toiletry-bag-sized cooler bag they'd be clutching when they arrived at their hotel. Many of them then quite openly went directly to the hotel bar with it. "May I have some ice cubes for this, please?" they'd ask the bartender, and fill their bags up with them before going up to their rooms. If you were mid-way through a course of EPO at the start of a stage race, you'd need to take your ampoules from hotel to hotel, which meant always having enough ice cubes, which would need refreshing a couple of times a day. The mini bars in the hotel rooms would often be full with ice cubes and ampoules. Personally, I was very careful about what I took, and recorded everything that I did. I had no desire to be careless, and neither did I feel the need to openly advertise what I was taking.

I'd buy the ampoules of EPO either with a prescription at the chemist, or through people I knew who could get hold of it for me through other channels. Because I was getting recognised more often, I didn't dare to actually go into the chemist myself to get my EPO. Instead, I'd ask people that I trusted to get it for me, even if it meant forging a prescription in order for them to buy it. In a few cases it was riders in the peloton who were selling doping products to other riders. My impression was that the teams' management turned a blind eye to what their riders were doing when it came to doping. I suppose that they knew what was happening but just didn't want to know any of the details. How they actually doped varied from rider to rider. On some teams it was organised by the team doctors and the soigneurs, while on other teams it might have been an individual rider who bought the products through his connections.

I was always very cautious about where I got my EPO from. Once, though, I was convinced that it was just water in some of the ampoules I'd bought from someone. As a rule, the lids on the small ampoules were sealed, but on that occasion they weren't. My suspicions seemed well-founded when, after a month of using that batch, there was no change in my haematocrit level at all. During a course of EPO, I'd measure my own haematocrit level using a little transportable centrifuge. All I needed to do was prick my finger and put a couple of drops of blood in the centrifuge, which spun for about five minutes, separating the blood plasma from the red blood cells, and then gave me a reading. As far as I'm aware, the highest haematocrit level I'd ever recorded was 54 per cent. On the days with a high level, my blood would be thicker and darker, although nowhere near as thick as cream or marmalade, as people have said it can be. As a precaution, I'd take aspirin during the periods I was taking EPO, which helped thin the blood and make it less risky.

Every year it cost me between 80,000 (£9,000) and 120,000 kroner (£13,500) to dope myself with EPO. It meant that I could train more – harder and for longer – and that I could recover better afterwards. The harder I could train, the better my form for the races.

Every now and again, there'd be rumours that there was a new and better drug on the way. At one race, I got a massage from a freelance soigneur who had a briefcase with him. It was open in the hotel room, and at one point I glanced over at it and saw that it contained all kinds of ampoules. Some of them even appeared to have the skull and crossbones symbol printed on them, indicating that they contained something toxic. I neither wanted to know nor try what was in those ampoules. I had no desire whatsoever to start experimenting with stuff that hadn't been tried and tested, and which could have all sorts of terrible side effects.

"Maybe you should try Prozac," a colleague suggested to me one day.

"What is it?" I asked.

"It's something that will make you feel more positive," they replied.

Prozac is an antidepressant. It sounded harmless enough, so I got hold of a blister pack of it and gave it a go in my next stage race. The pills made me feel much more positive, which allowed me to see possibilities rather than limitations. This really seemed to help at stage races, which could be very stressful mentally, and where maintaining a positive frame of mind could really help.

At the road race world championships in Sicily in August 1994, I let a group of riders get too far away from the peloton and finished ninth. Those world championships proved that I couldn't win on EPO alone. It was pointless being doped if I was going to be half asleep in the bunch when I should have been trying to read how the race was likely to develop. It required discipline, training and ability to win races. But the decision to continue to use EPO and cortisone through my career was mine alone, and was a choice I'd made having thoroughly thought it through. No one was forcing me to swallow the pills, or holding me down while they injected me with EPO. I was choosing to inject myself, and it was a consequence of me deciding that I needed to dope in order to race at the level I wanted to compete at. It was my responsibility and no one else's. I wasn't proud that doping had become part of my daily routine, but it took many years before I was ready to admit that.

7 STEPPING UP

My ears were screaming, and my head felt like it was going to explode. Gradually, I awoke from my deep sleep in the tiny, claustrophobic room. Disoriented, I looked around in the dark, and that was when the heat hit me like a hammer. Sweat dripped off me as I tried desperately to remember where on earth I was. Feverishly, I pawed at the panel of buttons to make the noise stop.

I was in the cellar in our house in Luxembourg, in the middle of the night, in a specially constructed altitude chamber. It was an elongated tube, like some sort of space capsule, and I'd sometimes be woken up by this horrific noise as the capsule lost pressure and effectively dropped me from 3,000m to sea level in the space of 30 seconds. And, believe me, that really hurts your ears. There was always a noise coming from both the compressor and the fan, but that was something I got used to after a while. If I wanted to get anything out of sleeping in the altitude chamber, I needed to use it for at least 10 days in a row. It would stimulate the growth of red blood cells, in a similar way to the effect of EPO. I'd already talked to Mette about converting our bedroom into an altitude chamber, just like I'd heard other riders had done. The compromise ended up being that I'd buy one and set it up in the cellar instead.

For my whole life I'd been obsessed with technology, and was always on the lookout for the latest piece of equipment or an alternative training method to help improve my performances. Meeting Doctor Luigi Cecchini had only helped bring that side of me out even more. He taught me a lot, and I was like his apprentice. We brought out the best in each other when we were working on developing new or different methods of treatment, training programmes or cycling equipment – anything that could help us to steal a march on the competition.

As a youngster, I'd often spend whole Saturdays taking my bike apart to clean it. Every last piece of it needed to be polished; even the chain got a good going-over with a pipe cleaner. I spent hours out in the garage getting to know every last little detail of my bike. And as I put it all back together again, I'd study and adjust everything I could. Nothing could be left to chance, which resulted in me learning everything there was to learn about bikes – how every component worked and how I could adjust everything to make it perfect. This knowledge came in very useful later on when I turned pro, as I was able to get involved in conversations about what equipment we should use, and could hold my own when it came to talking to the team mechanics about my bike's set-up.

Rumours about my interest in both equipment and alternative treatments got around in the world of cycling, and it turned out there were a number of like-minded people. They had heard that I had an open mind when it came to new methods that could improve my performance, even if it was something that would only help by a few hundredths of a second. The way I saw it was that a few small improvements could add up together to make a big difference.

I'd often have people getting in touch with me – inventors, people who practised alternative medicine and general cycling-mad enthusiasts – trying to offer me their latest product. They were pretty inventive, too, and no one seemed to hold back when it came to different methods and ideas. And I didn't often have the heart to say no when they contacted me, either. Soon, I was notorious for turning up at races with a suitcase full of prototypes of every kind, and I was more than happy to talk any team-mates or room-mates who would listen through the different inventions, training methods or supplements I had brought with me. They'd listen patiently to my lectures on my latest discoveries, and sometimes they even showed a genuine interest. But to actually join me in trying whatever it was I'd brought along always seemed a step too far for them.

My room-mate seemed particularly interested when, following a stage in one race, I carefully rolled out a special mat on my hotel bed. It was covered in loads of little plastic nails which, when pressed down with your thumb, were actually pretty sharp. It was a real fakir's bed of nails – albeit a plastic one. My room-mate said nothing, but wore the kind of expression on his face that said that he thought I was mad. Eventually, he could contain himself no longer.

"Are you really going to sleep on that?" he asked.

"That was the plan," I told him.

"Good luck," he replied, and shook his head.

I explained that an eastern European soigneur had recommended it to me as a form of acupuncture, with the little plastic nails stimulating different zones on my body while I relaxed on it. I'd been told I only needed to use it for 20 minutes at a time to get some benefit from it, and that had convinced me enough to give it a try. Short of having an acupuncturist travelling with me to races, it seemed like the next best thing. And this modern, plastic version was a little more forgiving than a real bed of nails you might see in India. The pressure from the nails was supposed to help free up any blockages and dilate the blood vessels, giving better circulation and increasing the oxygen content in the muscles. It was also said to help the body to remove waste products and release endorphins – the body's natural painkiller. It was exactly what I was looking for as a bike rider.

My room-mate remained unconvinced, though. To him, it still looked like an incredibly uncomfortable and downright painful mat. I'd tried it a couple of times before for the recommended 20-40 minutes, but on this occasion I fell asleep on it.

When I woke up the next morning, having used the mat for just a bit longer than I was supposed to, my room-mate asked me how I was feeling. "Really good, thanks," I replied. "I barely felt a thing." That wasn't entirely true: I was in absolute agony, having had the equivalent of multiple weeks' worth of acupuncture in the space of one night.

In 1995 I was focused on nothing but the Tour de France, and I had been given free rein to base my season around it. I'd worked out that I'd ridden 36,000km during the 1994 season – the equivalent of 15 return trips between Copenhagen and Paris. But this year I was looking to take my year's total up to about 40,000km.

I was banking on my increased training distances and a strict diet to get me down from my normal racing weight of 73kg to 68-69kg by the time the Tour started. My new diet consisted of a breakfast of 50g of muesli or cornflakes with skimmed milk, a piece of fruit or two as a mid-morning snack, 80-120g of rice or pasta with vegetables and tomato sauce for lunch, and then more fruit in the afternoon. Dinner was 150g of lean meat, or 250g of fish, with vegetables or bread. Cake, sugary soft drinks, alcohol, sweets and ice cream were all off limits. Each time I was tempted to eat something I shouldn't, I simply reminded myself of the formula: each extra kilo could mean losing a minute to the top riders over a 10km-long climb. This little reminder to myself kept my hand out of the cookie jar, but it was an extremely strict diet plan, and I did find myself occasionally putting just a little extra pasta on my plate.

While racing, I began to watch my opponents in a different way. I'd try to see whether they were trying to lose weight like me – a sure sign of their intentions later in the season. I'd look at their faces in particular: were they struggling? Their calf muscles, buttocks and thighs also gave away their weight and form. I was always watching: were they battling against extra kilos, or were they heading into form?

As well as dieting, I was taking Herbalife supplements, which had a good effect on my body. A special herbal green tea, in particular, had become a favourite of mine, and something I considered to be my secret weapon. I'd use the tea in a water bottle, and drink it just before the finish of a race. It would give me a quick energy boost, much like taking a caffeine tablet would. Sometimes I also used to take a few spare teabags in my jersey pocket with me to races. Having the tea directly from the bag was a lot easier than trying to mix it up in a bottle of water. I'd take out the teabag, open it up and swallow it down in one. But at one race, I hadn't taken into account how windy it was. Most of one bag ended up in my ears, with very little of it making it to my mouth. The American rider George Hincapie was behind me, witnessing first hand my Gone with the Wind impression. He rode up next to me, and smiled. "What the hell was that, Bjarne? Gun powder?"

"Not far off," I smiled back.

Herbalife became one of my personal sponsors, and paid me a not insignificant amount of money to use their products. When the lorry delivering the products came to our house, they left behind two big pallets full of it: protein powders, vitamins, energy drinks and tea. Mette wasn't exactly thrilled. "Where on earth are we going to store all this?" she asked. I'd been told to expect a delivery that would keep me going for a while, but I had no idea just how generous an amount it was going to be. They ended up going in the garage, which meant that I just had to nip out to get what I needed as I went along.

The spring of 1995 didn't go to plan at all. I trained hard, but always felt quite empty of energy. I also had some kind of stomach flu, which saw me having to sit out some of the early-season races. My stomach felt really swollen, and I felt as though the food I was eating wasn't actually giving me any energy, and was instead just sitting in my stomach filling me up. I saw a number of doctors, but no one could tell me what the problem was. As time ticked by, and I continued to try to trudge through my training programme designed to help me hit form for the Tour, I began to get more and more frustrated. It took its toll at home with Mette and the boys, too, as I whinged and complained. "If things carry on like this, I'm just going to quit," I told Mette one day.

"Fine – you just give up, then," she replied, fed up with having to listen to me.

My directeur sportif, Bombini, had been counting on me riding the Giro, but had to accept that I wasn't going to be in good enough form for it, even if the doctors were able to find out what was wrong with me. "We need to have you examined properly," he said, and sent me to an Italian stomach specialist, where they discovered that I was suffering from helicopter bacteria – a nasty bacterial infection. It was a type of stomach ulcer that had completely knocked me sideways, and which I had possibly had since as long ago as the previous year's Tour, the specialist told me. I was given a course of strong penicillin, and supplemented it with some sessions of acupuncture. I soon felt a lot more energetic, and was hopeful that I could reach good form in time for the Tour after all – which Gewiss were very pleased to hear.

Gewiss, the team's main sponsor, were Italy's largest producer of electrical appliances, with approximately 600 employees, and put around 30 million kroner (£3.4 million) a year into the cycling team. For that kind of investment, they wanted their money's worth in terms of exposure. As a Dane, I was of particular interest to the company. Denmark was one of the countries that Gewiss exported their products to, and if I could get everyone talking about me at home it was going to help them sell more products. The company's marketing department actually kept a scrapbook of clippings from the Danish press about me in order to demonstrate Gewiss's exposure. They expected results from me, and also expected me to make myself available to the Danish press as much as possible. So they were pleased that there was plenty of interest in me back home.

Originally, the only journalist who showed much interest in me was Mogens Jacobsen from the newspaper *Politiken*, who would call me up to hear how things were going. But as the results came, things changed, and journalists from all sorts of magazines started to want to come and interview me at home and get pictures of me and my family. There were a lot of interview requests, and I was also invited to appear on various television shows. But even though I'd started to get used to being interviewed and to being on TV, I really didn't enjoy it. I thought too long about my answers, and fighting against my shyness was a constant battle. I preferred being in situations where I wasn't the centre of attention.

After my good results at the 1993 Tour, people had started to know who I was. "That's Bjarne Riis," someone would shout when I was out and about, and then everyone would turn and stare at me. Other people would talk to me as if we were long-lost friends. I didn't make a conscious effort to hide myself away, but I was happy to try to keep a low profile and just be a part of the crowd when I could. After a couple of days of being in Denmark, it was always nice to go back to Luxembourg or Italy where no one recognised me on the street.

The Gewiss team headed to the 1995 Tour de France under a cloud of uncertainty: no one knew whether the sponsor was going to continue with the team for the following season. We'd also lost one of our best riders, the Latvian Piotr Ugrumov, who had finished second at the 1994 Tour but had injured his ribs after a crash at the Tour of Switzerland. It meant that Bombini was left unsure as to who the leader was for the Tour. He eventually named Evgeni Berzin as the team's best hope for the overall classification, although I disagreed. I felt that I was in much better form than the Russian.

At the final medical test before the start of the race, the photographers were falling over themselves to get a picture of me and Berzin together. The Russian sat bare-chested on a treatment table, while I stood with a stethoscope pretending to examine him. He clearly didn't like this little set-up, and looked at me while I smiled for the cameras. Apparently, Bombini had told the press that Gewiss were actually there with three team captains – Berzin, me and the Italian Ivan Gotti – but that Berzin was the priority. I had a problem with this, and wasn't afraid to tell the journalists. Berzin was nowhere near to being a threat to Miguel Indurain, while I was in top form, having just won the Danish national championships the week before the Tour. I'd decided that I needed to be a lot more selfish than I had been, and would take more risks and be more aggressive, too. I'd had enough of playing it safe.

In the build-up to the Tour, I'd worked hard on trying to increase my anaerobic threshold – the amount of time I could ride at a high speed before reaching the point where my legs would get heavy due to lactic acid. The longer I could ride at my threshold without blowing up, the stronger I'd be, and the longer I'd be able to keep a high tempo in the mountains. My training had brought me to the race in fantastic form, and so I'd thought that Bombini would have backed me as the team's leader. But with Berzin leading the team, I was going to make damn sure that I wasn't going to be riding for him, even though he'd asked for the team's full support.

In the days leading up to the race, I spent a lot of my time talking to the team mechanics. My enthusiasm must have driven them crazy. They were happy to do what I asked of them, but their own experience told them that me asking them to put even more air in the tyres went against conventional wisdom. "Now, are you sure this is a good idea, Bjarne?" the mechanic asked me.

"I need the tyres pumped up so that they're rock hard and right on their limit, yes," I insisted.

"It's your choice, but it's a big risk to have them pumped up quite that hard," he offered.

Now he'd ensured that the responsibility lay with me if my tyres caused me to puncture, crash on some gravel or have a sore back after the race due to my bike being too stiff.

"It'll be incredibly uncomfortable to ride when the tyres are pumped up so hard," the mechanic told me.

"Forget comfort," I said.

It was almost a religious topic in cycling, comfort. But, for me, comfort didn't come into it when it came to tyres; I rode best on tyres that were tight as a drum. Tyre pressure is an extremely important consideration in cycling. The higher the tyre pressure, the better they roll.

Some mechanics were actually pleased that I showed an interest in my equipment and the way my bike was set up for a race. They weren't used to riders occupying themselves with tyre pressures, how much a screw was tightened, a precise-to-the-millimetre setting-up of a saddle or checking the gears. The smarter mechanics took advantage of my interest in their work to work together and develop ways to improve our performances. Others just thought I was mad for being so fixated on the details, and that I was simply a nuisance to them and their work. My opinion was that it was a joint effort to get the bike ready for a race so that I could perform to the best of my ability, which in turn brought success to the team, and ensured there was a team for everyone to work on.

Lying on my hotel bed on Tuesday 4 July, I yet again studied the list of participants. The Tour was already under way, but that afternoon was the team time trial, which we were one of the favourites for. Of the other podium candidates – Alex Zülle, Laurent Jalabert, Miguel Indurain and Tony Rominger – none had a team strong enough to match our Gewiss squad. If we could all work together, and if everyone gave it everything, then we'd win the stage. And everyone was going for it when we set off on the 67km route to Alencon. We were flying, and it felt like we were one, smooth unit. Everyone was taking their turn, riding with the will to win. "You're riding brilliantly," Bombini shouted from the team car behind us. "Come on!"

The intermediate times looked good: we were faster than ONCE, who had Jalabert in the yellow jersey, and were faster than Indurain's Banesto team. If we could beat ONCE by more than 45 seconds, we'd take the yellow jersey for Gotti. The clock stops on the fifth man in a Tour team time trial, which means that you can afford to lose four riders from your nine-man squad along the way. At the speed we were going, there were a few team-mates who were struggling to stay with us, but they were managing to hang on. We were riding at an average speed of 55km/h. "This is unbelievable!" the French TV commentators were screaming. The other teams were certainly going to have to ride insanely quickly to beat us. Frothing at the mouth, I came across the line with my team-mates to take the stage victory. We'd done a fabulous ride, beating ONCE by 35 seconds and Banesto by 59 seconds. It wasn't quite enough to get us the yellow jersey, but I moved up to third overall, just nine seconds behind Jalabert. There have been few better performances in team time trials than ours that day, and we were dubbed "the blue tornado" thanks to our blue skinsuits. My team-mate Ivan Gotti was now in second place, but few journalists knew who he was.

"I don't know him too well yet either," I told them, "but I know that he's a climber." I may have come across as slightly arrogant, but I wasn't too interested in Gotti. I was thinking about the yellow jersey myself.

"What did you have for breakfast that you can beat Indurain's team by almost a minute?" a French journalist from RTL asked.

It was meant as a perfectly innocent, just-for-fun question, but that wasn't how I took it. I heard it as an accusatory question about doping. "What kind of idiotic question is that?" I answered angrily, and gave him the kind of stare that would put an end to questions like that.

The next day, Gotti did take the yellow jersey, and led the race for the following couple of days, with me just a second behind him. Even though it was my dream to wear the yellow jersey, I had to remain loyal to my team-mate and help protect his position. The sixth stage was pretty uneventful until the closing few kilometres, where it became a real fight for position at full speed, with elbows and pushing and shoving. I got involved right up at the front, with Indurain just in front of me. I watched him try to close a gap in front, so I made sure I went with him. Behind me, I knew that we'd made a bit of a gap ourselves, but I was concentrating on staying in the mix. German sprinter Erik Zabel won the stage, and I finished 13th.

After the finish line, the Danish journalists swarmed around me. "I'm tired of using up so much energy on thinking about the yellow jersey – whether I'll be able to get it or whether I'll continue to help Gotti defend it," I told them, and headed off to the team bus to get changed. It surprised me that the few seconds' gap behind me back to the others hadn't changed anything much in the overall classification.

I'd just started to get dressed when there was a knock on the bus door. It was two Tour officials. "You need to come to the podium," they told me. "You're in yellow." I quickly finished getting dressed and followed them to the podium.

Finally, I'd done it. Climbing the steps up to the podium was indescribable. This was what I'd dreamt of. Nine years after my professional debut, and six years after I'd first ridden the Tour, I'd done it. I enjoyed every minute of it as they presented me with the yellow jersey, handed me the sponsor's toy lion, the podium girls kissed me on the cheek and the crowd cheered. Now I'd join Kim Andersen, Jørgen V Pedersen and Rolf Sørensen in the history books as Danes who had worn the yellow jersey. Pleased as punch, I proudly waved to the spectators as the Danish fans there sang my name. It was then off for handshakes with Eddy Merckx and King Albert II of Belgium.

After the protocol, a group of journalists asked me how I felt about having taken the yellow jersey from a team-mate. "It's a shame for Gotti, of course," I told them, "but we're also pleased to have kept it on the team. It wasn't my fault that that gap opened up at the finish, so I couldn't help taking the jersey." It meant that I'd wear the jersey for stage seven, when Mette and the boys were due to come and visit me on the race. Mette had played a huge part in me getting to wear the yellow jersey, standing by me when I'd been a nightmare to be with due to my stomach infection.

That night at the hotel, I stared at my yellow jersey and tried to imagine what it could mean for me financially. My contract with Gewiss ran out at the end of the year, and we'd arranged to renegotiate it in the next couple of weeks. Other teams had shown interest, too, and I'd already talked to a number of them. Having worn the yellow jersey meant that I'd be able to ask for a substantial amount more money, and I'd decided to make the most of it. This next contract, whoever it was with, was going to give me some real financial stability. I knew that I was likely to lose the jersey again in the coming days, but that didn't really matter. I now felt as though I'd deserved to experience the feeling of leading the world's biggest and best bike race.

The next morning, it was thrilling to come to the stage start wearing the yellow jersey. Everyone wanted a piece of me, and the Tour "speaker", Daniel Mangeas, interviewed me in front of the crowd at the start. "This feels like a dream," I told him, as in all honesty that's exactly what it felt like. Laurent Fignon turned up with his wife, too, to say hello and congratulate me, with a hint of pride, I like to think.

Once we were under way, Laurent Jalabert rode up alongside me, and we had our photograph taken together. The Frenchman smiled at me, and I later understood why: he was hoping to take the yellow jersey for himself. Jalabert and his ONCE squad did everything to try and take the bonus seconds available at each intermediate sprint. I got no help from my team-mates, however, and unsuccessfully had to try to defend my jersey on my own.

Twenty-five kilometres from the finish, Indurain attacked and took Johan Bruyneel with him. The two of them built up a good lead, and Bruyneel won the stage and took the yellow jersey. I was furious at my team-mates who had left me to my own devices, and so had contributed to me only getting to spend one day in yellow.

My mood soon improved when Mette turned up in the finish area in Liège, though.

"I'm proud of you, darling," she told me, and gave me a hug. There was nothing better than when my family could help me to get over my disappointment.

On the morning of the next day's stage – an individual time trial – I looked over my TT bike again to check that the mechanics had set everything up properly. In my head, I was already thinking about how I could beat Miguel Indurain. The Spaniard was undoubtedly the best in the world against the clock, and had thrashed all his rivals in the Tour's time trials for the past four years. Such dominance ensured that he had such a buffer at the top of the general classification that no one was able to make the time back on him in the mountains, where he was pretty useful himself, too. The 54km between Huy and Searing would be key to helping to decide the race later on, and I was only too aware of this as I headed off on my ride.

The first time check – bellowed at me by Bombini from the team car following behind me – had me as the third best time so far. I felt like I was riding well – really well – and that I still had more to give. I was completely "in the zone", oblivious to what was going on around me. It hurt, but that didn't matter, and I concentrated on trying to give it everything. Indurain had started behind me, so I expected him to come flying past me at any moment, but it began to irritate me that Bombini wasn't shouting any useful information at me. Yes, I was getting my own time splits, but what I really wanted to know was how I was doing compared to Indurain. Seeing as that information wasn't forthcoming, I decided to knuckle down and get on with it. If I allowed myself to get too irritated about not getting the info I wanted, then it might start affecting my concentration.

With 15km to go, I began to really go for it, almost certain that Indurain must be right behind me. At the feed zone, I missed my water bottle, as the soigneur who was trying to give it to me had just taken it out of a cooler box, so it was soaking wet and slipped through my fingers when I tried to grab it. Out of the corner of my eye, I also saw one of Indurain's Banesto team helpers, which made me think that the Spaniard must be right on me. When I looked back, I could see what I thought were some cars not too far in the distance. He was coming all right – I was convinced. But I was still going well, and caught and passed the Spanish rider Melchior Mauri who had started ahead of me, which gave me even more of a boost.

With 5km to go, I was really beginning to feel my efforts. My morale began to drop a little, and again I felt as though Indurain must be almost on top of me. A look back revealed that the cars I'd seen before were even closer. I didn't want to let him catch me, though, so again I knuckled down to trying to empty myself in the last part of the stage. I frothed at the mouth, my lungs were screaming for more air and my legs were heavy with lactic acid. I was going into the red, but was not going to stop until I crossed that line.

When it finally came, I almost collapsed off my bike, but ended up slumped against a crowd barrier. "What was my time?" I shouted above the noise of my heaving lungs and short breath.

One hour, four minutes and 28 seconds.

"Water," I gasped at my soigneur, exhausted. I was completely dehydrated having done the whole last section without a drink. What I really craved was an energy drink to help try to repair the damage I'd done to myself. Every single muscle in my body hurt.

"You were second, Bjarne," someone said. Indurain had won.

"How much did he win by?" I asked.

"Twelve seconds," came back the reply.

"What did you say?"

I was shocked. I couldn't believe it. Just 12 seconds behind Indurain. Then a number of people told me that with 5km to go I'd actually been beating him by five seconds.

"Why the hell didn't anyone tell me that?" I asked.

There were all sorts of excuses: the radio didn't work properly, there was too much noise from the crowd . . .

Never in my wildest dreams had I dared to hope that I could beat Indurain, but I knew that on a good day I may be able to finish second to him. But had I known that I was leading by five seconds with 5km to go I would have found something extra from somewhere and would have made damn sure that I'd beaten him. Just being told that I was winning would have given me the extra impetus I needed to sprint the rest of the way to the finish. Instead, I'd spent most of my time waiting for him to come past me. It turned out that the cars I'd seen in the distance before hadn't been anything to do with Indurain – they'd been press cars, attracted by my good performance. "What the hell happened?" I angrily asked Bombini. It had been the first time in years that anyone had got anywhere close to beating Indurain in a time trial. "I'd expected more support," I fumed.

Sensing that they might be able to get some good headlines out of this, the Danish media surrounded me. "I'm happy to have been able to show what good form I've got, which must mean that I'm now the rider the team will ride for," I told them. "They need to ride for me in the mountains now – the team directors need to recognise that." I was now second overall, just 26 seconds down on Indurain.

The next day was a rest day, and Bombini had to make the decision as to who the team was going to ride for. But he didn't want to choose between Berzin and me, and so made us co-captains. On the first mountain stage the following day, the plan had already fallen to pieces. I stuck close to Indurain, although Alex Zülle broke away on his own. My legs were feeling heavy after the time trial, and it took everything I had to hold Indurain's wheel. I was worried that he could tell I was having a bad day. Berzin, though, was having an even worse day, and had to let us go, proving that I'd been right: his form wasn't good enough for the mountains.

Indurain continued to turn the screw, and it was killing me trying to stay with him. Eventually, I had to let him go. It was better to shift to a lower gear and try to stay calm in the hope that I'd feel better again than to panic and risk losing everything.

Zülle won the stage, while I hobbled home, exhausted, in 18th place, seven-and-a-half minutes after the Swiss. My soigneur had to hold me up after I'd crossed the line. "What about Indurain?" I mumbled.

"He came in five-and-a-half minutes ahead of you," he told me.

It hadn't been a great day. Zülle had leapfrogged me to second place overall, but I was still third. Indurain remained untouchable in first place. I had no excuses. I simply wasn't strong enough on the day.

On 12 July, we attacked one of cycling's most famed climbs – Alpe d'Huez – with its 21 hairpin bends that led up to the ski resort at the top. It was a costly stage for Gewiss, as Berzin finished the stage sitting silently beside Bombini in the team car. The Russian's race was over. I stuck close to Indurain and Zülle all the way up the climb, while ahead of us a group had gone clear, which contained the little Italian climber Marco Pantani. On every single hairpin bend were huge groups of supporters with Danish flags, cheering me on. It gave me the extra motivation I needed to hang on to Indurain, who was setting an uncomfortable tempo on the climb, which had already dropped some of my closest rivals, such as Laurent Jalabert, Tony Rominger and Richard Virenque. At one point, I tried to attack, but Indurain patiently reeled me back in, so after that I was just happy to stay with him to the top and retain my third place overall. "I hope to finish on the podium in Paris," I told the gathered journalists.

The 15th stage to Cauterets took us over the legendary Tourmalet in the Pyrenees. Frenchman Richard Virenque went away in an early break, but I was more interested in watching Indurain, Zülle and Jalabert. I tried multiple times to try to get away from them on the Tourmalet, but each time they brought me back. On the final climb, I attacked again, and this time it stuck. I crossed the line in fifth place, having put two minutes into Jalabert – my closest rival for third place in the general classification.

"I really took the race to them today," I snorted, proudly, at the finish. But I couldn't help noticing that everyone seemed a bit upset, as though something had happened.

"Casartelli's dead," someone said. "He crashed on one of the descents and hit his head on the road. He died in hospital." It was tragic. Fabio Casartelli was just 25, and was a former team-mate of mine at Ariostea. I knew him as someone who was happy and carefree, and now he was dead. I struggled to hold the tears back. I suddenly felt physically awful.

"What's your reaction to what's happened?" a journalist asked me.

"I can't even think about it," I replied. Casartelli was married and had a four-month-old son.

"I don't want to say any more," I said, and refused to answer any more questions.

At the hotel, I learned more about the awful accident. Casartelli had crashed along with five other riders on the descent of the Col de Portet d'Aspet while going 80-90km/h. He'd hit his head on a concrete block at the edge of the road and suffered multiple fractures of his skull. He was flown to hospital by helicopter, but there was nothing they could do to save him. Just like the rest of us, Casartelli hadn't been wearing a helmet.

The bunch was united by grief the next morning. Casartelli's team, Motorola, had chosen to stay in the race. Between us, we discussed whether the day's stage should be ridden in memory of the Italian. A lot of the teams wanted for us to show our sympathy and solidarity to Casartelli's family by riding the stage neutralised, and not as a race. Personally, I was torn. I really felt for the Italian's family, friends and team-mates, and was devastated about what had happened to him. But at the same time, Motorola had decided to continue in the race, which meant that we should probably ride the stage as though it was any other.

From a sporting perspective, it was my last chance to try to overhaul Zülle for second place. The stage was to take us over a climb that was even tougher than the Tourmalet, where I'd planned to attack the Swiss rider. But the stage got under way and, after a few kilometres, the decision got round that the stage was neutralised, and that no one would be racing. Who it was that made that decision, I don't know, but of course I was in agreement. In a situation like that, the peloton acts as one, and I would never have dreamt of going against it. But while we rolled silently on, I thought about my missed opportunities. I couldn't understand why we were riding the whole stage. This was a symbolic gesture, so why were we riding for the whole day through the mountains?

The Motorola riders rode across the finish line side-by-side in honour of Casartelli. Afterwards, the press asked me what I thought about riding the stage in memory of the Italian. "I think that it would have been best for everyone if we'd either raced the stage properly over the full distance, or just ridden slowly for 100km," I said. "I think a lot of the other riders think the same thing, but someone had clearly made the decision beforehand how the stage was going to be ridden." There were others who thought it was a beautiful stage and the right thing to do, but everyone was entitled to their opinion, and I was sticking with mine.

The Tour's penultimate stage was a time trial over 46km, where I again rode strongly to finish second to Indurain. My third place overall – and a podium place in Paris – was assured.

The last stage to the French capital's Champs-Elysées tended to finish as a bunch sprint, but I fancied giving it a go myself. I kept myself near the front of the bunch, and ordered my team-mates to the front with a couple of laps of the finishing circuit to go. But the sprinters' teams were never going to let us have it our way, and the sprint was won by "The Tashkent Terror", Uzbekistan's Djamolidine Abdoujaparov. I rolled across the line with a lump in my throat. There were Danish fans everywhere.

I found Mette, who was hiding behind a pair of sunglasses. We gave each other a big kiss, and I could tell that there were some tears behind the glasses. A couple of officials found me to tell me that it was time to go to the podium. Suddenly, Bombini appeared beside me clutching a Gewiss jersey. "Do you think you might be able to put this on?" he asked me. I was already in my Danish champion's jersey, but I knew Bombini was still fighting to convince the team's sponsors to stay on board to assure the team's survival.

"Okay," I smiled.

As I stepped up onto the podium with Indurain and Zülle, I was brimming with pride and happiness. We waved to the crowd, and I could clearly hear the Danish fans cheering for me. The Spanish national anthem boomed out of the loudspeakers, and it made me realise just what an achievement my result was after three weeks of hard work. I remember thinking what a special moment this was as I waved at the people waving their Danish flags. Over the loudspeakers, the race announcer was telling the crowd that I was the first Dane to have ever stood on the Tour podium.

Indurain asked us to stand up on the top step with him for some photos, and we took the opportunity to congratulate each other on a great race. On the way down from the podium, an elderly Spanish man embraced me and congratulated me. This man in a slightly crumpled suit also gave Mette a hug. "That's Indurain's dad," said Mette.

Danish television channel TV2 stood ready to interview me. "What are your goals now going forward?" came the question.

"The next step, of course," I smiled. The next step up – or, rather, the next two steps up, to the top of the podium.

My team-mates and I congratulated each other. We'd done well – financially, too: third place had secured the team almost a million kroner (£112,000), which, in keeping with tradition, would be shared among the riders and team staff.

Next, I took part in the Tour of Denmark during the first week of August. It was a real lap of honour, as thousands of spectators lined the route, cheering my name as I raced past. The organisers estimated that there had in fact been a total of a million people on the roadside that week – which isn't bad for a nation of just five-and-a-half million people. It was overwhelming to have so many fans cheering me on. I won the race, which was celebrated by tens of thousands of people at the finish in Copenhagen.

My future still hadn't been decided, but there were a number of offers lined up. Cyrille Guimard – my old directeur sportif at Castorama – had been chasing me to try to get me to join his new team, Indurain's Banesto squad had shown interest and Deutsche Telekom, who Brian Holm rode for, had made me an offer. And Gewiss were keen to retain my services, too. But the most serious offer of all had come from former French pro Marc Madiot, who was setting up a new team called Française des Jeux. They were offering big money, on a two-year contract. Madiot was trying to attract both me and Rolf Sørensen: me for the Tour de France, and Rolf for the Classics. We met up to talk things through over dinner at the Eiffel Tower, and more or less came to an agreement.

With my future all but secured, I headed to the Tour of Spain with the intention of winning the race. However, it wasn't long before good old French politics managed to get in the way, and both my contract and the setting-up of the team for 1996 fell through. The frustration of having to start contract negotiations all over again helped me focus even more clearly on trying to win the Vuelta.

Stage seven was a 41km time trial. I was already well-placed in the general classification, and my decent TT results at the Tour made me one of the favourites for the stage win. I was on a specially built time trial bike, too, and soon found a good rhythm. I felt as good as I had done during the Tour de France. But with 1.5km to go, approaching a small roundabout, I hit a hole in the road, which caused my front tyre to blow up. I was out of control, and smashed into a crowd barrier, back first. As I fell to the floor, I actually had flashbacks of my life so far, all in the space of a hundredth of a second. I could taste blood in my mouth as I groggily got back on my feet, and a mechanic stood ready with a new bike and helped me onto it. The pain in my chest and my back was killing me. I have no idea how I made it to the finish, but I collapsed soon after crossing the line, and was helped into the shade of a tree. I found it difficult to breathe, I had a banging headache, and blood was dripping from my various injuries. When I'd crashed, I'd had the best time checks, and was on my way to winning the stage. I was helped over to the ambulance, where the race doctor took a look at me. "It's hard to say how bad it is," he said, although he could tell that I'd done some damage to my ribs. I returned to the hotel, feeling beaten up and in pain, but was able to start the following day.

I went through the next day in immense pain, but that night Manolo Saiz – the manager of the Spanish team ONCE, who were staying in the same hotel – pulled me to one side. "We've got someone who may be able to have a look at your back for you," Saiz told me. That person was a practitioner of alternative medicine, who the Spanish team always had with them during races. He was blind "but effective" Saiz said. The man felt my back, and finished by giving it a twist.

"Jesus!" I yelled. It had made it even worse, and I filled the air with the kinds of words that made it quite clear that I wished Saiz had never recommended this guy.

After yet another painful stage, our own team doctor had had enough. "We need to get you X-rayed," he said.

We had some X-rays done at the nearest hospital, but the results didn't show anything in particular.

"This doesn't make sense," I said. "There's definitely something wrong."

A 3D scan eventually brought some clarity.

"You've ridden for two days with a broken vertebra," the doctor told me.

And that was that. I left the race, and my dream of winning the Vuelta left with me. It was about the worst news possible to be given right in the middle of contract negotiations with a number of interested teams. And on top of that, there was an important

Six-Day track race that a number of people were counting on me being at – in just a month's time. "Perhaps John Boel can perform a miracle," Mette suggested. John Boel was an acupuncturist who Mette's parents had introduced me to. He had his own acupuncture clinic in the little town of Aulum in Jutland in western Denmark. I was hoping that the alternative treatment might be able to help me get back on my bike in time for the Six-Day.

"I'll come down to see you in Luxembourg, and we'll see what I can do," John told me over the phone after I'd explained my injury to him. And the next day, there he was, together with his wife, Bodil, and a bunch of acupuncture needles ready to go.

I had two sessions of acupuncture a day for half an hour at a time while lying on a treatment table. John put needles in my legs and my neck: the legs to relieve pain and remove the build-up of liquid around the fracture, while the ones in my neck were to accelerate the healing process. And it really worked. After just three days' treatment I was feeling well enough to ride on my home trainer. We decided that I'd travel back to Denmark with the Boels so that I could continue to get daily treatment in the run-up to hopefully doing the Six-Day. Back at the clinic, we supplemented the acupuncture with a treatment of Chinese herbal medicine, as well as some swimming so that I could maintain some muscle strength and endurance without putting my body under so much strain.

After a week's bombardment of needles, herbal medicine and swimming, I was ready to get back out on my bike. I was ready for the Six-Day, too: I won it, and then was ready to negotiate a contract, injury-free, for the coming season with the interested teams. One thing was already certain, though: John Boel was coming with me to the 1996 Tour de France to help give me that little extra something that was needed to try to win the race. He had a toolbox that contained all the right tools to help improve my performance.

With the sheer volume of training I was doing, often out in the cold and wet, plus the stress of dieting, I was – like all pros – susceptible to the colds, flu and small infections that can often cost a good couple of weeks' hard training. Whenever I felt like I was about to come down with something, or I'd had a period of hard training, either John would come to visit or I'd fly to see him for a session of acupuncture. A season with or without illness could mean the difference between success and failure, and John had a few jokers to pull out to help things in the right direction. Before one race he purposefully sought out an area just below my knee where he placed a couple of needles. My reaction to it was almost instantaneous: it gave me a real boost of energy. "That's the 'three-mile point'," John explained. In China, the story goes that acupuncture in that part of the body gives you a new source of energy, and will allow you to go another three miles beyond the point where you would otherwise have given up. It wasn't something I wanted to do too often, as apparently it would lose its effect, so we decided that the three-mile point would only be "activated" for big races and before important stages. It would be one of my secret weapons for the Tour.

My colleagues in cycling would have called such treatment superstition, witchcraft or hocus pocus, but the three-mile point and the mat of plastic nails could perhaps make the crucial difference between me and those competitors who stuck to more conservative methods.

The contract negotiations began to fall into place, with the German team, Telekom, coming to the table with a good offer for the coming season. I met with the team owner and manager, the Belgian Walter Godefroot, who commanded a lot of respect in cycling circles. He seemed very keen to work with me. "I have three requirements," I told him. "I want the team to work for me, and me alone, in order to try to win the Tour de France. Secondly, my whole season needs to be organised around the Tour. And lastly, the best equipment and know-how needs to be made available to us," I concluded, and sat back in my chair. He didn't flinch – not even when I added my financial demands.

Telekom was one of the smaller top-level pro teams, and had taken part in the 1995 Tour as part of a composite team with Italian squad ZG Mobili. But I thought that there was real potential in the team. They had everything to play for, as there was a risk that the 1996 season could be their last if they couldn't get some better results in the bag. My gut feeling was that it was a team hungry for success, and when they said that they could meet my demands, I signed with them.

With a contract in place, I was looking forward to a bit of quiet time at home with Mette and the kids in Luxembourg, when suddenly the phone rang. "It's Jens from *Berlingske Tidende*," came the journalist's voice on the other end.

"What is it?" I asked.

After a long conversation, I put the phone down. "What was that about then?" asked Mette.

"I've just been voted Dane of the Year," I smiled.

8 VICTORY

New Year's Day, 1996. Bottles from the previous evening's festivities with our friends stood on the table still at our summerhouse in Søndervig. The kids were already up, of course, followed soon after by one of our guests, and one of my best friends, Georg Sørensen, who wandered around the house, looking for something. "Where's Bjarne?" he eventually asked the boys.

"Out training," they told him.

"Surely not in this weather," Georg said, looking out from the lounge window at the half-metre deep snowdrifts idyllically setting a winter scene in the countryside surrounding the house – making it impossible to ride. But there were other ways to train.

Like Rocky Balboa I was out there running in the snow. While doing so, I had flashbacks to my childhood, when I used to run in the snow to the gym in order to make my workout as hard as possible. Running in the snow makes for some very hard interval training, too, when it comes up to your knees. I could feel my pulse hammering away as I sweated out the previous evening's overindulgences. The cheerful chatter had inevitably turned to New Year's resolutions, but I had only one plan for the year, and that was the mammoth task of trying to win the Tour de France. It was a promise to myself I wasn't going to quickly give up on, either. I was deadly serious, knowing that to follow my training programme would require willpower and compromise. I was the only one who knew whether I had what it took to make all the sacrifices necessary to reach my goal, and I knew that if

I wanted to achieve an extraordinary result, then it would require extraordinary effort. On Christmas Eve, while the others were at church, I was out doing a five-hour training ride. I was already on a strict diet, too, watching everything I ate, knowing that every extra gram would reduce my chances of performing in the mountains. Georg looked at me and shook his head as I stumbled sweatily in through the door, treading snow all over the floor. "You're crazy," was all he said.

It was a pretty crazy time when Mette and I met up with my new Telekom team-mates for dinner at a castle in Germany. As the team's new star rider, I wanted to make sure that they saw me in a good light and that I was the kind of person they could trust. I turned up to meet the rest of the team for dinner in a nice Italian suit, and one of the first people I saw was my old friend, and now new team-mate, Brian Holm. "You're a bit overdressed for this, aren't you?" he said. Mette and I looked around at the other couples, and saw that most of them were just dressed in their normal clothes. "Surely you don't want to get what you're wearing ruined," he added, before heading off again, leaving us really quite confused.

After a number of seasons with structured, well-organised Italian teams, it was a real culture shock to come to a German team which turned out to not really be any of the above. Mette and I sat politely at the table as the cooks served us big lumps of meat, mediaeval style, along with big glasses of beer. It wasn't long before we understood what Brian had meant about us having worn the wrong clothes. People were downing the beers at quite a rate, and the dinner quickly descended into a chimps' tea party. As disciplined as these German riders were when racing, it was a whole different matter when it come to behaving themselves. The riders were soon play-fighting with each other, throwing food, climbing on the tables and falling off the chairs, drunk. My nice Italian suit was soon covered in splashes of food thrown by my new team-mates. They'd then laugh manically and just carry on. "What did I tell you?" laughed Brian, and went back to the party, leaving me to think about my time on the Italian teams I'd ridden for, where it would have been absolutely unthinkable for my team-mates to have behaved like this.

Mette had had to take cover to avoid her dress suffering the same fate as my suit. "If they're as good at riding as they are at partying, then you've made a great decision," she told me.

At eight o'clock the next morning, I stood ready to go mountain-biking. Gradually, my team-mates began to appear, exhausted-looking and hung over, but trying their best not to leave their new captain waiting. "You're looking perky," Brian said.

"A gentleman in the evening is still a gentleman in the morning," I told him.

If you think you're capable of partying all night, then you need to make damn sure you're also able to train the next morning.

At first glance, there was little to demonstrate that the Germans were as good at riding as they were at partying. Out on the road, they behaved like a bunch of happy, worry-free tourists, demonstrating absolutely zero logic or structure. Their philosophy seemed to be: get out on your bike, ride a couple of hundred kilometres, and then head back for a good, solid German meal. I was shocked that the team's training philosophy was this unstructured and badly thought through. It was like being back in the Seventies or Eighties. What it did mean, though, was that I had the opportunity to make my mark on the team and introduce them to my own theories and my way of doing things. It would require them to be open to new methods, though, and to try to forget their bad habits. The team's star riders, Germans Olaf Ludwig and sprinter Erik Zabel, weren't too sure about me. Not only was I joining them at the top of the hierarchy, but I was also preaching my ideas and opinions about how they should be training to them.

"I want to win the Tour," I announced at one of our early-season training camps. There was no point in me being modest about my goals. I needed to make sure that my team-mates knew where I stood, for them to understand why Walter Godefroot had signed me to the team, and why I was planning my season the way I was. Almost immediately, it seemed as though laying out my plans had the desired effect, especially among those riders who were well in with a shout of making it onto the Tour squad – riders like Rolf Aldag, Udo Bölts and up-and-coming German talent Jan Ullrich, who was fighting for a place with the Dane Peter Meinert. Whether they genuinely believed that I had a chance of realistically winning the world's biggest bike race was a different matter, though. At that point, they didn't really know me, but I knew that I had half a season to convince them to trust me.

In the first few races of the 1996 season, I rolled around in the "wrong" half of the peloton, looking like I was "blowing a balloon up", as Brian Holm liked to describe my way of gasping for air when the racing really got going. My team-mates were more than a little sceptical about the team's new "star", and were no doubt thinking to themselves, "He's got no chance of ever winning the Tour." But that was because they had a different way of looking at things compared to me. My season was entirely focused on reaching top form for the Tour de France, so I had no reason to be firing on all cylinders for these spring races at all. I was keeping my powder dry. I tried to explain the reasoning behind this to my team-mates, but a number of them had grown up cycling in the former East Germany. Their kind of training philosophy was deeply ingrained in them, and they still trained the way they always had – by way of long, monotonous training rides.

"Look at them – they're like machines!" Brian laughed when we were out on a ride with our German team-mates one day. They didn't say a word to each other for six or seven hours, and just rode along at a constant tempo.

"See that guy there?" said Brian, pointing to Erik Zabel. "He trains around 50,000km a year." Their training methods were hopelessly out-dated. My approach was far more scientific. I was able to upload data from my training rides onto my computer in order to analyse it and see where there was room for improvement when plotted against the form curve I'd worked out with Doctor Cecchini ahead of the season. Cecchini had taught me to work with watts. It was a very scientific method of doing things, and one I'd used for many years, but for the Germans it was a completely new approach. Watts are measured per kilo – that is, how much power is being produced per kilo that you weigh. The more watts per kilo, the better. It's the perfect tool for measuring a rider's performance level: as you increase your watts-per-kilo figure, you know you're going in the right direction.

Slowly, the other riders on the team began to become more interested in my training methods, although it was obvious that they wanted to see that it actually worked for me before they'd be convinced that they should be doing it too. I was equally suspicious as to whether their methods were doing them any good. They'd be training for six hours without a single interval, while I'd do four hours and incorporate a number of intervals. The data afterwards would show that I was burning just as many calories in four hours as they were during six, and the advantage of doing things my way was that I wasn't getting anywhere near as worn out. Riding six hours day after day starts to take its toll.

At a training camp in Spain, a small group of us were out doing intervals. A couple of the riders were German. "Let's have a little break," I suggested, and headed to a café I'd seen on our route.

"What are we doing?" one of the Germans asked.

"We're just going to have a quick coffee," Brian told them. "It'll give us a rest, and give us a bit of energy."

Three of us – me, Brian and Swedish rider Michel Lafis – sat down at a table outside the café and ordered ourselves some coffees. The Germans stayed in the car park, still on their bikes, riding figures of eight in order not to stop. I sat there and smiled, while Brian and Michel couldn't help pissing themselves laughing at their German team-mates who were unable to relax even for a minute. "What's wrong with you?" Michel laughed at them. "Either come and join us for a quick coffee or carry on without us." The two Germans looked at each other, thought about it for a second, then gave us a wave and went on their way.

Before I joined the team, Brian had warned me about the little cliques. The Germans certainly banded together, and if you weren't in their good books, they were likely to talk about you behind your back. But my goal-oriented way of doing things seemed to appeal to them, and I didn't really have any problems. Jan Ullrich was the rising star of German cycling, and had been the amateur road race world champion before joining Telekom. He kept a low profile, but was always looking out for ways to make himself a better bike rider. After just a couple of training rides, it was plain to see that he was something special, and if his ambition matched his ability, then he had real potential. But it was obvious that he had zero interest in what bike he was riding or what equipment he had; he was more than happy to just accept what the mechanics gave him. I, on the other hand, would spend hours with the mechanics, adjusting, improving and changing all sorts of bits and pieces on my bike. I insisted on adjusting my own gears myself, as I knew how to do them so that they were just right. The majority of the Telekom mechanics were thrilled to have someone show so much interest in their work, but I'm sure a couple of them were a little irritated by me being quite so anal about everything. Clearly, none of the riders had ever shown any interest in what the mechanics did before I came along, but soon some of them came to see what it was I was up to, and gradually the mechanics acquired a few regular visitors coming to check over the bikes. Whether they were just trying to do the right thing in my eyes, or whether it was genuine interest in their equipment, I don't know, but it certainly helped foster a better feeling of teamwork and professionalism.

As the Tour approached, I was more and more focused on being ready for it. "Hello! Anyone there?" Mette clicked her fingers to get my attention after I'd drifted off into my own world again, thinking about some detail or other in preparation for the Tour. "Don't forget the rest of us," she smiled.

We were sitting in the living room, having a nice time with the boys, but the reality was that all I was thinking about was the Tour. I'd find myself thinking about things like a new pedalling technique that would ensure that the chain was always fully under tension. Everything I did was with a view to July. If I went to the gym with Mette, I'd set up the stair-climbing machine to do intervals to test out my maximum heart rate. I scared myself sometimes. When I was out training on my own on the bike, doing interval work, I'd sometimes get myself into an almost trance-like state, and ride at my maximum heart rate as though I was from another planet. My muscles would scream with pain, but it was as though I almost enjoyed it, and that it acted as some kind of meditation. I was permanently in pain, but would ride anyway, oblivious to anything else. I think I was in the cycling equivalent of what in running is called a "runner's high" – a feeling of being at one with yourself,

and being able to enjoy feeling every fibre of your body. I'd sometimes train in the evening, and it would get dark while I was out,
stuck in my trance, not knowing or caring what time it was or
where I was. It was just me, my body and my bike, and nothing
else mattered. I used Cecchini's words almost as a mantra: "Whoever
can ignore the lactic acid for the longest will win the Tour de
France." And then eventually I'd snap out of it, stop, and not know
where I was for a moment. I'd be so focused, so lost in my own
world, that I wouldn't even notice which way I'd ridden. Luckily,
by now I knew every single road in Luxembourg, so it never took
long for me to find my bearings and head home in the right
direction.

"You're crazy," Mette would tell me when, after a quick bath,
I'd tell her all about my time out on the bike.

On Friday 28 June, Godefroot drove me to the obligatory medical
check prior to the start of the Tour de France, which in 1996 was
setting out from Holland. "How's your cold?" he asked me before
we got there.

"Yeah, fine thanks," I replied. "I feel great."

In the lead-up to the race, I'd been suffering with bronchitis and
sinusitis but, thanks to a few sessions with John Boel, I'd quickly
got over it, as my performances at the Danish national championships a week before the start of the Tour proved. I'd won both the
road race and the time trial, which meant that I'd be in the Danish
champion's jersey for every single stage of the Tour. Unless I was
wearing yellow, of course.

Godefroot was the Telekom team boss, and also the one who
owned the company that actually ran the team. The Belgian was
someone you could trust – the kind of man who kept his promises,
and was always up front if there was anything wrong. He never
really interfered, either, which suited me. Tactically, he was very
smart, but he was rarely that demanding or proactive when it came
to the riders. Rudy Pevenage was his right-hand man – a skilled
directeur sportif who knew what he was doing, and who was capable
of running the team if Godefroot was called away to attend business
matters.

"Let's see how much you weigh," the Tour's race doctor said, motioning for me to stand on the scales. This medical check was a brilliant gauge of which riders had hit top form for the race, and which riders risked having a lovely three-week holiday at the "wrong end" of the peloton. The scales never lied. Turn up too heavy for the Tour, and it revealed that you'd got your training wrong, or the discipline just hadn't been there, and it gave your competitors a real psychological boost. "Sixty-nine kilos," confirmed the doctor. I nodded, satisfied. Just like I'd planned. I'd hit top form at just the right time. My weight alone could tell me that I'd got it right, but it had apparently gone unnoticed that I was coming into form. A number of cycling magazines had left me off their list of riders to watch in the 1996 Tour. According to the magazines, the favourites were Tony Rominger, Alex Zülle, my former team-mate Evgeni Berzin and the two Frenchmen, Laurent Jalabert and Richard Virenque.

The evening before the start of the race, I decided to hold a speech at the dinner table, to ensure that everyone knew what the plan was. "I'm here to win the general classification," I said, loud and clear, leaving a pause afterwards so that I was sure that everyone had heard what I'd said. "And I consider it a realistic goal," I added. I noticed a couple of my team-mates give each other a look of doubt. But let them doubt me, I thought. Once we got under way, they'd know then that I was serious. I felt relaxed and mentally balanced, and I was brimming with self-confidence in everything I did. If I wanted to win, I had to dare to take risks, and I felt ready to do that. And I dared to say out loud what I wanted to do, even to those who didn't believe in me.

At the last moment, Godefroot had decided to put Jan Ullrich in the Tour squad instead of my compatriot Peter Meinert. It was a shame for Peter, but it would possibly make the team even stronger, as Jan had been riding amazingly ahead of the Tour. "He's going like a motorbike," as Brian had said. The better my team-mates were riding, the better my chances were of winning the race.

The rain was pouring down when, on Saturday 29 June, the Tour got under way with a 9.4km prologue around the Dutch town of 's-Hertogenbosch. The wet weather made the roads extremely slippery, so I was sure not to take too many risks this early on. I soon found my rhythm and, although I took it carefully on the bends, I tried to give it everything I could on the straights, which were not actually that much safer than the corners. I covered the route in 11 minutes four seconds, which was enough to get me sixth place – my best-ever prologue result – and lose me just 11 seconds to stage winner Zülle, and put me a second up on Indurain.

I knew that some of the Germans on the team had their doubts about my Tour-winning credentials, and that could perhaps lead to some kind of mutiny if the clique around sprinter Erik Zabel was allowed to grow. So I decided that it was in my interest to try to help get him into a good position for the sprints on the flat stages. If he could see that I was prepared to do some work for him, then he was sure to back me up for the overall victory. If he could get a stage win or two, it would help to keep everyone happy as well as give everyone some real confidence. I knew that I could definitely count on Brian's support, whatever happened. "I think it's great that you've dared to say that you're here to win," he told me. Brian's support was extremely important to me, as he was well-liked by everyone on the team and someone the others listened to.

Zabel missed out on victory on stage one, and complained to the press that "everything's all about Bjarne". However, he managed to win stage three, and this time I complained to Godefroot about him having slagged off his team-mates to the press.

"It's bloody amateurish," I told him, and Godefroot promised he'd sort it out.

Saturday 6 July, stage 7: Chambéry – Les Arcs, 202km

As soon as we hit the race's first mountain, on the road to Les Arcs, I attacked. I'd decided that I wanted to test out my nearest opponents by riding offensively to see how they'd react. Each time I put in a little dig, they struggled to react to it. I was in complete control on the stage, and was able to cause havoc. Indurain showed signs that there were cracks in his armour, Zülle actually lost time, and Jalabert was already well out of the picture.

On the descent off the Col de la Madeleine, I was completely in my own world – focused and in total control on the dangerous corners, which meant I was going extremely fast. I was in ridiculously good shape and was keen to prove it. At one point on the descent, I looked behind me. No one was there. They weren't able to keep up with me, and by the bottom I'd taken half a minute out of them.

"You can stop now," Godefroot said from the team car next to me. "There's still a long way to the finish, and it will cost you too much energy to ride on your own.

"But you'll get your chance soon," he grinned.

I'd shown them what was in store for them: that I was going to take control of this race.

Sunday 7 July, stage 8: Bourg Saint Maurice – Val d'Isère, 30km time trial

For a number of days, Brian had been suffering with stomach ache and a cold. Each stage was almost a battle for survival for him. We were room-mates, but Brian was keen that his coughing and spluttering wouldn't disturb me. That morning, I woke up and could tell that there was something missing. I looked around the room and, sure enough, Brian's bed was empty. I thought that maybe he'd already gone down to breakfast, but then remembered that while he'd been feeling ill, he hadn't exactly been hungry. When I opened the door to the bathroom, there was Brian, asleep on the floor. He'd spent most of the night in there throwing up in the toilet. "Why on earth didn't you just wake me up?" I asked him, concerned.

"Because you're trying to win the bloody Tour de France!" he told me. "And I certainly wasn't going to wake you up ahead of a time trial."

This was Brian all over: loyal, thoughtful and unselfish. Berzin won the time trial, and kept the yellow jersey, while I was second on the stage, 35 seconds behind him.

Monday 8 July, stage 9: Val d'Isère – Sestrière, 46km

"There's a lot of snow out there," I told Brian. I was looking out of the hotel room window, and could see the snowstorms up in the mountains where we were headed on the day's stage. This was the race's "queen stage" – the big one – over 190km. But the weather had become a problem. On the day when we had planned our tactics to the smallest detail, the race organisers were trying to decide what to do about these "unforeseen problems".

Overnight, the summit of the Col de l'Iseran – one of the day's major climbs – had been battered by snow and wind, and things weren't looking good for taking a bunch of bike riders over it. The message soon came that the stage was to be shortened, and that the race convoy was going to be transported to the other side of the Iseran and the stage would start there. That would shorten the stage by 45.5km – quite a large chunk of it. We put on some warm clothes, and were then driven in the team cars over the Iseran, following a snow plough. As we drove, I started to think about a new plan, now that the stage had changed character. Things didn't get any better when some new information came through, this time from the top of the Col du Galibier. "There are gusts of up to 100km/h here," the race radio told us. Combined with the snowstorms and rain, the organisers decided that it was too dangerous to go over the Galibier, too, and that the stage would be shortened even further. The length of the stage had been an integral part of our original tactics, but now both the Iseran and the Galibier were off the menu. I'd wanted to wear my competitors down, exhaust them, and then attack them. Now our best-laid plans were buried in the snow.

As we drove over the climbs, Godefroot and I were in agreement that we wouldn't have been able to race in such conditions. "There's no way you could have ridden up here. It would have been far too dangerous," Godefroot said. I just sat there and smiled, remembering my run on New Year's Day in the half-metre deep snowdrifts. The shortening of the stage left us with just 46km to race, and two climbs: the Montgenèvre and the climb up to the finish in Sestrière. Some of the riders were saying that it was the kind of stage that just needed to be got through – that we could just take it relatively easy. That wasn't my way of looking at it at all. For me, there were still two climbs, and therefore still two opportunities to put my rivals on the back foot, and two chances to try to get the yellow jersey and the race lead.

I wrapped up warm in my Danish champ's jersey, arm warmers and knee warmers, and we headed away from the start at three o'clock in the afternoon. There was no time to waste, but it was the Festina boys who were the first to push the pace on the lower slopes of the Montgenèvre. They seemed keen, as I was, to make every kilometre count and shake up the general classification. My rivals were gasping for air thanks to the high pace, and I could see that Berzin was already struggling in his yellow jersey. A lot of the other riders were riding in the small chainring, while I was still in the big ring, which gave me extra confidence. "Set a hard tempo," I ordered Ullrich and Bölts, who set about taking it in turns to crank up the speed. "Then I'll do the rest," I added. It was soon going to be time to start to do some real damage.

First, I went to the front and raised the tempo a bit more – just a little test to see how they would react, and to get them working a little harder and show me what they had. Zülle, sweating and huffing and puffing, was, I could tell, already in trouble, while Rominger didn't look good at all.

Another little dig from me, and then the signals started to come: the facial expressions and the swaying of the upper body, betraying their condition. It was hurting them, and my small accelerations were doing damage to the right people.

I let myself drop back to about 10th or 11th position, just to check on them one more time. And then I unleashed everything I had, rocketing past them all at full bore. By the top of the Montgenèvre I had 19 seconds over Luc Leblanc, and 23 seconds over Virenque, both of whom had tried to come after me. More importantly, though, I had a 31-second gap over the group containing Berzin, Indurain, Rominger and the Spaniard Abraham Olano. Descending was something I was good at, and enjoyed, and I set about increasing my lead as I plummeted down the other side of the Montgenèvre and on towards Sestrière. Once onto the final climb, I put absolutely everything into keeping everyone behind me. But the main goal was to take the yellow jersey from Berzin, as well as take as much time as possible out of Indurain and Rominger in particular.

Later, I found out that Berzin had really suffered on the climb up to Sestrière. He had no team-mates left to help him, and the other riders left it to him to set the pace, as he was in the yellow jersey and had everything to lose. He was forced into driving the group along, while the others sat behind him and saved energy. It was one of those days where I felt invincible. Everything came together perfectly: my self-confidence eliminated any doubt, my legs felt strong, and each time I checked where my rivals were it gave me extra self belief that I'd made the right move. During the last kilometre to the finish, I experienced a real rush of euphoria, oblivious to everything around me, and felt only positivity and pride about the way things had gone. Mette had told me that she'd be somewhere at the side of the road cheering me on, but I was completely in my own world and didn't see her. However, I was almost spent after 25km in the lead on my own, and remembered Mette's words as I neared the finish: "It's got to hurt for it to be good."

Just before the finish, I zipped up my Danish champion's jersey and, as I crossed the line, I threw my arms up in the air. There was no huge celebration, though, as every second counted, and out of the corner of my eye I noted my time: one hour, 10 minutes and 44 seconds. I got off my bike, tried to get my breath back, and waited for Berzin to finish. The yellow jersey came home, exhausted, a minute and 23 seconds behind me, which meant that I'd done enough to take the jersey. I was thrilled, but was quickly ushered to the podium by the organisers, who made a ring around me to hold back the crowd. I'd never been so proud as I was standing up there on the stage in yellow. This race was now mine for the taking.

I tried in vain to find Mette. I wanted to give her a hug and share my happiness with her, but it was impossible to see her amongst the huge crowds, and I was soon set upon by a bunch of Italian, Danish, German and French journalists. "Do you think you can hold the yellow jersey all the way to Paris?" one of them asked.

"I haven't got a crystal ball, although it would make things easier if I did," I told them. "But yeah, what I did today would suggest that I've got a good chance of winning."

I was asked whether I was particularly pleased to take the yellow jersey from Berzin, as our relationship had been quite strained when we'd both ridden for Gewiss. It was in these kinds of situations that I needed to stay professional. "If you think there's any kind of problem between me and Berzin, you're very much mistaken," I replied.

Instead, I took the opportunity to explain how the hierarchy at Telekom worked now that the race was entering its decisive phase. There was to be no more infighting, or upset sprinters. "Bölts and Ullrich are riding so strongly that they should also finish high up overall by the time we reach Paris. In fact, they're so strong, they're almost rivals," I told the press. "I'm joking, of course, but they are riding really well, and will be a great help when we're trying to defend the jersey."

When I went up to the TV area to do some interviews, I ran into my old team leader, Laurent Fignon, who was doing an interview with Denmark's TV2. He had a tear in his eye, and gave me a big hug and a heartfelt "congratulations" because he was so proud of me.

During my massage, I phoned Doctor Cecchini to talk through the day's events. Having the yellow jersey now changed everything. I needed to defend it, and I wanted to speak to Luigi about the best way to do that. Doubts and insecurities had already started to creep into my mind as it dawned on me what responsibility I now had. "What if I have a bad day and lose five minutes on a climb?" I asked him. "Can I trust my team to ride for me now?"

Luigi listened, and then the calmness of his voice in his reply helped to calm me down and allow me to pull myself together. "Bjarne, you're leading the race because you're the strongest," he reassured me. "You don't get the yellow jersey by accident." Everything he said filled me anew with self-confidence.

"You're the main man in the peloton now. You're the one who decides what happens."

Back in the hotel room with Brian that evening, we decided we should celebrate winning the stage and getting the yellow jersey. We emptied the mini-bar – of chocolate and nuts – then turned off our mobile phones so that we could chat in peace.

Tuesday 9 July, stage 10: Torino – Gap, 208.5km
Rolf Sørensen was out after a stage win, and with 26km to go he attacked alone, and it looked like he might have done enough to

get what he was after. However, we had other plans. We were trying to help Zabel to a stage win, so I had to ignore the fact that it was a fellow Dane who was out in front trying to win the stage.

Just a few hundred metres from the line, we caught Rolf, and Zabel screamed across the line as the stage winner. I signalled to Rolf that I was sorry that we'd reeled him in, but he understood that I was only working for my team.

Godefroot had some good news. Because of the enormous interest surrounding the team, our stage victories and my yellow jersey, our main sponsor, Telekom, had decided to continue with its backing of the squad to the tune of around 30 million kroner (£3.3 million). Prior to the Tour, the company had considered halving its investment, but our results had persuaded them not to. The questions in the press conference were mostly about how I was going to set about defending my jersey all the way to Paris. "The Tour will be won in the Pyrenees," I smiled, without giving away any secrets as to what our plan of attack actually was.

Monday 15 July, stage 15: Brive-la-Gallarde – Villeneuve-sur-Lot, 176km

Just a few kilometres into the stage, I needed a piss and signalled that I was going to stop. It was an unwritten rule in the bunch that no one attacks if the yellow jersey needs to stop for the toilet or if they have a mechanical issue. However, on this occasion, around 30 riders took the opportunity to slip away, and we had to use a lot of energy to reel them back in again. When we did, they got a real earful for not having shown more respect. It's just something you don't do.

The next day's mountain stage was being planned down to the last detail. The script had been written, and the mechanics had been briefed as to how I wanted my bike set up. Or, rather, bikes, as I was going to swap to an even lighter bike for the final climb. Godefroot knew exactly the point on the stage where that was going to happen, as well as the precise points where I was going to get fresh water. Everything was planned.

I spent a long time with the mechanics that evening, making sure that my secret gear ratios were set up properly. We were going to "cheat" in that, when I was in the large chainring, I'd actually be in a gear that corresponded with what most of the other riders would be pushing in their small rings. The idea behind it was to trick my rivals into thinking that I was managing to push a huge gear on the steep climbs, while they'd be struggling in their small chainrings. It would give me a psychological advantage over them, if it worked.

I also spoke to Fignon, as I really respected his thoughts and opinions. He told me that I should do what he used to do when he was leading a race: "Attack!" Rather than just sit back and defend the race lead, letting everyone else do the work before securing the race in the final time trial, I should make sure that the race was mine, he said. "The yellow jersey should be laying it all on the line in the mountains," he told me.

Tuesday 16 July, stage 16: Agen-Lourdes – Hautacam, 192km
Zülle, to me, seemed restless, and I watched him as he looked around all the time, jumpily, as though he was about to attack. We were about to hit the 13.5km-long Hautacam, with its average gradient of 7.8 per cent. It was going to be the hour that decided this Tour de France – just 13km of climbing, during which I had to beat my rivals by making the decisive move that would prove that this was my race, and that I deserved the yellow jersey.

The inevitable attack from Zülle had no effect, other than it encouraged Indurain to up the pace even higher to try to get rid of the weaker riders in our group. I put Bölts and Ullrich at the front to crank the pace up even higher. "Just go as fast as you can for as long as you can," I told them, "and then I'll take over."

I let myself drift back into the group to check on how my rivals were looking. I studied their gear clusters – what gear were they riding? – and watched to see if they were shifting gear quite often, which was a tell-tale sign that they couldn't find a good rhythm. Were they getting up from the saddle more than they usually did? Did they still have more to give? I identified that everyone was riding in the red – all riding at their maximum pulse rate, which is stressful and can put you over the edge. Like this, not many of them would be able to carry on before the lactic acid took over in their legs. Now was the time for me to make good use of all the tricks Fignon had taught me about reading my rivals' condition and effort. I knew all the signs to look for. A large part of my job was to study the competition. Were they sitting strangely? Straining their neck muscles? Were they gritting their teeth, and how was their breathing? I could recognise the smallest signs that they were in trouble. And Rominger was in trouble. So was Berzin.

I attacked, and forced them to work even harder. It made Rominger hunch on his bike even more. It made Olano move even further forward over his saddle, and Berzin was left trying to push too high a gear. Indurain's shoulders were beginning to slump. It was a good sign that he was about to blow – just as my intention had been ahead of the stage. The changes of rhythm had worn the defending champion down, and had put him into the red for a long time. I still hadn't put in an attack at 100 per cent effort, so I knew that I still had a lot more to give, but I was the only one who knew that. I quickly attacked again, and it was enough to drop Berzin and Olano. It was over for them after riding for too long at their limit. After a few more accelerations, I virtually stopped and dropped my chain down onto the small ring to make it look like I was suffering. But then I quickly whacked it back up to the big ring and accelerated again, and this time Indurain cracked.

It was that "secret gear" that did it for them – I could see it in their eyes. Each time I'd attacked, I'd done so in the big ring, while they struggled in their small chainrings. It made them think that it was easy for me to be in the big ring, and that I was too strong for them. With plenty still left in the tank, and completely in control, I accelerated one last time, and was on my own. None of them could follow me. This was it. Now, having broken them with my earlier attacks, I gave it everything I had, satisfied that none of them were going to be able to follow me.

For the final 7km of the climb, I was on my own, and it was up to me to win the Tour. Virenque, Leblanc, Laurent Dufaux and Leonardo Piepoli tried to organise a chase group, but it was too late, and they were too worn out to stand any chance of catching me. My efforts had taken their toll on me, too, though, and the last few kilometres were painful. Very painful. I'd given it everything, and my legs began to burn and I gasped for air. I had to will myself on, focus and concentrate on the fact that every single second would bring me closer to overall victory. I had to let pain be my friend, accept it, and not let it overtake my thoughts or my body. I pushed it in front of me, convincing myself that I could hold out for just a couple more minutes.

I actually continued to increase my lead over the last 5km of the stage thanks to being able to keep my speed up, ignore the pain and force myself up to the finish. As I rode into the last 500m, I was filled with joy, and the adrenaline rush dampened the pain in my legs. "You've got over a minute in hand," Godefroot shouted to me from the team car. I let myself be overtaken with happiness and pride, and allowed myself a proper victory salute, kissing my index fingers and pointing them to the sky in celebration.

"Now I can call myself the best," I told myself. I'd retained the yellow jersey and increased my lead over the second-placed rider, Olano, who was now two minutes 42 seconds behind me.

Thanks to his five consecutive Tour victories, between 1991 and 1995, Miguel Indurain had been the undisputed leader in the peloton. In my eyes, he'd always be a big champion, and he took his demise in 1996 with dignity. Lesser riders in the same situation would have let their ego and pride get the better of them, and would have quit the race rather than prolong their suffering, but Indurain wasn't like that and vowed to keep fighting. I wanted to recognise the class of the man the next day when we finished in his home town of Pamplona. Besides Spanish, Indurain only spoke a little Italian and French, so we were limited as to how much we could talk, but he seemed to me like a genuinely nice guy.

Wednesday 17 July, stage 17: Argeles-Gazost – Pamplona, 260km
As the race leader, it was all about remaining humble. It was up to me to look out for the other riders and make sure that they were okay. And it was far better to be generous than greedy; those were the attributes that defined a champion. And that was why I wanted to try to help Indurain win the stage to his home town, if he could. Unfortunately, the Festina boys were like wild animals and were constantly on the attack. Dufaux and Virenque shot off the front,

while Jan and I gave chase. It was too fast for Indurain, so I shouted to Jan to follow Festina while I dropped back. The young German had no trouble getting across to them, and they were joined in the front group by four or five others. I tried my best to get Indurain across to the lead group, too, and, while at first he fought hard to hold my wheel, eventually he had to give up. I'd done what I could, so I had no choice but to leave him while I rode up to the breakaway.

At the top of the next climb, there were still hundreds of kilometres to the finish, so we had to really knuckle down if we wanted to stay away, and we put our heads down and got on with it. One by one, my rivals were eliminated, so with a few kilometres to go I asked Jan if he wanted me to try to lead him out for the stage victory. He shook his head, as he clearly didn't have enough left in the tank, but by staying away in the day's break, we'd managed to get him up into second place overall.

I decided that I'd try for the stage win myself, and only Dufaux looked like he was going to try to stop me. But just then, a load of tomatoes and eggs rained down on me. It was the crowd throwing them at me, because I'd dared to beat their hero, Indurain. It was disappointing, as I'd felt as though I'd done what I could to limit the damage in his own backyard. I opened my sprint early, and tried to just keep going, but I felt Dufaux come up beside me. It was going to be close, but then Dufaux pushed just a little harder and came past me on the line for the stage victory, which led to some swearing from me while the Swiss rider celebrated. Indurain, Rominger and the others finished more than eight minutes down, while Jan was confirmed as being second overall.

I asked someone on Indurain's team whether it was possible to get him up on the podium with me when I went up to collect my yellow jersey, and whether I could give him the bouquet of flowers to show my respect for him. I let him go out onto the stage first to receive the public's applause. "Now it's your turn," the organisers told me, bundling me out onto the stage after Indurain. I quickly took my turn up on the steps of the podium, but just as quickly stood down again and thrust Indurain's hand into the air. It was his moment, and he'd earned it. It wasn't about me. I could tell that the chance to be cheered by his home crowd had meant a lot to him.

That evening, Indurain went onto Spanish radio, and told the Spanish public that they needed to respect me and treat me nicely – which meant not throwing tomatoes at me any more.

In the hotel room I tried to prepare myself mentally for the time trial, which was taking place on the penultimate day of the race. The mountain stages had taken a lot out of me, but I was confident that I had a good buffer over Jan in second place, almost four minutes behind me. Of course, it was always possible to have a bad day, or to crash or get a puncture, and a combination of any of those could cost me victory. I knew that anything could happen in a time trial like this, and I was reminded of the final time trial of 1989 when Fignon lost the Tour by just eight seconds, even though he'd been the best rider that year. I knew that you could never take anything for granted.

Saturday 20 July, stage 20: Bordeaux, 60km time trial
I was having real trouble with the zip, desperately tugging at it to get it to do up. The clock was ticking, with my start time for the time trial getting ever nearer. The Tour organisers had had a skinsuit version of the yellow jersey made for the time trial, but it was made out of some cheap, crappy material, with a rubbish zip. Frustrated, I gave the zip a hard tug, and promptly broke it. With a couple of minutes to go before the start, we'd found a safety pin to fix it with, but the whole idea of the tight-fitting skinsuit making me as streamlined as possible had been kind of ruined by a big safety pin holding it together.

Out on the road, my time trial wasn't going too well. Fatigue had really grabbed hold. My legs were not feeling as good as they had been earlier in the race. My muscles were tired, and my pedal stroke had lost some of that silky rhythm it had had before. Instead, it was sheer willpower that allowed me to carry on and keep my spirits up. On the other hand, Jan – who had started just ahead of me – was apparently flying, although I was still confident that my lead of 3:59 over him was enough to ensure that I held on to the yellow jersey.

I had a new time trial helmet, which was designed to minimise drag and so help me go faster, but it was big, heavy, too hot and irritating, so at one point I took it off and threw it to the side of the road. I was annoyed that I wasn't having a good day and that I wasn't able to show what I was capable of. "Come on, Bjarne," Godfroot shouted from the team car, as though he could tell that I was frustrated.

Then: "You're a minute and 25 seconds down on Jan."

I needed to snap out of it – it would be crazy to let it all go on the second-to-last day of the race. I managed to find my rhythm again, my legs felt better, and mentally I was back on track. "This is my race," I told myself. "No one's going to take this jersey from me."

Jan rode a fantastic stage – enough to win it – while I finished fourth on the day, 2:18 down. I congratulated Jan on his victory, which was well deserved, but I'd done enough to defend the yellow jersey, and still led the German by 1:42, which made losing the Tour on the final stage virtually impossible.

Sunday 21 July, stage 21: Palaiseau – Champs-Elysées, 145km
As a team, we led the bunch into Paris, and I was so proud of what we'd achieved. Zabel had won the green points jersey as best sprinter, while Jan was going to finish second overall. And Brian, Bölts and the others had done everything to ensure that I'd stand on top of the podium in Paris. Riding into Paris together was almost symbolic. We'd been the team that had really grabbed hold of the race, and here we were leading it to the finish. On the finishing circuit, there were Danish flags everywhere, and I enjoyed every minute. Unfortunately, we weren't able to secure victory for Zabel on the final stage, but we all celebrated as we crossed the line anyway.

As soon as I'd got off my bike, the TV cameras stood ready to capture our celebrations. Rolf rolled by and was one of the first to offer his congratulations. Brian found me and gave me a huge hug. "We did it!" he laughed. The rest of the team all hugged me, too, and it felt like I was floating on air as I made my way towards the podium. It was all just so overwhelming. And then, to top it off, I spotted Jesper and Thomas in their yellow jerseys in one of the grandstands. Mette was there, too, wiping away tears of joy. I rushed over to them and kissed Mette. This was the moment I'd been waiting for for so long – to be able to celebrate with them. The tears streamed down Mette's cheeks, and I began to cry, too. Mette knew exactly how much work I'd put in to getting to this point – how much pain and sacrifice it had taken to get here.

I could hear the Danish fans singing our national anthem over and over, and I just managed to grab a couple of gulps from a can of soft drink before I got called up onto the podium. And when I stepped on to the very top step, the Danish fans erupted. The national anthem came on over the loudspeakers, and then everything just went by in a blur – too quickly for me to take it all in properly. I realised that what I was most proud of was the fact that I'd dared to believe in myself, all the way from that run I'd done in the snow at the summer house at the beginning of the year.

From there on in, it all went by in a bit of a blur. I remember flashes of being congratulated by people, but it was all so emotional and so much was going on that it was impossible to take it all in.

Back at the hotel, my father was waiting for me with a huge smile on his face, and gave me a big hug. He'd been there on the Champs-Elysées, too, and had seen all the support the Danish fans had given me. "When you rode across the finish line, it gave me goosebumps, and I couldn't help shedding a tear," he admitted.

That night, we celebrated my victory, Ullrich's second place and Zabel's green jersey at a restaurant in Paris. As well as the whole team, Mette, Jesper, Thomas and my dad were there, along with my good friends Kim Eriksen and Georg Sørensen. At one point, Zabel stood up and tapped his glass to get everyone's attention. "I just want to say sorry, Bjarne, for not believing you when you said that you were going to win the Tour de France. But you did it, so congratulations," he smiled.

The party wound up at about four in the morning, which meant that we only had a couple of hours' sleep before travelling to Bonn, in Germany, to Telekom's headquarters. The Telekom directors offered their congratulations, as did a number of politicians who were also there. Before we knew it, we were on our way again, this time home to Copenhagen, where I knew they had prepared for us to be driven to Tivoli gardens, in the centre of the city, from the airport.

During the flight, Mette and I chattered excitedly about how many people we thought would come out to cheer us on the route to Tivoli. We landed at Copenhagen's Kastrup airport at about three in the afternoon, and were then driven in an open-topped Lincoln towards the city centre.

People had come out in their thousands to line the route all the way there, clapping and cheering, and waving flags and home-made banners with my name on as we went past. Mette and I just looked at each other while, in the back, the boys thoroughly enjoyed the attention. "This is madness," I told Mette as we drove. It was truly overwhelming – I was being treated like some kind of hero.

"It is crazy," Mette smiled. "But shouldn't we wave like members of the royal family?"

I hadn't really believed them when the organisers of the celebrations at Tivoli had said that people would come out to celebrate my Tour win, but they had been absolutely right.

"They're here for us," I said to Mette, disbelievingly. It was hard to believe that winning a bike race could move people enough for them to come out to see me. It was incredible.

"We should just try to enjoy every second of this," Mette said.

There were people as far as the eye could see when we stepped out onto the stage in Tivoli, with me having been introduced as "possibly this century's greatest sports person". Mette and I nervously held each other's hands, with both our sons held tight in the other hand. There were stools for us to sit on so that we could enjoy the show that was put on for us.

First of all, the Danish prime minister, Poul Nyrup Rasmussen, gave a speech. "I am in no doubt that your name will stand as the biggest individual triumph in Danish sports history," he said. "That there are so many people here, and out in the streets, is down to the fact that you are a man who can. If you're not able to move mountains, then with enough willpower you can conquer them instead. What you have given us, and proved to us, is what we now want to say thank you for."

There was then an afternoon and evening of entertainment for us, including a song that a Danish band had written about me, which they played in front of the 40,000 people who were there in the park enjoying the show.

The next day, the celebrations continued in Herning, where I was greeted by all my old friends from Herning Cycling Club, including Alex Pedersen. The party took over the town centre and the town hall, and on more than one occasion I managed to catch a glimpse of my father, who was beaming with pride.

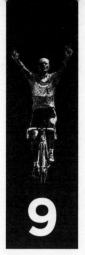

9 DRIFTING APART

I went off to the Olympics in 1996 with the belief that my Tour form might be able to win me a medal. I'd come to Atlanta just four days after winning the Tour in Paris. This being the USA, everything had to be bigger and better than anywhere else, as you would expect, but I was finding it difficult to enjoy it as much as I probably should have. What I really needed was time to digest and reflect on my victory at the Tour, and to think about how all the attention affected me and my life.

The race itself turned out to be very tactical, and I could tell that I just didn't have the legs or the head for it. I finished down in 86th place, while Rolf Sørensen luckily held the Danish end up by taking the silver medal. As I was also riding the time trial, it meant that, rather than head straight home, I got to stay even longer in the athletes' village, where I'd started to get to know some of the other Danish athletes pretty well. We were staying in the same block as the women's handball team, and they were quite a lively bunch. They were always up to something, and had virtually taken over our common room, so there was always something fun going on. We'd chat to a lot of them at the Olympic village's huge athletes' restaurant, and Anne Dorthe was one of those who was often around. She was playing in the team when one of my colleagues, Lars Michaelsen, and I went to watch the women's handball final between Denmark and South Korea on the last day of the Games. It was a good way to try to forget what had been a disappointing Olympics for me. That same day, I'd ridden the time trial, and it went about as well as the road race. But the atmosphere for the handball final was electric. The South Korean fans were crazy, and the game itself was riveting, right up to the final whistle. In the dying seconds, the two teams were tied, but then Denmark were awarded a penalty throw. Anja Andersen missed it, and the game went into extra time. But the Danes eventually came good, winning the match and the gold medal.

That evening, a party was arranged to celebrate the victory. It was a pretty informal affair, with the girls wandering around in their tracksuits with their medals around their necks. Lars and I were invited along, too, and had a great time sharing in the victory. It was good to have a few glasses of wine and a couple of beers without feeling guilty now that the Games were over. At one point in the evening, I found myself sitting next to Anne Dorthe, and we started chatting. We got on really well, and had a lot in common. Time seemed to fly by as we sat and enjoyed a glass or two of red wine. Soon there weren't that many people left at the party; most of them had gone off to explore Atlanta's bars and nightclubs. We decided to get a taxi back to the athletes' village together so that we could change out of our red-and-white tracksuits and put something a bit more appropriate on for going into town and finding the others. Having chatted together for so long, we'd built up quite a bond, and were clearly attracted to each other. We ended up sharing a kiss in the taxi.

We found the others in the centre of town, where the athletes, staff, journalists and members of the public were all mingling and enjoying themselves. After so many weeks of hard work, everyone was ready to party hard. But later, Anne Dorthe and I again found ourselves locked in conversation, sitting on a curb, while various Danish people wandered around nearby. At that moment, we didn't think at all about how bad it must have looked.

Back at the village, we went to my room, and sat on separate beds across from each other, in silence. But it wasn't an embarrassing silence – it felt more like we were just enjoying each other's company. We both seemed surprised by how much we liked each other, and how well we got on.

As the effect of the alcohol started to wear off, I sat thinking about how it had come to this: these feelings we both clearly had for each other and how serious they might be, despite not really knowing each other.

Without either of us actually saying it, we decided that nothing more should happen between us, and we said good night to each other, with the feeling that it was best for everyone if that was that. The next day, I travelled home to Denmark. I felt like I had plenty to think about. On the one hand, I had a very guilty conscience over what had happened the night before when it came to Mette and the boys. Even though it was just an innocent kiss, it still wasn't the kind of thing that a family man like me should have been doing. But on the other hand, I could tell that the experience had thrown up a number of questions, such as why I was having these feelings about Anne Dorthe, and whether that meant there was something wrong between Mette and me.

Thinking about it all the way home didn't really help make anything any clearer, either. In fact, I began to get worried that someone might have noticed Anne Dorthe and me together and put two and two together.

I'd decided that I wasn't going to tell Mette what had happened. In my own mind, I was already trying to play it down as a moment of madness.

But my worst fears began to manifest themselves at the Tour of Denmark shortly after I'd got home. Rumours were going around about Anne Dorthe and me.

It was nothing short of a disaster, and it affected my mood, so much so that I was unable to enjoy all the support I was getting from the public, still so keen to cheer me on after my Tour win.

I tried to pretend that everything was fine, but inside I was feeling extremely guilty. I couldn't help thinking about Anne Dorthe and what had happened, and couldn't help asking myself why it had happened. Even though we'd only got to know each other for a relatively short time, it had made me want to know more about her. There was no doubt about it that she was good looking, but I knew that there was a lot more to her than that, which also attracted me.

While I'd managed to win the Tour of Denmark the year before, this time round everyone was out to try to beat the Tour de France winner. The route really wasn't tough enough that I could make my mark on it, and it was the Italian sprinter Fabrizio Guidi who won, with me in third place, over a minute down. It was during the race that I heard that some of the gossip magazines were working on some articles about what had happened between Anne Dorthe and me during the Olympics. To try to temper the situation, I talked to Mette about how I'd heard that these magazines would do anything to try to get a story, and she was both sad and angry about it, not knowing what she should believe. The accusations and rumours made for a tough few weeks for Mette and me, and I was ashamed to have brought in this doubt about the love we had for each other, as we'd always stuck together and supported each other in order to make a safe environment for ourselves and the boys.

In the autumn, one of the magazines published an article in which it said that Anne Dorthe and I were actually together, which of course wasn't true at all, and made Mette, and me, extremely upset.

Through a friend, I managed to get hold of Anne Dorthe's phone number. On my training rides, I'd go through what I wanted to say to her over and over, without actually being able to pluck up the courage to ring. I wanted to be sure, too, that it wasn't her who was talking to the press about us, and wanted to make sure that she knew that nothing could come of it. I called, and the friend she lived with answered the phone. She misunderstood who I was, and thought I'd said that I was Lars Friis, who was Anne Dorthe's handball trainer. "Hi Lars!" Anne Dorthe said when she took the phone from her friend.

"It's actually Bjarne Riis," I said, probably a bit too gruffly.

"Hang on a second," she said, and closed the door behind her.

It was the first time we'd talked to each other since Atlanta, and I couldn't help some of my frustration from coming out. "What have you been saying to people about that night?" I asked, accusingly.

"Nothing," she replied, calmly. "We both agreed that it was nothing, didn't we?"

I quickly calmed down myself, as her reaction had completely thrown me. The conversation was going nothing like I'd imagined it would.

"How are you?" she asked me.

"Okay," I replied.

"And how are things at home?"

"A bit up and down," I told her. This wasn't supposed to turn into a proper conversation.

We spoke for a few more minutes, but then I ended the call. The plan had been to try to stop all the rumours and speculation, but it seemed like I'd made things even worse. I was left feeling more uneasy than I had been before ringing her. There was definitely something special about her, and it felt to me like the feelings we'd had for each other in Atlanta had been there again on the phone, albeit well hidden. In my training sessions following our chat on the phone, I spent all my time thinking, and found myself steadily becoming more and more unsure of myself and my own feelings.

A week after having called her the first time, I rang again – just for a chat. That then led to another phone call, and another and another. We talked about anything and everything: how our days had been, our thoughts and feelings, and life in general. She understood what it was like to be an elite athlete, and so we shared our stories and experiences about that, too. We had a relationship that was developing over the telephone. Our respective careers made it virtually impossible to meet up, so we had to make do with these long, quite emotional, phone calls. My talks with Anne Dorthe began to make me more and more critical of my marriage with Mette. In order to try to justify what I was doing – to try to help make it okay that I needed to have these conversations with another woman – I tried my best to convince myself that there was something wrong between Mette and me. I told myself that the two of us had grown apart, that I didn't get enough of my own space, that we didn't want the same things any more, and that Mette didn't want to follow the same path in life as me. When you start to think like that, it very quickly gets tough to go back to how things were and see the positive side of your marriage, which just a few months before had worked perfectly and seemed like the most natural thing in the world.

Mette and I knew each other so well that she knew something was wrong. Every time she tried to talk to me about it, I'd get angry and try to change the subject. I could tell that I was being a lot quieter than I normally would be, and I craved solitude, which meant ignoring the boys and only seeing the negative side of everyday life together. Inside, I felt torn, and spent all my time feeling miserable. I'd never been much good at pretending, and yet there I was doing what I had to do to try to get through everyday life with my family.

Anne Dorthe and I arranged to meet up in Copenhagen that October, as I was going there for a Six Day race. It would be one of my last events of the year, and although track racing wasn't one of my better disciplines, as the reigning Tour de France champion there was some good money to be had from the organisers, so I'd said yes to taking part. I knew that, like at the Tour of Denmark, everyone there would be out to beat me, so I wanted to make sure I was well prepared for the race. That meant training on the track beforehand, and it was by using that as an excuse that Anne Dorthe and I managed to meet up. We went for a walk together, and talked a bit about the Olympics before discussing everything that had happened since. We were both keen to try to find out what it all meant for us now. It was so easy to talk to her – just like it had been at the Olympics. It didn't seem to matter that so many weeks had gone by since we'd talked face to face. We said goodbye knowing that we wanted to learn even more about each other. We didn't arrange another meeting there and then, but it was pretty obvious that we were going to remain in touch.

Come the end of the year, I decided that I needed to try to pull myself together. The 1997 Tour de France was only another six months away, and if I wanted to defend my title I needed to be mentally strong and ready to live a life dedicated to training for July's race. I needed to get my private life under control, too. Common sense told me that I should commit myself to Mette and the boys, but my feelings were trying to push me in Anne Dorthe's direction – to try to get to know her better and try to find out whether there was anything more between us than the obvious attraction and the mutual understanding that we seemed to have.

Anne Dorthe and I arranged to meet up again, and all the old feelings were soon there again. In fact, they were stronger than ever, as we'd got to know each other so much better during our many telephone conversations. It was clear that we had something very real between us, but the situation was complicated. Did I really want to act upon this? Did I really want to destroy the picture of the Tour winner and his loving family? I could tell that the boys knew that their father wasn't very happy, and Mette could sense that I just wasn't the same any more. Since I was 16, I'd been convinced that Mette was the love of my life. We'd made a family together, and all our friends had become mutual friends. My former team-mate, Kim Eriksen, who I'd known since I was a boy, had married Mette's sister, for example, and Mette's parents had always given me all the feelings of security that I felt I'd missed out on as a child. They were the kind of people I could always turn to for advice and support. Mette had always been there for me, too, and I could always rely on her thoughts and advice. And our boys – the most important and precious things in our lives. Were their parents really going to get divorced, like mine had? Hadn't I always promised myself that that would never happen?

Again, I used my training sessions on the bike to try to make sense of it all, but it hurt so much to think about it that I couldn't make a decision. On the rare occasions that I thought I'd worked it all out, I'd get off my bike and the doubts would immediately return.

10 A CHAMPION IN PAIN

The atmosphere in the car was nothing short of awful as Mette and I drove to Rouen in northern France for the pre-race press conference ahead of the start of the 1997 Tour de France. Mette stared out of the window, while I drove, lost in my own thoughts. Inside, I was feeling a mix of emotions: confusion, irritability and nervousness. I was confused, plain and simple, about my private life. I was irritated about the current situation at Telekom, where I had the feeling that a lot of people were unsure about whether they wanted to ride for me or for Jan Ullrich. They said that they were working for me, but it was clear that there was something going on and that it was in fact Jan who was being set up for the overall victory. And then I was nervous because I felt under pressure to try to show that last year's victory hadn't just been lucky. I was the rider with the number one on my back, which meant I was the one everyone was gunning for. It was a totally different feeling being the one having to defend my crown compared to the year before when I was the one chasing my first Tour title. There was also a nagging feeling that my form wasn't good enough. Did I still have what it took to win the Tour or, by winning Amstel Gold and getting second in the Rund um den Henninger Turm that spring, had I peaked too early? Psychologically, I definitely wasn't ready for the world's hardest bike race. I was feeling fragile, vulnerable and unsure over my private life.

Mette soon woke me from my thoughts with an entirely practical question, but we managed to misunderstand each other, and it quickly descended into another argument, which we had had far too many of in the past few months. When we finally made it to Rouen, we were both still in a foul mood. Mette dropped me off at the press centre, where in just a few minutes' time I was going to have to take part in a press conference. I was in another world when I met up with my team and the media. Even though I tried to be professional, I was certain that people would be able to tell that I wasn't feeling myself. Everyone wanted a piece of me, to ask what my plan of attack was, and what my expectations were. The questions were fired at me from all angles.

"Can you defend your title?"

"Who are your main rivals?"

"Are you feeling well prepared?"

"Who's the leader at Telekom – you or Jan?"

We hadn't so much ridden a metre of the race, and questions like that last one had already been brought up. There was a lot more Danish press there, too, with many of them there to do nothing more than follow me to get whatever information they could about me. All of this was part of the job, and was fair enough with me being the defending champion. But right then, I wanted to be anywhere other than there.

Back at the team hotel, everyone was beginning to feel nervous. The pressure had begun to get the better of some people, and my mood wasn't helping, either. Our directeur sportif, Rudy Pevenage, was checking over my time trial bike, which had been specially designed for me, and which I was hoping to use for the prologue. "Any news?" I mumbled.

"No," Pevenage replied, not sounding very optimistic.

"This simply isn't good enough," I snarled.

It was Friday 4 July, the day before the race started with a 7.3km time trial, and yet we still didn't know whether the International Cycling Union (UCI) was going to approve my bike for it. The UCI jury was going to make its decision that evening. It was totally unprofessional that we hadn't had it approved a long time ago. The UCI had strict rules surrounding bike design. Mine had been designed to cheat the wind, and had been built by the

Italian bike manufacturer Pinarello at a cost of around 400,000 kroner (£37,000). Little more than a week before the start of the Tour, I'd ridden it at the Danish time trial championships, where the UCI had been fine with it. At the Tour, it appeared, things were different, but I still blamed my team for not having got it sorted out.

Bike trouble aside, I was already annoyed with Pevenage. I felt as though he hadn't made it clear enough that I was the one the team was supposed to be riding for, but he seemed to be more interested in talking Jan up, which was creating unrest on the team. As things were, I had no real proof that he was actively acting against me, but I felt far from convinced that he was doing everything he could to help me. Brian had warned me about Pevenage, who he called the cookie monster. It was a nickname he'd been given following a training camp in Mallorca, where Pevenage had gone into the riders' rooms while they weren't there and gone through their things to check whether they'd brought any biscuits with them from home. Brian didn't trust him at all. "He's two-faced," Brian told me. "One moment he's really friendly, and then the next he's working against you."

Since the previous year, Walter Godefroot had had less to do with the daily running of the team, and it was Pevenage who had taken up the reins. "Godefroot's definitely on your side, Bjarne," said Brian, "but Rudy's only interested in Jan, so watch him."

I'd first had my suspicions that not everyone on the team was behind me at the Tour of Switzerland in June. The time trial bike had been specially designed for me, but at the Swiss race, two of them had turned up: one for me and one for Jan. No one had told me that they were making him one, too. My bike wasn't quite right in Switzerland, either, while Jan's seemed to be working properly. I'd helped develop it, yet here was the German profiting from it.

So after that, I made sure that I kept an eye out for any little signs that the team was trying to prioritise Jan over me.

According to the press, I was the favourite to defend my title, while Banesto's Abraham Olano, Luc Leblanc and Richard Virenque were among my biggest rivals. Jan had only been named as an outside bet. But, despite that, the media's interest in whether the team might be backing Jan instead of me was irritating, as it wasn't something that had been addressed internally. I took it upon myself to clear up any confusion in the interviews I gave. "Having Jan on the team is an asset for me, not a problem," I explained. "Besides, if I'm riding at my best, I can't see there being anyone who can beat me." It was a strange state of affairs for everyone on the team when the biggest obstacle appeared to be this uncertainty over who the leader was. But for me, I was the captain and the defending champion, and Jan was simply my lieutenant, and that was that. At least, I hoped it was.

The next morning, I was out riding the course when the news came through about the UCI's decision. I wasn't going to be allowed to use my special time trial bike. That afternoon, on a different bike, I had to settle for 13th place. It meant that someone else had the responsibility of defending the yellow jersey – Chris Boardman in this case, after the Briton won the prologue – and that suited me fine. I needed a bit of time to quietly ride myself into the race before things got serious, so I was pleased that the press would, for now, go after other riders.

On the next day's stage, I made sure I stayed up near the front of the bunch to lessen the chance of being involved in a crash. Despite that, a rider in front of me hit the deck when the road narrowed at one point and brought down half the peloton, including me. I was quickly on my feet again, and luckily there was no real damage other than having lost a bit of skin. But the crash had caused chaos, effectively cutting the peloton in two. Vital seconds were being lost, so I jumped back on my bike and began to give chase. I looked around to see which of my team-mates were here to help me, but there wasn't a single one. Instead, they were all up in the front group trying to help our sprinter, Erik Zabel, to a stage victory. And that didn't work out, either. The Italian, Mario Cipollini, won the sprint, while Zabel was fourth.

A minute later, I crossed the line, fuming about what had happened. The Tour had only just begun, and I had already lost time. Most of the main contenders, including Jan, were around 20 to 30 seconds off the yellow jersey, while I – no thanks to my team-mates – was almost a minute and a half down. Anyone with the slightest understanding of how bike racing works knows that you don't keep driving onwards to try to win the stage when your team leader has been delayed by a crash.

I was going to have to explain that to my team-mates later on, it seemed. I just hoped that they had a good excuse. Losing the time I had wasn't a huge problem – there was still a long way to go, and I hoped I could make it up again. The problem was the message it gave to me as the team leader – not to mention to my rivals and everyone following the race. It looked like I didn't have the team's full support. Perhaps my team-mates weren't as confident that I could win again as they were saying they were. Perhaps, when push came to shove, they just weren't as loyal as they should have been.

The journalists stood ready to try to find out. "Were you satisfied with the support your team gave you today, Bjarne?"

"There was sod-all support from them today," I replied, before Godefroot could skilfully lead me away so that I couldn't answer any more questions. He knew that my rage needed to be controlled. If this all blew up completely, and got all over the papers, it could be very bad news for the team.

"Go and get changed. There's no need to talk to the press today," he smiled, calmly.

I slammed my bike against our team camper van, and went inside to change out of my cycling kit, slamming the door behind me.

"Bjarne is still the team leader," Godefroot assured the journalists outside.

Back at the hotel, it was clear that my team-mates were well aware that they'd abandoned me. "What the hell happened?" I shouted at them. Rolf Aldag said that he'd seen me get up again, and thought that everything had been under control.

Udo Bölts, who was the only one who had radio communication with the team car, said that he hadn't heard anything, as the crash had caused so much chaos. He said that there hadn't been any information about what had happened to me. The other riders said that they hadn't realised that I wasn't still in the front group, so had continued trying to set Zabel up for the stage win. "That's completely unacceptable," I told them.

"We made a mistake, Bjarne, and we're genuinely sorry," said Godefroot, trying to placate me.

At the start in the town of Saint-Valéry-en-Caux the next day – ahead of the race's longest stage – some of my rivals couldn't help noticing that Jan was now better placed than me in the overall classification. In fact, everyone seemed to have an opinion. Rolf Sørensen said that it was "a luxury problem for a team manager, but not so great for Bjarne or Jan as individuals, as how are they supposed to play it? Bjarne can't very well chase Jan if he attacks, but then he can't really just let him go, either".

US Postal's Danish directeur sportif, Johnny Weltz, said that "it would never have happened to Miguel Indurain", implying that the Spaniard's team-mates would never have left him behind.

Both Danish and foreign journalists flocked after me with their predictable questions about the power struggle at Telekom. One Danish paper's journalist pressed me on what had happened the day before. "How do you feel about the fact that one of your biggest rivals, Abraham Olano, is already a minute in front of you?" he asked.

"What do you reckon?" I answered, irritated.

"I don't know," he replied, "but then I'm not a pro bike rider."

I'd never had the warmest of relationships with the press, but it seemed to be getting even worse.

Alone in my hotel room one evening, I suddenly felt the need to hear Anne Dorthe's voice. Eventually, I had to give in, and gave her a call. She asked me how I was, but I preferred to hear about what she'd been up to, and about her lust for life, which was the opposite of how I'd been feeling of late. The telephone calls with Anne Dorthe became longer and more frequent. She could tell that I was a bit all over the place and unselfishly listened to all my frustrations and innermost thoughts, which really helped me.

Bastille Day – Monday 14 July – was the signal for the sprinters to take a step back, and for the climbers to come to the fore. Because it was Bastille Day, the French riders were out of control. As early as the first climb, Festina's Didier Rous, Neil Stephens and Pascal Hervé came to the front to set a vicious tempo for Richard

Virenque. Their intention was to try to shake Olano. We were in on it, too, and Jan helped them to set the pace. However, Festina had other plans as well, and soon began to take it in turns to attack, trying to grind us down. The Col du Tourmalet was the kind of climb that filled everyone with dread, so I sent Jan, Udo and Georg Totschnig to the front. Jan was riding effortlessly, but seemed happy to do his job. Soon, the fierce pace caused us to drop Olano and Luc Leblanc.

The stage's final climb, the Col de Val Louron-Azet, would prove to be decisive. It had come down to a duel between Festina and us. Jan set the pace, which was doing more and more damage behind, while Virenque was riding strongly and tried to get away multiple times. Each time, though, Jan would calmly reel him in, with me on his wheel. But I was struggling to hold my young German team-mate's wheel, while Jan continued to look very comfortable and clearly had a lot more to give. Dehydration and cramp were both beginning to take hold of me, and when Virenque attacked for a fifth time just before the top of the climb, I had nothing left to respond with.

Up until this point, Jan had proven to be nothing but 100 per cent loyal, but now he had no choice but to follow the Frenchman, as did the little Italian climber Marco Pantani. It looked as though Jan would easily have been able to overhaul both riders and take the stage victory, as well as the yellow jersey, but he didn't want to upset the apple cart when it came to our relationship, and so just followed his rivals' wheels. The three of them caught Laurent Brochard, who had been up the road on his own, and the quartet then continued to ride away from the group I was in.

So then it became all about limiting my losses to Virenque, Pantani and Jan to prevent my situation from becoming unmanageable. In the sprint, Jan held back and let the others fight it out, with Brochard winning the stage. I came home in eighth place, losing 41 seconds to the lead group.

Overall, it meant that Jan moved up to second place, just 13 seconds behind the yellow jersey, while I was fourth, one minute and 43 seconds down.

The press thought they could smell blood, and gathered outside our team camper van. They wanted to know whether I was still the team leader and the one everyone on the team was riding for. Godefroot dealt with the first questions, with a big smile on his face, while I got changed in the van.

"Riis is still our main man, and if our tactics have to change, then that's something we'll discuss later," he said.

The stage had prompted some questions about my form. "I'm actually quite satisfied," I told the journalists once I'd got changed, and then chose to address the "problem" that was Jan Ullrich myself. "I'm pleased about the way Jan let Virenque do most of the work, as he knew that I was just behind. If Jan had attacked himself, I would have lost more time, which he obviously didn't want to happen."

"But what happens if Jan takes the yellow jersey?" a journalist asked.

"The Tour's a long race," I said, "so let's see how things look in a week's time after the mountains. This race is still wide open, and I don't know whether Jan will be able to take the yellow jersey."

There was no need to speculate too much.

Each evening, I'd talk to my adviser, Luigi Cecchini, who was at home in northern Italy. "You're too stressed and are burning up too much energy unnecessarily," he told me.

"It's all the attention I'm getting," I told him. "Everyone's constantly talking about what's going to happen on the team."

"Well, you'll just have to show them who makes the decisions tomorrow," Cecchini said.

The next day's stage took us over five climbs in the Pyrenees before climbing up a sixth to the finish at Andorra-Arcalis. It's impossible to hide either strength or weakness when climbing six mountains in the space of 252km. Jan and I didn't talk about what might happen during the stage; we had to just wait and see how things developed, and then decide what to do when the time came. The likelihood was that our legs – and how good we were feeling – would make the decision for us, and we'd ride for whoever was in the strongest position come the end of the stage.

We rode the stage defensively, and let other teams and riders take the initiative. On the second climb of the day, the Col de

Portet d'Aspet, we all stopped to remember my former Ariostea team-mate, Fabio Casartelli, who had died after a crash on the descent of the mountain at the Tour in 1995. After that, the racing got under way, and a few riders immediately decided to try their luck. We simply wanted to keep an eye on the Festina boys – Virenque and Dufaux, in particular – as well as Marco Pantani, who was one of the strongest climbers in the race. Olano struggled on every climb and lost time, looking far from a man we needed to fear and use our energy up on.

On the penultimate climb, Jan rode up next to me. "How are you feeling?" he asked.

"A lot better than yesterday," I replied, then added, "Set a high tempo, and let's see what happens."

When we got to the last climb, Jan went to the front of the group and looked back at all of us. Everyone expected that he'd now turn the screw to make the race even harder and set me up for an attack. But that wasn't Jan's plan at all. He attacked from the group, and Virenque tried to go with him, while the rest of us were left virtually standing still. Jan looked over his shoulder to see whether I was still there, and hesitated a moment. He then attacked again, and again Virenque tried to go with him, but didn't have enough in the tank to stay with him for long. I had no intention of trying to follow Jan's move, and set about settling into my own rhythm instead, with Dufaux locked to my wheel. Jan reeled in lone breakaway rider Cédric Vasseur along the way, and crossed the line alone as the stage winner. A minute after him, Virenque and Pantani limped home, while I managed to drop Dufaux and finished fifth on the stage, three minutes and 20 seconds down on Jan. Jan took over the yellow jersey, while I ended the day fourth overall, a good five minutes behind my German team-mate.

When I found him at our camper van afterwards, all I could do was congratulate him on his fantastic ride. The team's hierarchy had been decided, as it had been impossible to follow Jan in such form. It was a relief for him, too, as it at last spelled an end to what had seemed like endless speculation. There was no reason for me to show any bitterness when I talked to the press. "Jan was the strongest," I told them, then added, "and no, it hadn't been planned. I simply couldn't keep up with him. I'm pleased that he was able to show how strong he is, and that no one else could follow him. It was great to see, and now I can just be pleased that we've been able to keep it in the family," I smiled.

There was no need to make a song and dance about it all. Jan had won convincingly, but I was sure there were still going to be some opportunities for me. The Alps were still to come, there was still more than one time trial, and a podium place was realistic, too. "Nothing much has changed," I continued. "My role remains the same. No one's taken anything from me. Jan has always been loyal to me, and now it's my turn to show my loyalty to him."

The German journalists were thrilled with Jan having got the yellow jersey, and besieged our hotel that evening. As a result, a small press conference was called by the team, which I took part in, too. I genuinely wasn't bitter in any way, and was careful not to take the bait when the press still pushed for stories about the supposed rivalry between Jan and me. "Will Jan having the yellow jersey mean that you won't get as much help from the team any more?" someone asked.

"I don't know," I replied. "On the climbs it normally ends up just being Jan and me left, so we'll just have to see who's strongest when we get to the Alps."

"Did the fact that there were no real transitional stages between the flat stages and the first mountain one cause you problems?" came the next question.

"I think you can always find some kind of excuse," I said, "but I've not got one this time. Jan was ready, I wasn't, and that's it. Right now, Jan is in a class of his own. He's riding effortlessly and, if he can keep it up, then of course I'd be very pleased if he won.

"But I still think that anything could happen in this race," I added.

The balance of power had shifted in the team for now, but saying what I did at the end was to let both the competition and Telekom management know that I was far from beaten, and that I wasn't just going to lie down and become a domestique. In my experience, just one bad day can turn everything on its head. One day when your body wouldn't do what your head wanted, or when your legs felt like concrete blocks, was all it took. I left the press conference having conveyed, I hoped, the message that no one should write me off yet.

My "ghost bike", as the press had dubbed my time-trial machine, had finally been approved by the UCI, and I was going to use it for stage 12's 55km-long time trial. We had planned that I would change to the special bike after the main climb on the TT route. The few seconds it would take to swap bikes would soon be cancelled out by the time the bike would save me.

I'd worked out that, in total, switching bikes would take about 15 seconds in total, but when it came down to it, it took considerably longer. Still, I rode strongly, and finished third on the stage.

Jan, though, did little to dispel the rumours that he was from another planet. He destroyed us all, winning the stage by over three minutes. It meant that it was now a race for second and third place. Jan led the race by more than five minutes, while I was over eight minutes behind him in fourth place overall. I now hoped to make it onto the podium in Paris, and targeted the stage to Alpe d'Huez as a good occasion to try to move up the classification. Cecchini and I had identified that stage as one to really go for it on, and so we fine-tuned our plans the evening before, over the phone.

My team-mates did everything by the book, delivering Jan and me to the foot of the climb of Alpe d'Huez. It was then up to us. As expected, the little Italian climber Marco Pantani went straight on the attack, and Jan and I gave chase. The Italian attacked again and again through the hairpin bends that led us up towards the summit, and one by one we fell off the pace. Only Jan could follow him. I decided that I'd do best just to try to keep my own rhythm and hope that Pantani would get tired and have to slow down. That didn't exactly happen, though. The Italian won the stage and moved up into third place overall. I finished in fifth, and remained fourth overall.

On the 14th stage, to Courchevel, I received a message from Godefroot: "Jan's in trouble." The German had found himself isolated between the front group, led by the aggressive Festina duo of Richard Virenque and Laurent Brochard, and the group I was in, which also contained our team-mates Udo Bölts and Georg Totschnig. The race organisers hadn't let Godefroot drive through to Ullrich to tell him what to do, so he was left to his own devices with the choice between trying to reel back the Festina group on his own, or dropping back to our group and hoping that we could all work together to try to close the gap. He chose the latter, and soon we were united in chasing Virenque up the Col de la Madeleine. "You made the right decision," I assured Jan.

I worked hard to pace Jan up the climb, and for the first time in the race, I felt like I'd rediscovered the same form I'd had the year previously. I tried to keep Virenque's lead to a minimum, sacrificing myself for Jan, although there was something in it for me, too: I was showing everyone that I still knew how to ride a race. After the descent, Virenque still had a few minutes' lead, so I gave it everything through the valley to close the gap almost single-handedly. We approached the final climb together, but Virenque was soon on the attack again. Eventually, I had to let him go, but Jan managed to cling on to his wheel, and followed him home as the Frenchman took the stage win. Pleased with how things had gone, I crossed the line in fifth place, and ended the day in third position overall. "I'm feeling better and better," I told the journalists at the finish.

But that night, things took a turn for the worse. I had stomach ache and was vomiting, and the next day I was still feeling ill when we set off for Morzine – the last mountain stage. I still had stomach ache, felt drained of energy and as a result just couldn't find my rhythm, and on the day's tough climbs, Ullrich, Virenque and Pantani found it easy to ride away from me. Pantani won the stage again, while Jan managed to hold on to Virenque. I lost time – and lost my third place overall.

The next day's stage was a complete disaster for me. I simply felt burned out – as though my muscles just didn't work any more. Mentally I wasn't in the right place, either, and that only served to make things even worse physically. Basically, I'd lost it. My stomach pains were getting worse, too, and I lost valuable time when it came to chasing that third place. On this stage in particular, it went so badly that I finished over six minutes down on the lead group, and plunged down to seventh overall. I was extremely frustrated after I'd come across the finish line. Immediately the Danish journalists swarmed around me, and I felt like a caged animal.

"Leave me alone, for God's sake!" I snarled, as they pushed and shoved each other to try to get near me. My relationship with the press had come completely off the rails. I didn't want to answer any more questions, and couldn't cope with any more stress. I shut myself away in my hotel room that night. Feeling frustrated, I called Anne Dorthe, just wanting to hear her voice. We talked for ages, although it was mainly her talking and me listening, and that's how I preferred it. Afterwards, I tried to work out why it was that the Tour had gone so badly for me. I decided that I probably should have listened more to Cecchini and taken a break after my win at Amstel rather than desperately trying to keep my form all the way up to the Tour. And I should have taken control of my private life. Every time I thought about how my life had changed so dramatically, the stomach pains got even worse.

The penultimate stage was a 63km time trial around Disneyland Paris. It was my last chance to try to better my seventh place and move up again in the general classification. At the start, I was having problems with my "ghost bike", and it was annoying me. I'd asked the mechanics to make a few changes to it for me, including removing the front derailleur, as I only wanted to run one chainring.

After signing on for the stage, I rode to the start ramp, where I swung my leg over the saddle to get off. However, I'd forgotten that my water bottle was attached to the back of my saddle – so that it was in a more aerodynamic position – and caught my leg on it, which knocked me off balance and sent me crashing embarrassingly, and in slow motion, to the ground. "Fuck!" I snarled through gritted teeth.

I'd managed to break my rear derailleur in the fall.

"Fix it," I snarled at the mechanic.

"It'll take a while," he protested.

"Get me my spare bike, and then fix the other one," I ordered him.

I started the stage on my spare bike while the mechanic worked on my other one in the team car, and after a few kilometres I asked whether it was ready again. "Not yet," came back the reply.

"Just get it done!" I shouted, which left no uncertainty as to how I was feeling about it.

A few kilometres further on, it was ready, and we did a very quick bike change. If I was going to spend six months developing a special time trial bike, then I was going to make damn sure that I used it. Just another few kilometres further on, though, I punctured. The mechanic sprinted out of the team car with a new wheel, and quickly swapped it in. I quickly got going again – and then my chain came off. Presumably, it was because I'd removed my front derailleur, which would normally help to hold the chain on. It had got stuck in the frame, and I had to stop yet again. I couldn't believe what was happening and, frustrated and furious, I stared at my bike in disbelief. "Now what the hell do you do, Bjarne?" I asked myself. A split second later, I took hold of my bike and hurled it into the field behind me. I'd had enough. Rudy Pevenage had got out of the team car, but didn't dare come any nearer to me. He knew that I would have gone mad at him, so didn't see the point in getting involved.

The mechanic ran up with my spare bike, but I told him that I didn't want it. "I want that one," I told him, pointing to my special bike that was now lying in a heap. The mechanic told me to take it easy, and went to collect my bike while I wiped the oil off my fingers onto the grass. My bike was quickly ready again, and I jumped on it. To add insult to injury, Abraham Olano, who'd started six minutes behind me, soon caught up with me. Olano won the stage, and I finished almost 10 minutes slower in 93rd place.

The next day, we rode into Paris with Jan in the yellow jersey as a worthy winner. He'd beaten second-placed Virenque by a massive nine minutes. "Congratulations," I told him after we'd crossed the finish line. He'd thoroughly deserved to win.

"Thank you, Bjarne, and thank you for all your help," he smiled. He knew that I'd been up against the ropes, and how disappointed

I really was, and as a result he didn't celebrate his victory in front of me. Jan was a nice guy, and none of what had happened was his fault. I remained seventh overall, which was a long way off what I'd hoped for at the start of the race. But after what had happened over the three weeks – stomach problems, stress, in-fighting and a mess of a private life to think about – I probably couldn't really have expected that much better.

11 A FALLEN CHAMPION

Sitting on the bed in our bedroom, Mette and I looked at each other with tears in our eyes. "Are we sure?" she asked me. I nodded, silently.

It was December 1997, and while most people were putting up decorations and looking forward to Christmas, it wasn't the happiest of times at our house in Luxembourg. "Well, we'd better tell them, then," said Mette. Long conversations, marriage therapy and a holiday to Lanzarote hadn't been enough to change our decision, and now we needed to tell the boys.

"Jesper, Thomas – could you come in here, please?" I called to the boys. Excitedly, they raced into the bedroom, but it didn't take them very long to realise that Mette and I were upset. No doubt they'd understood that something hadn't been quite right in the previous few months, too; children tend to be able to sense that kind of thing.

"There's something we need to tell you," we began, once we had them sitting up on the bed with us. Neither of us could hold back the tears. Even though we'd agreed how we were going to tell them, it was almost impossible to actually say what we had to say to our beautiful little boys. But we had no choice now. We'd taken too long to come to the decision, so now it was best just to get it over with. It was so painful: all the good things we'd built up together had fallen around our ears. Perhaps all along we'd hoped that somehow there was a way to save our marriage and our family, but too much had happened to be able to go back.

There had been many sleepless nights where I'd gone over it all in my head, repeatedly asking myself the same questions: had we done enough to try to save our marriage? Had I given Mette enough of a chance? But the decision to end our marriage had been mine alone. I couldn't ask Mette to be anyone she wasn't, or ask her to understand why I wasn't happy any more. It had been a miserable last few months, and it simply couldn't go on. I couldn't keep living two lives, either: the one with Mette and my family, and then the other, secret, one with Anne Dorthe. It had got to a point where it was hurting everyone involved. I couldn't do it to Mette and the boys any longer. I'd have to learn to live with the fact that my decision would pull the rug from beneath Mette, and completely change her life, and that it would affect my boys for the rest of their lives. After my own childhood experiences, I'd sworn that my children would never have to experience the heartache of divorce. But now here I was sitting in our bed with seven- and five-year-olds Jesper and Thomas, breaking my promise. "Daddy's not going to live here with you any more," we told them through the tears. The boys started to cry, too, as we explained exactly what it all meant: that we wouldn't be living together any more, and that Mum would live with them while Dad lived somewhere else and would come to visit.

All four of us sat on the bed, hugging and crying. "Can't you just go to the doctor's, Dad?" Jesper asked, hoping that it was something I could be cured of.

December should be the month where families come together and are happy, enjoying the approach of Christmas, yet my family was in tears and unhappy. Silently, I packed a bag ready to fly to Denmark. We'd decided that Mette would stay at the house in Luxembourg with the boys, while I went to live in our summer-house in Denmark. With tears in my eyes, I said goodbye to Mette, Jesper and Thomas. During my trip, I had mixed feelings. I was so sad to have hurt Mette and the boys in the worst imaginable way, and it upset me, too, that it was going to be a while before I would see my sons again. But there was also a sense of relief in that I had finally made a decision, and that I was no longer living an existence that was making the people I loved most so unhappy. I was also looking forward to being with Anne Dorthe without feeling guilty – learning to get to know her better and letting our relationship develop. It was finally the end of living a double life. I rang her to tell her that I'd left Mette. She was at the handball world championships in Germany, where the Danish women's team was one of the favourites. She could tell that I was both upset and relieved. "Once I'm back from the world championships, we can be together," she told me.

I still had one horrible task ahead of me once I arrived at the summerhouse. I unpacked my things and tried my best to pull myself together before wandering down to see Mette's parents, who lived nearby. I wanted to see them to try to explain in my own words why I'd made the decision to divorce their daughter. I'd always enjoyed a close relationship with them, and they'd supported me all the way through my career.

We sat down in the living room. "If there's anything you want to say to me or ask me, then please do so," I told them once I'd tried my best to explain myself. They were, of course, enormously disappointed about my decision, but otherwise they didn't say very much. All three of us knew that our relationship would never be the same again, and I knew, too, that a lot of Mette's and my mutual friends and contacts would end up having to choose sides.

"Goodbye, Bjarne," Mette's parents said to me, and shook my hand, as I left their house.

I sat at the summerhouse thinking about how the public might react to the news about Mette and I once it was published on the front pages of the papers – whether it would be met with condemnation or understanding. Until that point, the recognition I'd got for having won the Tour had made me proud. People seemed to associate me with something good and positive, whether that was when they saw me in the street, read about me in the papers or saw me on television. But that was possibly all about to change. Perhaps they wouldn't be able to see my side of the story, and would simply see me as someone who had left his wife and family for a younger woman, who also happened to be a sports star. I really didn't know what the consequences would be. It just felt so wrong to be sharing such a personal, private and unhappy decision with everyone, especially when by far the majority of them were strangers, who had nothing to do with either my life or my feelings. I didn't like having to try to justify the decisions I'd made in my private life.

When it came to bike racing, I'd happily speak up and explain why I chose to do this or that during a race, but what I did or didn't do in private surely wasn't anyone else's business just because I'd won a big bike race.

Later that week, Anne Dorthe played in the handball world championships final against Norway in Berlin. She played brilliantly, inspiring the team in her role as captain and scoring a number of important goals. The Danish team thrashed the Norwegians, with Anne Dorthe having put everything into the game in order to ensure that they won the world championships for the first time. As captain, she was the one who got to lift the trophy, too.

While Denmark celebrated the handball team's achievement, I quietly left the country and flew to Mallorca, where I borrowed former Danish pro rider Ole Ritter's summerhouse. I wanted to get away from it all to try to get over my break-up from Mette. Anne Dorthe and the team were welcomed back to Denmark as heroes, just as I had been after the Tour, and I was thrilled for them.

The next day, Anne Dorthe flew out to join me in Mallorca, where we had decided to spend Christmas together. But the next few days would turn out to be a real mishmash of different emotions. The sadness I felt over my split with Mette was difficult to escape from. The prospect of not spending Christmas with my sons just felt worse with every day that passed. On the first evening after she'd arrived, Anne Dorthe opened up one of the windows to lean out and pick some fruit from one of the overhanging trees. But as she did so, she noticed that there were people outside the house. A number of Danish magazines had clearly found out where we were staying, and they'd sent photographers to try to snap some pictures of us together. "God, I hope they didn't see me at the window," said Anne Dorthe. But we needed to go out to buy some food, so crept out of the back door. Once we'd got our shopping, we tried to sneak back in unnoticed, but this time the photographers spotted us.

"Can we just get a few pictures of you?" they asked.

"No," we told them, and hurried back into the house before they got some anyway. If we were going to have to spend our whole stay with them waiting for us outside, it wasn't really going to be much of a holiday.

I got in touch with Ole Ritter to explain the situation, and to tell him that we thought we'd need to move out of his summer-house. Instead, we rented a different house a little further away, and actually managed to move to the new place without the photographers noticing. But the media continued to ring me. I didn't want to speak to them, but one journalist from *Ekstra Bladet* did manage to get a few words out of me. "How are you feeling?" he asked me.

"How do you think?" I replied.

"What's it like not being with your family at Christmas?" he continued.

"Not that great," I told him.

And that was pretty much the extent of the short interview – nothing really was said. Yet inside it did trigger a reaction in me. It all came rushing back, and was overwhelming: the confusion, the unhappiness, the awkwardness of it all. And, most of all, the pain I felt from missing the boys so much. It was no doubt the reason that I suddenly came down with a bad cold, or flu, and spent the next two days in bed feeling terrible. Anne Dorthe was very understanding about my reaction. She, too, was feeling a little flat after such a hard and intense handball world championships. We only spent a week in Mallorca before heading back to Denmark to stay with Anne Dorthe's parents at their summerhouse in Sallingsund in the north west of the country for new year. We spent our time there hidden away, and I got to know Anne Dorthe's parents, who were extremely accommodating and welcoming.

Later that month, I met up with the rest of my Telekom team for our 1998 pre-season training camp, where I got the opportunity to discuss the internal problems we'd had during the past season.

Jan and I agreed that we needed to stick together for everyone's sake. The press were always asking us what the hierarchy in the team was going to be for the coming season, and Ullrich tried to assure the media that there weren't going to be any problems. "Bjarne and I both know that, if our friendship fails, it could be catastrophic for the whole team," Ullrich told them. "I think, therefore, that we'll both just have to wait and see what kind of form we have come July. I'm convinced that Bjarne will help me to win the Tour again if I'm the strongest, as much as I will help him win again if he's the strongest."

We also tried a new communications system at the training camp for the first time. Each rider was given a mobile phone with a hands-free earpiece and microphone so that Godefroot could sit in the car and ring each rider up to talk to them. It seemed like a great idea, although it didn't really take into account those moments when we didn't have any signal, which kind of hampered things a little.

Telekom still expected a lot from me, and I'd been named at the team presentation as the leader for the Tour de France, alongside Jan. I was the one with the most experience, and so I was being relied on to lead the troops. That was a huge pat on the back for me, despite everything that had happened. Godefroot knew what was going on in my private life, and could see that I had lousy form, but left me to my own devices when it came to training anyway. He was confident that I knew what I had to do if I wanted to arrive at the Tour in top form. Besides, it appeared that I wasn't Godefroot's biggest problem. That honour fell to Ullrich, who had apparently celebrated his Tour win a little too much, and had piled on the pounds as a result.

"He's a good 10 to 15kg overweight," a team-mate told me one day. And if that was true, he had a good amount of dieting ahead of him if he wanted to make it to fighting weight in time for the Tour. I could hardly talk, though: I was also a handful of kilos heavier than I should have been at that point and was struggling to recover from a training crash that had fractured my hand. The truth was that the amount of training I was doing really didn't match the quantity and quality that was needed to make it as a top-level pro rider. It was time to call in my dad to help.

The exercise bike weighed at least 90kg, and even for two strong men it was a real effort to heave it up to the fifth-floor apartment. "I certainly hope that you're actually going to use this bike after all that," my father told me, exhausted, after we'd finally got it into the flat. But, despite my best intentions, the exercise bike stood unused for quite a while. It acted almost as a reminder to my guilty conscience that I didn't have the energy to train. It was around that time that I really began to wonder whether it was the end of cycling for me – that it was time to hang up my bike and just admit that that was that. I'd been injured before, and had been out for even longer than I had been with my hand, but I'd never had any trouble with motivation, like I seemed to be experiencing now. It wasn't looking much better for Anne Dorthe either, who was also having a tough time. She hadn't played handball since the world championship final in December, and had already had three operations on her injured knee. As soon as she tried to run on it, it hurt, so she had to stick to cycling and strength training in the hope of it getting better.

All this meant that Anne Dorthe and I had some long, deep conversations about what we might do with our lives if we both had to put an end to our careers as professional sportsmen.

In one last effort to try to motivate myself again, I'd had an idea. I found the VHS cassette of my 1996 stage win at Hautacam, turned the exercise bike towards the television, and put the tape into the video machine. Sweating like mad, I pushed the pedals round as I watched myself win the Tour stage. It was one of the few times that I'd actually seen it, and it seemed to reawaken something inside, reminded me that I was a good rider, and showed me that this was what my career was all about. I didn't want what had happened to me in my private life to affect me so much that it ruined something that had given me so much joy since I was a kid. The video had given me new inspiration, and I knew that I couldn't stop my career just like that. I was convinced that I still had what it took, and that I could rediscover my motivation for long training rides and reach good form in time for the Tour de France. I set to work and began to feel the speed returning to my legs. I started on a strict diet again, and was soon losing weight. The spring gave me a new zest for life, and I was able to enjoy being with Anne Dorthe. I was back in the game.

In the middle of April, I made my season debut at Spanish stage race the Tour of Aragon. It was my first race since October, so there were a few cobwebs that needed shaking out. The first stage should have been 174km, but a number of the climbs we were supposed to cross were so covered in snow that there was no way that the race convoy was going to be able to get through, and the stage got shortened to 82km. "Pretty lucky, eh Bjarne?" Godefroot laughed. I was still a good few kilos too heavy, and I had form to match.

The stage went well enough, although I had to really fight my way up the last climb to the finish. But it was good to be racing again, and I felt that my motivation was there. I finished the stage in 49th place, while Jan fought his way home in 71st. Godefroot was worried with just three months to go until the start of the Tour. His two podium candidates looked like two blokes who had just got up from the Christmas buffet. "Neither Riis nor Ullrich are riding anywhere near as well as they were at this point last season," he told the press. "Ullrich is too heavy, and Riis is simply overweight."

But I was sure that I'd be able to shed those extra kilos and hit good form in time for the Tour – mainly because Anne Dorthe had introduced me to a practitioner of alternative medicine called Ole Kåre Føli who, through his combination of chiropractice and massaging of the body's energy points, gave me a much-needed service of body and mind. Stress, pent-up frustration and the emotions I'd gone through after my divorce had all taken their toll on my body, but he worked on me and helped loosen me up. During one course of treatment with him, I decided that I wanted to take him with me on the Tour.

My form began to improve from week to week, and in mid-May I took part in the Grand Prix Midtbank in Herning. With 50km left to race, Rolf Sørensen and I looked at each other as if to say, "Let's do it," and attacked. The move worked, and we got a gap, and in the sprint for the line I got the better of Rolf to win it for the third year in a row. It was an indication that I was on the right track. Later that month, I went to the Bicicleta Vasca – another Spanish stage race – and again I had Jan as one of my team-mates, who was also on his way back to race weight. The fifth and final stage was a 110km mountain stage, and a perfect opportunity to test myself against some of the better riders on the climbs. Things went well, and my self-confidence returned, the power was still there and my ability to read a race was still intact. The spark had come back. I crossed the line first, ahead of Abraham Olano and Ullrich. Overall, I was outside the top 10, but that didn't really matter. The stage victory was enough to prove that I was back, and that I could still compete with the best.

After the race, I travelled to France to scout out some of the Tour stages, and my training there indicated that everything was going in the right direction. From there, I travelled to Lucca in Tuscany, Italy, where Doctor Cecchini was waiting to test my form and help plan my last few weeks' training up to the start of the Tour. Luigi's testing facilities were pretty modest, and the journalist from *BT* who had come along to see it was clearly surprised that they weren't more luxurious. There were a couple of static training bikes that were wired up to a machine and a computer screen. And that was about it. On the walls hung pictures of a number of the riders that Cecchini had worked with over the years – among them a picture of me at the 1996 Tour de France. It's a result that the Italian remains proud of to this day.

Prior to the Tour de France, I rode the Tour of Switzerland together with Ullrich, and we came under a lot of scrutiny from the press, not least because Godefroot had revealed that he wasn't sure which of us would lead the team at the Tour. Jan's weight problems had held him back, while my form seemed surprisingly good, despite the extra kilos Cecchini had told me I was still carrying.

As early as the first stage, I was able to ride away from Jan when the road went upwards. On the following stages, on which there were a number of steep climbs, I continued to progress, and felt as though I had what it took to be able to follow those riders who had taken part in the Tour of Italy, and so were in top form. On the sixth stage, in particular, I was going really well, and finished over a minute in front of Jan. I finished ninth overall, and the German journalists began to get the impression that Jan was going to have to play second fiddle to me at the Tour. Our directeur sportif, Rudy Pevenage, who was Ullrich's biggest fan, made a fool of himself in his opinion of what the race had demonstrated when it came to the way to play things at the Tour. "Bjarne's going better than last year, and I'm sure Jan would have no problem riding for him if he proves to be the strongest of the two of them at the

Tour," Rudy said to the amazement of the gathered journalists, before quickly adding, "or the other way around."

Back home in Denmark, Anne Dorthe and I managed to enjoy some quality time together before I headed off to the start of the Tour in Dublin, and we arranged that she would come and visit me on the race. Maybe it was going to be a good Tour de France after all.

12 "I'VE NEVER TESTED POSITIVE"

I was in a good mood when I turned up to the pre-race medical check-up two days before the start of the 1998 Tour de France in Dublin. A lot of the press attention was on Jan as he stepped up onto the scales. He'd fought hard to get down to his racing weight and, with his new, short haircut, he wouldn't have looked out of place in the military. The doctor examined me while the Danish press looked on. The scales showed that I was 70kg – just a kilo heavier than my ideal race weight.

Jan was the big favourite to win the race again, while I was considered an outsider. The pundits were predicting a battle royale between the two of us from Telekom and the Festina boys, Richard Virenque and Alex Zülle. But the day before the race, my mood was to suddenly and dramatically change. We'd just returned from a training ride, and I'd barely put my foot down before one of the team staff came running up to me. "Have you heard?" he asked me.

"Heard what?" I replied.

"One of Festina's soigneurs has been arrested after they found his car full of doping products," he told me.

The news spread like wildfire, and it quickly became all anyone was talking about. That evening, we held a team meeting at the hotel. Everyone had questions about what was going on, but it was soon clear that no one knew very much at all. We followed the latest news closely on TV, and were all ringing everyone we knew to try to find out more. We were particularly concerned about what it would mean for us riders. The media eventually found out that the soigneur's name was Willy Voet, and that he had been stopped at the France-Belgium border in a car full to the brim with doping products. I made eye contact with a couple of my team-mates, and our nods to each other seemed to suggest that this was not good. I knew Willy Voet by sight. He was one of those people who'd worked in cycling for a number of years. According to the media reports, the French police now had him in custody, and it was alleged that he had initially told the police that the drugs were for his own personal use – which was extremely unlikely, to say the least.

The Tour's start in Dublin should have been a massive celebration, but when the prologue got under way on Saturday 11 July, there was anything other than a party atmosphere, with the news affecting the riders, the press and the spectators. Everyone was just waiting to hear what the French police had found. Later, we found out that customs officials had confiscated 250 syringes containing EPO, and another 400 containing a range of products, including testosterone, blood-thinning medicines, anabolic steroids and amphetamines from Voet's car. The Festina team's *service course* – the squad's headquarters – was subsequently raided, and evidence was found that the team had been systematically doping. In the fridge, police found doping products labelled with riders' names. Each rider had a container with medicine in. The Festina team had some of the biggest names riding for them – Richard Virenque, Christophe Moreau and Laurent Brochard, among others – but the police said that they would be interrogated as soon as the race crossed back into France.

The news caused panic in the peloton. Everyone was suddenly unsure as to what to do – especially when it came to doing something with the doping products they'd brought with them to the race. There was no question in my mind; I knew I now had to be extremely careful. The press smelled a scandal, and with each day that passed, there were new revelations and allegations. In the newspaper *France-Soir*, for example, a Swiss doctor claimed that 99 per cent of the pro peloton was doped. When Festina soigneur Voet admitted to the police that the doping products found in his car were indeed for the team's riders, team manager Bruno Roussel was hauled in for questioning. The Danish journalists asked me for my reaction. "This doesn't look good for cycling, I must say," I told them.

On Wednesday 15 July we arrived back in France, and on the day's stage my countryman Bo Hamburger managed to gain enough time to take the yellow jersey. The race carried on, but the French police came down hard and, that night, gendarmes ransacked Festina's hotel. The riders were taken to the nearest hospital to be drug tested and were interrogated by police, while the team management was arrested.

When the news got back to the other teams about the raids and the arrests, panic broke out once more. Everyone thought that all the hotels were going to be raided by police and customs officials. And if they found any drugs, it would mean that you were going to be arrested and marched down to the police station like a criminal. That helped me make up my mind: the drugs I had with me were going to have to go, and quickly. Within just a few minutes, I'd gathered together all my syringes of EPO and rushed into my hotel bathroom. I squirted the lot down the toilet, and then set about carefully removing any evidence that it had ever existed. The rumours about the police raids turned out to be true, and a number of hotels were searched, although not all of them.

On Friday 17 July, ahead of stage six, almost all of the media's questions were about doping. "If this continues, there will be a number of riders who'll simply want to go home," I told the press. "I've ridden for so many years that I'd rather stop with good memories than have to ride the rest of my career with rumours hanging over me. It's not that fun to be a bike rider at the moment, as when people think about Festina, they immediately lump all the rest of us in with them, and that's not fair."

"You think that people suspect the whole peloton of doping?" a journalist asked.

"Just read the newspapers back home," I retorted. "It's not even just in the sport section any more – this stuff's all over the front pages now, and our sponsors are not happy, believe me."

No sooner had we crossed the finish line of the day's stage than Festina's manager, Roussel, admitted that systematic doping was going on at the team. "The objective was to improve the riders' performance while under strict medical supervision and stop riders doping themselves, therefore putting themselves at risk, as has happened in the past," Roussel's lawyer said.

With that admission, the rest of the Tour could only get worse for us. It was no longer about just a few individuals who had dabbled with doping for their own means, but a whole team. Here was the proof that one of the biggest squads had an organised doping programme, which meant that the hunt was only going to intensify, and both the police and the press would begin to investigate whether the other big teams were doing the same. The Tour's race director, Jean-Marie Leblanc, threw the Festina team – with all its big stars – out of the race that evening. Shortly afterwards, French television showed pictures of Virenque leaving the race in tears. The rest of us, who still hadn't been implicated, sat around in our hotels, feeling a mix of fear and worry for what would come next. The action taken by the police and customs officers seemed planned, as though it was part of a bigger investigation by the French government.

I began to find it difficult to get to sleep at night. I'd lie awake thinking about everything that had happened, and the fierce criticism the sport I loved was now being subjected to. The way people were judging us as criminals was fuel for thought. Maybe the critics were right when they said that, as pros, we lived in our own little bubble. Within the sport, most people knew that drugs were being transported around to be used during stage races, and very few hadn't been a part of it. But it had become an accepted part of the sport. It was an option that had become a necessity, but perhaps things had gone too far. Even so, it didn't justify the police's heavy-handed methods. It wasn't like doping was going to disappear overnight. That was completely unrealistic. As long as there were benefits and money to be had from taking EPO and other products, people were going to take short-cuts to get to the top. Doping in sport goes completely against the spirit of sport itself, but the difference between that and being treated like hardened criminals, thrown into solitary confinement, strip-searched and having your possessions taken away from you, is huge.

After another sleepless night alone with my thoughts and worries, I knew I had to pull myself together for the time trial on Saturday

18 July. Things didn't go well for me; I felt like I never really got going. Jan, on the other hand, won the stage easily, thrashing everyone, and took the yellow jersey from Hamburger in the process. I finished almost four minutes down on my German team-mate.

While a few journalists wanted to ask me about my performance, most were only interested in what I thought about the developments in the doping story. The questions had, I felt, become a lot more suspicious in their tone. The race was now drowning in the subject of doping.

On Wednesday 22 July, our attentions turned to trying to defend Jan's race lead on the stage finishing at Plateau de Beille. The small Italian rider with the pirate bandana and the sticking-out ears, Marco Pantani, seemed to have become Jan's biggest competition. He was a fantastic climber, and few could match his tempo in the mountains. He was having a particularly good season, too, and even though we were watching him for signs that he might attack, there was little we could do come the final climb. Pantani's attack splintered the lead group, and he won the stage – although it wasn't enough to take yellow from Jan. I was in 15th position overall by the end of the stage.

The talk had turned a bit more towards the race in the previous couple of days but, despite that, there was a feeling that it would be only a matter of time before new revelations came out. Sure enough, that was exactly what happened on the rest day the following day, when a number of riders and staff members were arrested by the police. Among them was the manager of the Dutch TVM team, Cees Priem, and the team's doctor. They were arrested because evidence of doping had been found when the police had raided TVM's hotel.

We wandered around in our own hotel in our tracksuits, feeling increasingly like we were part of a TV crime drama rather than sportsmen taking part in the world's toughest bike race. Everyone was worried and jumpy, expecting the police to burst in at any moment and go through our rooms and suitcases with a fine-tooth comb. We found out that doping was punishable as a criminal offence under France's drugs laws, which was why the police and the authorities were able to use such heavy-handed methods as the raids, interrogations and arrests continued. A number of riders were calling for all the teams to pull out of the race altogether and leave France in protest at what was happening, but there were just as many riders who wanted to stay, which caused many an argument. I was one of those against boycotting the race, as I thought doing so would just make things even worse for us. If times were changing and there was now an option not to dope, then we had to accept it, and not just bury our heads in the sand. And pulling out really wasn't going to do us any good. If there was a problem – and clearly there was – then it was only going to be destructive to behave like a bunch of spoilt children. I felt under huge pressure, so thank goodness that I had Ole Kåre, Anne Dorthe and my dad there with me.

At the start in Tarascon-sur-Ariège the next morning, there were some tense-looking riders. The opinion in the peloton was split as to what to do next. Ahead of us was stage 12's 222km route, but the French and Spanish riders were refusing to race. They were led by French star Laurent Jalabert, who wanted us all to quit the race, but it was difficult for anyone to keep a cool head when it came to discussions, as we were all stressed out and confused. No one knew how to handle the situation, with each team seemingly coming to the table with different goals. I argued that we should ride the stage, but show our discontent by riding part of the stage at an easy pace. Jalabert was having none of it, however, and wasn't scared to say so.

Despite everything, we all rolled out of town for the first few kilometres on the neutralised section of the course from the *départ fictif* to the start proper, where we all pulled to a halt. There was no way that we could carry on, with the unrest and disagreements that were continuing to go on.

We got off our bikes, with many of the riders plonking themselves down in the road, and waited. Each team nominated a rider to speak on their behalf, and I was Telekom's spokesman. Together with the others, I began to negotiate with race director Leblanc. We made it clear to him that we had had enough and were tired of being treated like criminals. But even though we were the spokespeople for our teams, there was no real unity among us. All sorts of accusations were flying about. Some teams were calling us Telekom riders selfish – that we were only thinking about our wallets and the bonuses that would surely come if we could keep Jan in yellow and win the Tour. "That's absolute rubbish," I told them. "The easiest thing would be to go home, but that wouldn't solve anything."

Suddenly, Jalabert got hold of the microphone from Leblanc's car, and began to speak like some kind of union boss to the others. "No one's talking about the race any more," he shouted. "All anyone wants to talk about is doping, but we've had enough. We feel like we're being treated like cattle by the press and the Tour organisation."

That just served to create total chaos. Each team representative returned to their team-mates to discuss the issues internally. It was impossible to get everyone to agree to your point of view.

Most of the Spanish and Italian teams had been given the green light to go on strike, but would it really do any of us any good to all sit down and cry about the situation? The best decision didn't appear to be to stick our tails between our legs. We needed to unite as a peloton, and make it all the way to Paris – not only for our sake, but for the sake of the race, the sport and our sponsors.

We had the full backing of our sponsor, Telekom, who trusted us and were confident that we were doing our best by them in what was a difficult situation. We were obliged to look at the bigger picture, and to the future, before making any hasty decisions.

Not everyone shared my opinion, though, and after an hour of futile arguments, I'd had enough, and marched over to Leblanc's race director's car and got in next to him to discuss how we could get going again. "We can't just stop here," I told him, and he agreed. The Frenchman looked at his watch. Time was beginning to run out. It had gone midday, and we needed to get going again from here by 1:00pm at the latest, as the roads wouldn't be able to remain closed any later than that.

Leblanc was clearly shaken by it all. "If we abandon this stage, then this year's Tour is over," he said, "as will next year's event be."

I explained the difficulty we were having as riders. "We don't want to be part of a witch hunt in which we don't have any say,"

I said. "If things continue like this, then we will just all have to go home, so you really need to do something."

No one wanted the Tour to have to stop, and so Leblanc promised that he'd do whatever he could to try to improve matters. "Okay – then we'll ride," I said, and went back to the others to pass on Leblanc's promise.

It wasn't as simple as that, however, and the arguments between us continued as time marched on towards 1:00pm and the deadline for getting the stage going again. While the bickering continued without any constructive suggestions for how we could resolve the situation, a group of us took matters into our own hands and took responsibility for making a decision on the peloton's behalf. "We simply can't stand here on the road – 180 of us – and expect to come to a decision," I argued. "We need to sit down properly and talk this through when we have time to do it."

But still a number of Spanish and French riders accused me of showing a lack of solidarity. "We simply can't have them going through the rubbish bins at the hotel," one of them shouted at me. "There need to be some boundaries."

A few days before, French television had gone to the Asics team's hotel in Pau and filmed what was in the dustbins from the riders' and managers' rooms. The TV programme showed that among the rubbish was some empty packaging for a banned product, and the journalists presented the packet as evidence that doping was rife in the peloton. The problem was that the Tour's race doctor had prescribed the drug to one of the Asics riders who had been struggling with a knee injury. There really did need to be a limit, as none of us wanted to be accused of anything we hadn't done. We all agreed that we needed to get together again once everyone had calmed down to talk things through. The compromise was that we would ride the day's stage but wouldn't talk to the police or the press afterwards. We also arranged a meeting for that evening, which all the teams would attend in order to try to reach some kind of long-term solution to cycling's doping problems. Leblanc also repeated his promise that he'd talk to his contacts, which included politicians, prosecutors and the police, in order to ensure that we weren't maltreated.

At 12:55pm, we were on our way again – five minutes before the deadline that could have spelled the end of the Tour de France. The deal reached with the race organisation to continue riding didn't exactly make me many new friends in the peloton, but I'd just have to live with that. Our whole team was now in the Spanish riders' bad books, and we certainly felt it for the remainder of the stage. The consensus was that if Telekom wanted to race so badly, then we were going to be made to race, and made to work hard to defend Jan's yellow jersey. Laurent Jalabert and his brother Nicolas, both from the Spanish ONCE squad, and TVM's Bart Voskamp attacked from the bunch and formed a breakaway group for us to chase. They knew that none of the other teams were going to chase them, so it would be down to us Telekom "scabs" to do all the work. We did have to work hard, too, and eventually brought them back, but it was the Jalabert brothers' way of showing the dissatisfaction with my decision. I'd certainly got the message. But the scandal wasn't going to go away any time soon, and there was soon more to come. The media were reporting that some of the Festina riders – Zülle, Brochard, Dufaux, Meier and Moreau – under police questioning had allegedly admitted that they had doped.

Virenque, on the other hand, maintained that he was innocent, while the story was that Zülle had broken down and said that he had doped in order to satisfy the sponsors' ambitions. Manager Bruno Roussel and the soigneur, Willy Voet, had explained to the police how the doping was organised at Festina, and how other teams had also been involved in smuggling doping products. It felt as though the sport of cycling itself was disintegrating, and that our whole future was being called into question.

In the meeting between the teams, we decided that we weren't prepared to answer any more questions about doping for the rest of the Tour. Journalists would only be allowed to ask questions about the race itself. Of course, it was completely unenforceable, especially not after the latest news in the Festina case. The press were never going to bow to our wishes about what could or couldn't be talked about. The tone of their questions made it very clear what they thought about what was happening. As one of the spokesmen, I'd put my neck on the line, which meant fielding even more difficult questions from the media – many of which I was totally unprepared for. "Are you doped?" or "Have you ever doped?"

were the kinds of questions thrown at me again and again. I felt as though the line was being crossed, and that they were just all out to get me. Each time I talked with the press, I was forced more and more into a corner – and one which seemed almost impossible to get out of with my honour still intact. So far, I'd managed to defend myself against questions about my own doping simply by lying. But in one interview for a Danish TV channel, I tried to be a little more truthful by answering that "I've never tested positive". It certainly wasn't a lie, and was the best I could come up with in what was a difficult and stressful situation. In principle, I hadn't said anything wrong. Had I answered "yes" to whether I'd doped, my career would be over. I didn't really have anywhere else to go; cycling was my bread and butter, and I had no desire to be one of the ones who had to take a bullet for all the others who had spent their careers doping. My "never tested positive" answer, though, caused a huge hoo-ha back in Denmark.

On the morning of Sunday 26 July, the shit really hit the fan for me. I was told that back home in Denmark *Ekstra Bladet* had called me a coward on its front page. The headline was based on Laurent Jalabert having seemingly spoken out about how dissatisfied he was with my role during the negotiations with the Tour organisers. The Frenchman had criticised me for what he saw as me only thinking about Telekom's interests, and continuing in the race because Jan had the yellow jersey. Calling me a coward, however, was crossing the line, and I wasn't going to stand for it. In addition, the president of the Danish cycling federation, Peder Pedersen, had told the media that he needed a much clearer and more definitive answer to whether I'd doped than "I've never tested positive".

When I arrived at the stage start in Valréas ahead of stage 14, the journalists swarmed around me. I was furious about the "coward" headline. My anger, plus the journalists' accusatory questions, made for a bad combination, and there was soon confrontation in the air.

"I think that Peder Pedersen should come to me himself with such remarks," I told them. "I've already given my thoughts on doping."

But the Danish journalists asked again whether I had ever doped. "I'm 34 years old, and have raced bikes since I was seven," I said. "I have never been more fit and healthy than I am now."

"Yes, but have you ever doped?" came the question again.

"Of course not," I replied, and turned my back and rode off into the safety of the peloton on the start line.

Afterwards, I felt very much like I was up against the ropes, up to my neck in something I had no control over and under pressure to answer questions I simply wasn't ready to answer. What had been said swam around in my head, and my anger built steadily over the course of the stage. I knew that it was the journalists' job to ask the difficult questions when they had to, but I also thought that it was unfair the way they seemed to distort every word I said, and would often take what I said out of context. I really felt as though they were walking all over me and treating me like dirt.

Back at the hotel in Grenoble after the stage, I began to hatch a plan. I'd decided that I was going to talk directly to the people watching at home and try to give them the answers they wanted. I rang TV2 and told them that I wanted to go live and talk directly to the viewers. Despite it being my idea to do it, I wasn't really ready when they immediately agreed. I hadn't really thought my message through, and didn't know what I was going to answer when it came to any questions about doping. On the grass outside the hotel, the crew began their live interview. "Bjarne, you specifically asked to come on television to talk directly to the Danish public, so what is it you wanted to say?" the presenter asked me.

"I'm just tired of this whole controversy about both me and the Tour de France, and in turn what that means for cycling," I said.

"And what is it in particular that you're tired of?"

"I'll tell you," I continued. "When I was asked this morning so many times whether I've ever doped, my answer was that of course I haven't. I want to completely distance myself from anything to do with doping."

"So you stand by what you said about never having doped in your career?"

"That's right," I said. "And now I just want to be left alone. I need to be allowed to get on with concentrating on riding my bike. I really don't think that it's fair that there are some people who are out to ruin my career. If things stay as they are, then that's it – the viewers won't be able to watch Bjarne Riis any more. I'll be gone."

"What is it you think that the press are doing to try to ruin your career?" they asked.

"I'm only talking about the Danish press here," I said. "I won't be called a coward. I don't want to be accused of doping. I want to be taken seriously as a sportsman. I've raced since I was seven years old. I'm now 34, and feel fit and healthy, and in fact have never felt as fit and healthy as I do now. Do I look like a junkie? Do I? I just want to be left alone now."

"Well, now the Danish public have got the answer they wanted," said the presenter. "And that's all this was about: getting a clear answer to the question as to whether you'd doped. Why was it such a difficult question to answer?"

"Listen – any situation like this is going to be difficult," I replied. "In cycling right now we've got a situation that is very delicate. Just one stray word here can suddenly become catastrophic. Everyone's walking on eggshells, and we cyclists are right in the middle of it all. It takes so little to say something wrong, and then suddenly we're all in it up to our necks."

I'd had an opportunity to air my frustrations and give some clear answers to the people watching back home in Denmark, without any of my answers being edited or taken out of context. Yet deep down, I still wasn't completely satisfied, because now there really was no way back. I'd said that I didn't dope, which was a step further than my previous, evasive answer about never having tested positive. I was always going to be remembered for having said that, but now I'd perhaps made things even worse: I'd lied on live TV.

The morning after the interview, on Monday 27 July, there was concern at our hotel. We were readying ourselves for the day's mountain stage to Les Deux Alpes, which took us over the Galibier along the way. We were expecting someone to go on the attack to try to take Jan's yellow jersey, and the prime suspect was the climber Marco Pantani. It was a cold, wet day. "We should have someone standing on the top of the Galibier with some dry clothes and rain jackets," I told the team management.

The Galibier was set to provide Pantani with the perfect place to attack us and, should he attack there, then our best bet would be to try to pull him back again on the descent – providing we were properly prepared, clothing-wise, and weren't freezing. "That won't be necessary," they said, explaining that, logistically, it was going to be too difficult to put someone on top of the mountain to wait for us.

"I disagree," I said, but the general feeling was that we were just going to have to wait and see whether Jan would have what it took if Pantani did attack.

Once under way on the stage, we seemed to have everything under control, but the terrible weather threatened to give anyone who could attack a big advantage over those who didn't enjoy such conditions and wouldn't be able to react.

As soon as we were on the Galibier, as predicted, Pantani attacked, and Jan tried to go with him. "Let him go!" I shouted at Jan, but he didn't listen and proceeded to hammer after the Italian at full pelt. It was suicidal on Jan's part. In that kind of situation, you need to be able to trust your team and use your team-mates in the best way possible. If Jan did lose just a minute or two to Pantani, then it wouldn't have been the end of the world when it came to the general classification, where he would still lead comfortably. But Jan clearly wasn't thinking that rationally when Pantani flew up the road, as he set off in pursuit without much hope of being able to keep up with him. The Italian steadily increased his lead over the rest of us, and was all alone at the top of the Galibier, having dropped Jan, who was now in no man's land with nobody to help him or look after him. He was demoralised and freezing, with no sense of what was happening in the race. A puncture then made matters even worse for him.

When Udo Bölts and I caught up with him at the bottom of the climb up to Les Deux Alpes, he was in an even worse state than I'd feared. He'd lost all momentum and was barely moving forward, and when I pulled alongside him and looked to see how he was, I could see that it was bad. His face was pale and swollen up due to the cold and exhaustion. He looked like a boxer, with an empty stare that told me he'd given up. He was shaking uncontrollably in his soaked-through yellow jersey, and hadn't eaten anything, so was completely drained of energy. We were going to have to push him the rest of the way home.

Nine minutes after Pantani had crossed the finish line as the day's winner, we hobbled in.

The yellow jersey had been lost, and Jan dropped down to fourth place overall, over six minutes down on Pantani, who now led the race. It meant that we'd lost the Tour de France – we all knew it, even though there were still two more mountain stages to go.

I was feeling a lot more positive about things on the day of stage 16. *BT*'s journalist had showed me a printout of readers' letters to the newspaper, showing their support for me. It seemed as though my live appearance on TV2 had been well received. Godefroot also told me that Telekom wanted to renew my contract, which was set to run out at the end of the year. On the stage itself, both Jan and I were keen to get back into the race. There were five mountains on the day's menu, including the Col de la Madeleine. We were riding well, and I could feel that my doctor's treatments had given me a real energy boost. Approaching the final climb of the day, the front group included Jan, Bobby Julich, Pantani, Michael Boogerd, Fernando Escartin and me. Jan seemed to be strong and, when he attacked, only Pantani could go with him. I chose to stick to my own rhythm, while the two of them disappeared up the road, with Jan being the most aggressive of the two. He won the stage, with Pantani finishing second. I came in seventh, just two minutes down. Overall it moved me up to 14th place, 15 minutes down on race leader Pantani. Jan was third overall, six minutes down, but just a few seconds behind Julich in second place.

This time everyone was in much better spirits on our way to the hotel – until yet another doping bombshell. Just after 6pm, police had entered TVM's hotel in Albertville, searching for drugs in the riders' hotel rooms. They'd also searched the team's bus and team cars. A number of the squad's riders were marched to the local hospital to have blood tests and hair analyses done. TV pictures showed the police escorting them away from the hospital again, with one of the TVM riders covering his face with his wind jacket so that no one could see who he was. It made him look like he'd been arrested for killing someone. Seeing the TV images made me angry again. How could they treat us like this? We were being treated like murderers. It seemed completely over the top.

1. My first season. My bike is my pride and joy.

2. Getting used to winning. In my first season, I won almost everything and my self-confidence was born.

3. In 1981, we won the Danish Junior Team Time Trial Championships, with my father as our coach. I'm second from the right.

4. Young and ambitious after earning my first professional contract with Roland Van de Ven.

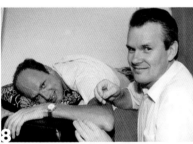

1. Brian Holm (centre) and Jan Østergaard (second from right) also rode with me on the Roland team. Manager Guillaume Driessens is far left.

2. In 1989 I got a contract with French team Super U.

3. I was Laurent Fignon's loyal helper, "gulping the wind" for the French star.

4. Winning my first Tour de France stage in 1993 ahead of Max Sciandri.

5. In yellow for the first time at the 1995 Tour de France.

6. Collapsing, exhausted, after finishing second in the individual time trial during the 1995 Tour de France.

7. Being greeted by fans before the 11th stage of the 1995 Tour.

8. Acupuncturist John Boel helped to boost my energy and strengthen my immune system.

9. Third place at the 1995 Tour made me the highest-placed Dane ever at the race.

10. Mixing it with Miguel Indurain and Alex Zülle in the Pyrenees at the 1995 Tour.

1. Crunch time on the Hautacam at the 1996 Tour. Everything had been planned down to the last detail, and I won the stage to Hautacam thanks in part to the "secret gear" on my bike, which helped to trick my rivals.

2. Gulping in the wind and stamping on the pedals.

3. A strong team. The Telekom squad supported me in my bid for victory at the 1996 Tour.

4. Surrounded by photographers after the final stage of my Tour victory.

5. On the final 1996 Tour podium in Paris, flanked by second-placed Jan Ullrich (right) and third-placed Richard Virenque.

6. Jesper and Thomas in their yellow jerseys at the finish in Paris in 1996, with Mette crying tears of joy.

1. Wearing the yellow jersey during the prologue of the 1997 Tour de France.

2. My trainer, Luigi Cecchini, had a scientific approach to training. Here, I'm trying a new computerised test programme ahead of the 1998 Tour.

3. Jan Ullrich was the strongest on the 1997 Tour, while I had to take on the role as the German's domestique.

4. At the 1998 Tour, no one could agree on whether we should leave the race. Emotions were high, as seen in this discussion with French rider Luc Leblanc.

5. A packed press conference for the day I admitted to having doped.

6. Riding a lap of honour with Carlos Sastre after his 2008 Tour de France win.

7. Sitting beside Alberto Contador during the press conference in Pinto after his suspension by the CAS.

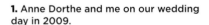

1. Anne Dorthe and me on our wedding day in 2009.

2. Anne Dorthe, me and all five of my sons.

3. Dad with Christian and Matias in Vejle. He enjoyed spending time with his grandchildren in the garden.

4. Three muddy little boys.

5. A great catch. Fishing with my two eldest sons, Jesper and Thomas.

6. Oscar and me outside the house in Vejle. I'm always on the lookout for new goals and opportunities, and the future hopefully holds plenty of both.

Wednesday 29 July was the day of the race's final mountain stage, and therefore our last realistic opportunity to try to wrest the yellow jersey from Pantani. The peloton, though, was ready to revolt. A number of teams were threatening to leave the race in protest at the methods still being used by the police. They wanted the rest of us to leave, too, so that the race would have to stop. However, consensus was still split between the riders as to what to do. Everyone had been worn down, and it only took a couple of misplaced words for arguments to break out and for riders to start shouting at each other, which served to divide us even further. But who would dare take the first decision? Riders stood there, bewildered, waiting for someone to make some kind of decision on a subject they themselves were confused about. Race director Jean Marie Leblanc tried his best to persuade us to get on our bikes and start the stage, and hopefully keep the Tour de France alive. The 149km to Aix-les-Bains was suddenly much more than just another stage; it was a day that could potentially decide whether bike racing survived at all.

In my mind it was clear: we needed to ride the stage, and I rolled away in front, while the others reluctantly followed behind. But shortly afterwards, there was more chaos. Everyone stopped again, and the negotiations restarted. Some riders peeled their race numbers off their jerseys in protest, which was tantamount to deciding they weren't going to race any more. The ONCE team – led by Jalabert – decided officially to leave the race, and other teams considered following suit. But we got going again and, in my role as just one of the spokesmen, I went to Leblanc's car and began to negotiate with him through the open window. We weren't going to put up with the police treating us so badly, nor did we want to be part of this witch hunt with no right to reply, which had been the case so far. Leblanc promised he'd try to do what he could when it came to the police's handling of the situation, and I let myself fall back to the peloton. We all stopped and huddled together in a circle. I told them what Leblanc had promised, but not everyone was prepared to accept it, and the arguments started up once more. My old team-mate, Luc Leblanc, in particular, was very emotional. We argued loudly, pointing our fingers at each other accusingly. We were no diplomats – that much was clear. We agreed to keep riding slowly until the race director could come back with some guarantees. Out of respect for the thousands of roadside spectators, we were going to ride the stage, but not at exactly what you could call race pace. On the day's first climb, we had trouble even getting through the crowds. Most of them cheered us on, but some gave us the thumbs down, or had ripped three of the fingers off the big cardboard hands that had been given out by a race sponsor from the publicity caravan that preceded the race so that they were effectively giving us "the finger" and showing us exactly what they thought of both doping and us. Along the way, Spanish team Banesto and the Italian squad Riso Scotti both decided to drop out of the race in protest. Neither of them believed in the promises.

Again I rolled up to Jean-Marie Leblanc in the race director's car to try to get a final answer on what would happen next. He told me that the authorities had given him their word that the police would only continue their investigation of us riders with "dignity and discretion". It was a welcome promise, as rumours had been going around the bunch that the police had gone as far as performing rectal examinations in a bid to find drugs. Such methods really were unacceptable.

Two hours behind schedule, we crossed the finish line. That evening, the rider in the polka-dot "King of the Mountains" jersey, Rodolfo Massi – who was one of Bo Hamburger's team-mates on the Casino team – was arrested. Police had raided his hotel room and found doping products, and he was also suspected of trafficking drugs. Some of the media were claiming that Massi was known in the peloton as "The Pharmacist", in reference to his alleged distribution of drugs. Back at our hotel, there were all sorts of crazy rumours doing the rounds – one being that Telekom were also about to pull out of the race, which meant that the hotel lobby was soon full of journalists. "Is it true that you're going to leave the race?" came the question in Danish, German and English. But I had no idea where the rumour had come from, and neither did Godefroot. It turned out that it had stemmed from a Spanish news bureau. When I crawled into bed that night, exhausted after another crazy day, it was as one of just 97 riders left in the race, with 189 having started.

The Tour's penultimate stage – on Saturday 1 August – was a 53km time trial. It was an opportunity for Jan to try to move up to second place overall, whereas my ambition was just to get through it. Earlier in the race I'd managed to pull the back of one of my thighs, and every pedal stroke caused considerable pain. Mentally, I'd also had enough. My passion for cycling had all but dried up over the course of the Tour, and I couldn't get home quickly enough. The three weeks that the Tour had gone on for felt like a year and, when on the last stage we rode the last few laps of the circuit in Paris, we just wanted it to all be over. Every single kilometre was a struggle for me due to my injured thigh, and my team-mates had to push me sometimes because it hurt so much to pedal. I finished the race in 11th place overall, while Jan ended up second to Marco Pantani.

The day after the Tour had finished, I left Paris feeling very unhappy. I realised that I needed to use the next few months to really think through my relationship with doping. My thoughts were that I never wanted to dope again, because it had become such a large part of my life, because it was wrong, and because now it would also be harder than ever not to get caught. But despite that, there were still reasons not to stop – the main one being that if I stopped, and the others all just carried on as before, then the chances of me being able to keep up any more would be extremely slim.

13 UNDER SUSPICION

Anne Dorthe paced up and down in our house in Italy. She was waiting for me to ring to say that I'd landed back in Italy after a trip to Denmark to be treated for a knee injury I had. Suddenly the doorbell rang, and Anne Dorthe opened the door to find two people standing there.

"Hi," one of them said. "Is Bjarne Riis in?"

"No, he's not," she told them.

"Do you know when he'll be coming back?" he asked.

"Who are you, and why are you so interested?" she asked them back.

"German doping control," he told her, and added that they would probably come back later.

As an employee of the German Telekom team, I was subject to German doping controls, which was the reason for their unannounced visit. Immediately, Anne Dorthe called me, but couldn't get hold of me because I was still on the plane. She was pacing up and down even more nervously then, checking out of the window whether the doping controllers were waiting in their car outside.

When I was able to return her missed call, she immediately asked me where I was.

"At the airport," I said. "Why's that?"

"There were two doping controllers from Germany here to see you," she told me.

"Are they still there?" I asked.

"Not that I can see from the window, no," she said.

When we saw each other later, Anne Dorthe was clearly still

badly affected by their unannounced visit. "We can't live like this any more," she told me. "I can't have it that we can be visited at any time of the day or night, and be worried that you've taken something illegal."

She was right that it couldn't go on – the fight against doping had really stepped up a gear. I'd tried to keep a low profile after the doping scandal at the Tour. While riders from Festina and TVM were being handed out bans for having admitted to doping, I'd used the time since the race to really consider whether I wanted to continue to dope myself or whether I wanted to stop and draw a line under it, and make the decision that this was the start of a new dope-free era. But the time I'd taken to think about it hadn't really made me any wiser or more decisive. If I was honest with myself, I really didn't want to keep doping at all, but my worry was over what my rivals were going to do.

Until this point, Anne Dorthe had tacitly accepted that doping was a necessary evil in professional cycling. Only on very rare occasions had she actually asked what the medicines were that sometimes stood in our fridge. I'd tried to explain what I took, what effect it had and how it worked. "I know it's something you do because you think that it's something you have to do to be at the top level," was her take on it.

At the start of January 1999, a journalist from Danmarks Radio, Olav Skaaning Andersen, called me with some bad news. "We've got hold of some information about doping that went on at the Gewiss-Ballan squad when you were on the team," he told me, "and we're making a programme about it. We wanted to ask you whether you want to be a part of it."

"What kind of information have you got?" I asked him.

"It's mainly about your haematocrit level," Olav told me, "and how much it changed in 1995."

"Come on," I said, irritated. "Do you think everything's to do with doping?"

For a number of years, Olav had investigated doping in cycling, but it was as though he'd forgotten that we trained like crazy and ate almost nothing to find our form. Bike racing was a lot more than just doping. There was also the strategy, the tactics, the mental strength and the ability to suffer. I tried to explain all that to him, but he wouldn't listen.

"It will all come out eventually, no matter what," he said. "But I think you'd be doing yourself a favour if you worked with us on the programme. Both the programme and the information incriminate you."

The information he was in possession of was print-outs of Gewiss-Ballan riders' haematocrit levels. The figures – including mine – were supposed to prove the use of EPO, he told me during our 45-minute conversation. "I'll think about whether I'll collaborate, and ring back," I promised.

In the hours after the conversation, questions kept popping into my mind. What exactly were these documents that they had? What could the programme do to my career? Should I refuse to be part of it, or should I go on and have my say? Anne Dorthe thought that I should do the programme, and I agreed with her. I called Olav back to tell him that I'd do it. "But I want to know what it is you've got," I said. We arranged to meet at Ole Kåre's clinic in Karlslunde the next day.

The atmosphere was tense when Olav and a cameraman arrived at Ole's clinic on the afternoon of 7 January. Before the interview, I was briefed on the haematocrit information, and was told that Olav and his mate, Niels Christian Jung, had also found some packaging from medical products in the rubbish at Gewiss-Ballan's hotel during the 1995 Tour of Denmark. While the cameraman set up his equipment, I got a chance to study the computer print-outs. They showed that I supposedly had a haematocrit level of 41 per cent during a training camp in January 1995, but another document showed that on the rest day at the Tour de France that same year, on 10 July, it was 56.3 per cent.

The figures, I was told, indicated that I had taken EPO. My name was in the documents, too, albeit written as "Rijs". When I looked closer at some of the other figures, it showed that one of my Gewiss team-mates had apparently had a haematocrit level of 62 per cent in August 1995, a few days after the Tour of Denmark. "That really is high," I said to Olav.

I still thought that it would do me more harm if I didn't take part in the programme, even though I wasn't convinced that the documents were genuine. I certainly had never seen the figures before. I knew that I was going to have to choose my words carefully, and the interview began. "Do you recognise these figures?" I was asked.

"No, I don't," I replied. "And they mean nothing, because I don't know where you've dug them up from, and don't know why I should believe any of what you're saying."

"What do you say to the figure of 56.3 per cent?" they continued.

"What do you want me to say? They're not my figures," I said. "Anyone can come along with some papers with numbers on them and say, 'These are yours.' Why should I believe it? There's no reason for me to."

"Were you tested on that rest day at the Tour in 1995?"

"I would say no," I said. "I don't recall having a blood test at all that year at the Tour. I think I only had blood taken by my team, Telekom, during the Tour."

During the 1995 Tour of Denmark, Olav's friend, journalist Niels Christian Jung, had worked as a masseur on the Gewiss-Ballan team, without us knowing what his motives were. During that time, he'd gathered together needles and ampoules from a hotel room in Kolding that another Gewiss-Ballan masseur was staying in. The ampoules apparently contained EPO. I'd been told about this before the interview, but suddenly Olav revealed during the interview that they'd tracked down the Gewiss masseur in question, whose name was Paolo Ganzerli. Olav repeated what Paolo had claimed – namely, that the team had used doping products, but that he'd never seen me take anything. I wasn't at all prepared for the questions that followed.

"It was in Paolo's room that the products were found in 1995. He told us that they were his, and that they were for the team."

"What do you want me to say to that?" I asked.

"You never used EPO at Gewiss-Ballan?" they asked.

"No, I've never used EPO," I replied. "That's enough now."

"He said that it was used by the team," they continued.

"I never saw it," I said. "But that's his account. As I say, if I always had to comment on things I don't know anything about, life would be too short."

"But Paolo said that EPO was being used by Gewiss-Ballan at that time," they replied.

"You know what? You can just say whatever you like, can't you?" I said. "You can just as easily say that you've seen me fill my car up with petrol and then drive off without paying. Where's this getting us?"

"So you never saw anything."

"No. Like I said, I never saw anything," I said.

During the interview I felt like I was being backed into a corner and judged without having even seen the supposed evidence. I got the feeling that it was only circumstantial evidence that they were in possession of. Once it was over, I thought that it had actually gone relatively well. I'd defended myself and hadn't said anything I shouldn't have done. However, I was annoyed that Olav hadn't told me that they had found Paolo.

Immediately afterwards I contacted my lawyer, Karoly Nemeth, and asked him whether we could take legal action against DR. I then talked to Paolo on the phone. It turned out that DR's journalists had found him in San Marino almost at the same time as Olav interviewed me, in doing so avoiding Paolo being able to warn me. He said that he didn't know that they were going to contact him, and that perhaps he'd said too much.

I thought it was completely unreasonable on DR's behalf, and called Olav again. "What the hell were you playing at contacting Paolo in Italy?" I asked.

Olav defended himself, and said that it was important that they'd done things in the order that they did.

"And what does Jung think he knows?" I asked.

Going after Paolo after we'd let Niels Christian Jung work as a masseur on the team, while what he was really most interested in was going through our rubbish, was, I felt, abusing my trust and was tantamount to setting a trap. But Olav didn't want to talk any more about it.

"You need to try to stop this programme being aired," I told Karoly before I headed off to the Telekom pre-season training camp in Mallorca. It felt like the sky was falling in.

On the grounds that what DR had was confidential doctor-patient information, Karoly tried to claim an injunction against the programme being shown, which had in fact now become two programmes which would be shown on consecutive nights. DR's lawyers, however, didn't agree, and said that the haematocrit levels were in the public's interest. Karoly called me in Mallorca. "We can't stop them from showing the programmes," he told me. All we could do was sit back and wait to see how much damage it all caused, and see what the public's reaction to the programmes was. I let Telekom know what was happening, and we waited.

On Monday 11 January, the first programme was aired – *The Price of Silence*, as it was called.

The accusations against me started with the 1995 Tour de France:

In the time trial, Riis surpassed himself. He was right up there at the same level as the then four-time Tour de France winner Miguel Indurain. At the finish, the Dane was beaten by just 12 seconds – a surprising runner-up to the Spaniard. The next day – 10 July – was a rest day on the Tour de France. Our print-outs show that all nine of the Gewiss-Ballan riders had a blood test that day, and that six of them showed haematocrit levels significantly over 50. Bjarne Riis's was at 56.3. Michael Friedberg is one of the country's leading EPO experts:

"56.3 is clearly very high. In fact it's ridiculously high: either the patient must be lying in the hospital, ill, or they've doped. It is not a level you would get in a normal, healthy human being otherwise. There is a considerable risk attached to such levels, and it can result in problems such as blood clots in the brain, in the heart or elsewhere. If it was one of my patients, I'd immediately stop them from taking EPO and would draw out around half a litre of blood."

In the space of just six months, Bjarne Riis's haematocrit level had rocketed – from 41.1 in January to 56.3 in July.

"When you're presented with such figures, it makes you think that there must have been a quite deliberate action to have increased the level. There is no natural way to increase the levels like that. I can conclude, therefore, that there is strong evidence to suggest this is due to doping."

In the days that followed, both the Danish and international press were filled with accusations against me. Telekom told me to say as little as possible and to just let the story run its course. But it was tough being the subject of what I felt was a smear campaign, and I really didn't want to be the only rider being held accountable for the doping practices of the 1990s. While I was at the training camp, my mobile didn't stop ringing as journalists fished for a comment from me. "Can you just provide us with a bit more information about your haematocrit levels?" they asked.

"Why should I?" I told them each time.

"It's the only hope you have of dispelling the doping rumours," a journalist from *Politiken* suggested. She meant that if I officially revealed my haematocrit figures, I could refute the circumstantial evidence.

A well-known lecturer in law, Jørn Vestergaard, told a newspaper that I needed to prove my innocence. But where was the justice in that? That I was guilty until proven innocent? That anyone could pluck wild accusations and allegations out of thin air, and then I'd have to try to prove that the accusations were false? It was a game I had no interest in playing. That would just mean that the media would be free to print whatever they liked, and then make whoever was embroiled in it try to prove that the story was made up.

In response, my lawyer went on the offensive. "I just don't get what the lecturer is talking about," Karoly told one newspaper. "Can he perhaps prove that it wasn't him who stole my bicycle three years ago? Of course he can't.

"My client is well known," Karoly continued, "but that shouldn't mean that the law works in a different way when it comes to him compared to anyone else. You're supposed to be innocent until proven guilty – that's how it's always been. This would be the first time in the history of law if suddenly things happened the other way around."

For the media, the doping scandal was just another story, and soon they'd be chasing a different one. There was always going to be the next thing for them to move on to, whereas it was my life, my career and my livelihood that was on the line.

But back in Denmark, there were people who were ready to distance themselves from me and walk away. Sponsors were pulling the plug, and stories about me – and doping – were in the papers on an almost daily basis. I was the once-feted hero who was now being cast as a serial cheater. The TV programmes and the subsequent negative publicity led me to hide myself away more than ever. I tried to concentrate on cycling, and to only talk about the sporting side of things, but I couldn't hold back when Mogens Jacobsen from *Politiken* came to interview me in Mallorca. "I really can't get my head around how, from one day to the next, people can almost turn their back on me," I said. "None of all those who think they're such experts have the faintest idea about my life. None of them know how hard I've really trained year after year, yet they seem to know exactly what I've supposedly done. I don't understand how people can be like that. I'm not asking for pity, but what I would like is some respect."

Back home again in Italy, I knuckled down to some hard training, but it was also time to have some serious talks with Anne Dorthe. She'd become worried about my relationship with doping after we'd watched *The Price of Silence* and was concerned about the extent of the side-effects. So far, she'd been non-judgemental, but now she needed some reassurances that I was looking after myself. "Are there any side-effects from what you take?" she asked.

"Don't worry – I am looking after myself. And I'm not sure whether I'm going to continue taking anything anyway," I reassured her, as I'd genuinely been considering whether I should stop taking EPO.

The TV programmes, the media reaction, the bans handed out to the riders who were caught or admitted to taking drugs and not least a court case in Italy – it was all plenty to worry about. In October 1998, a raid on a university clinic in Ferrara in northern Italy, run by Professor Francesco Conconi, resulted in the police confiscating the professor's computer. He was accused of masterminding a number of pro cyclists' systematic use of EPO. At the clinic, police allegedly found evidence of Gewiss-Ballan, and therefore me, having been doped in 1995. There was speculation that the haematocrit figures revealed on the Danish TV programmes had come from material seized by the police. The journalists had jumped straight onto the case, mainly because my own trainer, Luigi Cecchini, had connections to Professor Conconi at the start of the 1990s.

At the Tirreno-Adriatico stage race, five police officers came up to me one day with a court summons. "Will you testify?" they asked me.

"Yes," I replied.

It was yet more proof that it was far too dangerous to continue doping, and it meant that something had to be done.

Everything I owned at home that had ever had anything to do with doping needed to be got rid of, and I set about gathering it all into a pile. I dug out my training diaries from the 1990s, in which I'd recorded my heart rate, the weather, the distance I'd trained, my haematocrit levels and how many units of EPO I'd taken. I'd carefully noted down exactly what I'd taken, when and how much. There were diagrams and graphs covering the year and showing the improvement in my form in relation to what I'd taken. The entries had been written in code, but you wouldn't exactly have had to have been a rocket scientist to crack it. The pile on the floor took on the shape of some kind of monument to a period in my life that was about to end. Papers, ampoules, packaging – all of it was to be thrown away, disposed of from my life forever. For too long it had bothered me that I injected myself with doping products, living with a secret that was in danger of being discovered at any moment. Throwing everything out seemed like the right thing to do. I'd had enough of the lies and the constant threat of being found out, while the feeling of guilt had become overwhelming.

For the past few months, each time I went out training, my conscience had tried to convince me that it was wrong to continue doping. But it wasn't an easy process; each time I thought that I'd finally convinced myself to stop, there was always another little voice that piped up: "What about what the others are doing?" During those same training sessions, I realised what an integral part of my life doping had become. It was a habit and a lifestyle. But it just wasn't worth it. I didn't have the same spark or hunger for the job any more. I'd been in the game for too long and, especially on the days when the weather wasn't too great for training, it had become to easy to use excuses not to go out. "It won't matter if I don't train today," I'd convince myself. The thought of staying at home with Anne Dorthe had become far more attractive than spending three or four hours out in the wind or rain. Before, my life had revolved around bike racing. It had been about cycling 24 hours a day, with every little thing I did geared towards making me a better rider.

But I'd matured in every sense. My interests had changed. My thoughts had turned increasingly to the future, and what I was going to do once I'd hung my bike up. I'd begun to get more and more interested in business and commercial opportunities, and felt a need to broaden my horizons. Basically, I wanted to do anything other than cycling.

That spring, I rode a few races, which went okay – especially considering my lack of motivation and training. And on Friday 19 March, I stood in the witness box at the Italian court case concerning the university clinic in Ferrara. For five hours the judge questioned me in detail about what I knew about the use of EPO at Gewiss-Ballan. He tried to trap me in all sorts of ways, hoping that I'd crumble and give them what they wanted. The whole experience was nasty, aggressive and didn't feel right from the very first instance. The judge tried to make me feel like a criminal who had committed the world's worst crime. A Danish interpreter translated the judge's questions and my answers, and clips from *The Price of Silence* were shown. He tried to provoke me and scare me into admitting things. "We know everything, so you may as well tell us everything you know," he said.

"You'd better show me what evidence you have, then," I said.

Photocopies of the documents used for the TV programme were presented to me.

"Those figures aren't right," I said.

"We don't believe you," he replied.

The judge wanted me to hang my former team-mates out to dry. It was them he was going after. But I didn't want to be any part of it. I could be held accountable for what I'd done myself, when I was ready to do so, but until then I wasn't going to blow the whistle on anyone.

The next day, I rode the one-day Classic Milan-San Remo, but everything just felt wrong. Walter Godefroot could sense that I was severely lacking in motivation, and could tell that I was thinking of not riding the 1999 Tour. "Ride the Tour of Switzerland in June and then see how you feel," he suggested. Even though I stood at the top of the team's hierarchy and was one of the best-paid riders, Walter still wouldn't be prepared to let me take part in the Tour de France unless I was physically and mentally up to it. The stage race in Switzerland was the perfect way to gauge whether I still had what it took.

On Saturday 5 June I was in France to take part in the Classique des Alpes. I'd been following the Giro d'Italia on TV for the past couple of weeks, and all the old favourites were the ones animating the race. Laurent Jalabert, Ivan Gotti and Richard Virenque had all won stages, while Marco Pantani seemed more dominant than ever. He had won four stages along the way and was leading overall by more than five minutes going into the penultimate stage. But then we heard the news: "Marco Pantani is out of the Giro." Only later in the day, though, did we find out the reason why.

Pantani had been led away from his hotel by two Italian police officers. Anti-doping officers had paid him an unannounced visit at his hotel that morning and given him a blood test, which had shown he had a haematocrit level of 52. That was two per cent higher than the level allowed by cycling's governing body, the UCI, which was introduced in 1997, and so Pantani therefore had no choice but to leave the race, even though he was only two stages away from overall victory. The high presence of red blood cells were what the experts were looking for to indicate the presence of EPO. There would be only one thing that people would talk about from then until the end of the Tour de France, and that was doping. Everything would be under the spotlight once more, and the newspapers would come to the conclusion that nothing had been learned in cycling and that riders were doping, just as they always had done. And I'd simply had enough.

With just a few days to go before the start of June's Tour of Switzerland, I went to see Ole Kåre to try to relieve some of the tension I was feeling and to get some energy back ahead of the race. I was feeling irritable, as the German news magazine, *Der Spiegel*, had published an article claiming that there was systematic doping at Telekom. This new round of accusations, as well as the frustrations of the past few months, meant that I was tense and stressed and in real need of some treatment at Ole's hands.

During the final training sessions before the race, I'd felt heavy on the bike, and as though my energy was somehow being blocked. However, it did help make my decision easier, and I pulled Godefroot to one side one evening at the hotel.

"I'm not going to ride the Tour de France this year," I told him.

He knew that I was beginning to wind down towards the end of my career.

"That's okay," he said.

I felt a sense of relief immediately. It felt good to actually say the words out loud and to make a decision about something that had been nagging at me for a number of months. It felt good to acknowledge that, at the age of 35, I'd reached a point in my career where I had a choice between, on the one hand, joining a smaller team, where I'd be able to dine out on my previous results and be paid quite well and, on the other, being the one deciding when to stop and saying a dignified farewell to the sport.

Whether it was relief over having made a decision or the after-effects of Ole's treatment that hit me on the first few stages of the race, I don't know, but suddenly I was riding with a whole new energy and enthusiasm, and at a level much higher than I had up until that point in the season so far. There were almost signs of Tour form. Godefroot gave me a nod and a little smile one day that seemed to say, "Are you sure about not riding the Tour?"

That night while I was lying in bed, I couldn't help wondering whether I should perhaps ride the Tour after all. The first stages of the Tour of Switzerland had proved that I could still ride at the top level, as long as the motivation, energy and form were still there. Maybe I still had something to give, or perhaps it was nothing more than a crazy idea, borne out of the energy Ole had given me.

My form seemed to be improving with each stage, and it was clear that taking part in the Tour wasn't such a mad idea after all.

Ahead of stage four, and feeling full of enthusiasm, I went to see the team mechanics to see whether they could just make a few adjustments to my bike. They did their thing, and I jumped on it and rolled towards the start area, deep in my own thoughts. But there was something not quite right with the gears on my bike still, and as I rode along, I bent down to adjust the rear derailleur, just like I'd done loads of times before. Out of the corner of my eye, I kept a watch on the spectators, the other riders and the road, while I fiddled with the gears. For just a hundredth of a second I gave my full attention to the adjustment I was making, and then looked back up just in time to realise that my wheel had hit the curb at the edge of the cycle path. Even though I was going really slowly, it was fast enough that I lost control of my bike and lost my balance. I had no chance to take my feet out of the pedals and stop myself crashing and, trying desperately but fruitlessly to break the fall with my arm, I hit the ground hard, with my whole body weight falling on my arm.

Shocked and irritated, I looked up to see that a number of bystanders had rushed over. I could feel a pain in my elbow, wrist and shoulder, as the people helped me up. "Are you okay?" they asked.

"I'm not sure," I said. I could tell that something was wrong, and rolled carefully back towards the hotel nearby. Every single bump in the road made my elbow and wrist hurt.

In the car park, the bystanders helped me off my bike and called the team doctor, while I looked myself over. I'd certainly lost a bit of skin, and my elbow and wrist were already quite swollen. The doctor arrived and looked at my elbow, which was giving me the most pain. "It's broken," he said. He thought that my wrist was too, and decided to take me to hospital in one of the team cars.

The doctors at the hospital studied the X-rays they did carefully. "You've got a complicated fracture of your elbow, which will need an operation," they concluded. I'd fractured the radial head of my elbow in three places, while they also confirmed that my wrist was broken.

Less than an hour earlier, I'd been dreaming about the Tour de France, buzzing with energy and enthusiasm. And now here I was in so much pain that they'd had to give me painkillers. "You certainly won't be able to ride the Tour de France," the doctor confirmed. "In fact, it could be quite a few months before you can race again, if at all." At that moment, I didn't really know what "if at all" meant. But despite the pain, I felt a sense of relief that someone else had made a decision for me about the Tour, and that it was out of my hands. In fact, it felt somehow symbolic – as though it was actually some kind of higher power that had made the decision for me.

14 RUNNING AWAY

Anne Dorthe and I splashed around in the swimming pool while Jesper and Thomas relaxed on the side. It was these moments that we'd missed – the moments when it could be just us, on our own. The boys could get used to seeing Anne Dorthe and I together, and we were away from prying eyes. Our rented house just outside Lucca in Tuscany was a real refuge for us – far away from Denmark and the press. The house was well secluded and was once part of a castle that belonged to one of Napoleon's generals. We could relax, laugh out loud and not be bothered by anyone. We enjoyed every single day there with the boys and were happy that, despite only having spent a short time together, we had in fact come together as a family.

Anne Dorthe and I had had long, deep conversations about what we were going to do together in life, and when and how we should put our time as Tour de France winner and handball star behind us. Since she'd stopped her handball career at the end of 1998 due to a knee injury, Anne Dorthe had never really found exactly what she wanted to do next. My injury was serious, and the outlook was actually worse than first thought. The break in my elbow was an extremely complicated injury, and it remained to be seen whether I would be able to return to cycling at the top level. The question also was whether I actually wanted to – whether I would physically be able to train myself back up to that level, or whether it was actually nature's way of saying that this was actually the time to stop, reconsider our lives and then start something new together.

The house in Tuscany had been our sanctuary since we'd moved there from Denmark. Like any other couple, we needed to do things together without having to share them with the rest of the world or the public. As a "new family", we needed time to find our feet in our new roles and to get used to the way it all worked. If we were to start a new life together as Anne Dorthe and Bjarne, rather than the handball player and the cyclist, we needed to do it in a place where we could take our time and do it our way. "I want to be able to go down to the supermarket in jogging bottoms without worrying about what people might think," Anne Dorthe had said to me one day when we still lived in Denmark. "I want to be able to go for a walk with you, hand-in-hand, without there being a photographer waiting for us, and without people putting their necks out of joint to watch us."

"Let's move to Italy," I had suggested. The idea had been considered for quite a while, and seemed like a good idea as we were keen to get away. The only downside would be living so far away from the boys.

"I'm up for leaving if you are," said Anne Dorthe, and we did it – we moved away from the press and the public.

The view over the mountains, the silence and the anonymity were all the result of the freedom we'd been looking for. It gave the much-needed peace that Anne Dorthe and I needed to get to know each other properly, which we hadn't really been able to do in Denmark. Our relationship became much more relaxed without any interruptions, and we were able to be certain that the two of us were going to have a life together no matter what. We could finally be left alone. The local cyclists knew that I'd moved to the area near Lucca, and they often recognised me in the street, but they didn't hassle me in any way at all. And when Anne Dorthe went out, there was no one who stared at her because she'd been a handball player.

My injury from the crash at the Tour of Switzerland, on the other hand, was far more complicated, and had left me in a lot of discomfort. The elbow hadn't healed at all as planned, and returning to training had been hampered by the fact that I couldn't really sit properly on my bike due to not being able to fully stretch out my arm. The strange position it put me in then in turn gave me problems with my back and one of my knees when I rode. Walter Godefroot called me up one day to ask how things were going. "Not great," I told him.

He asked what the chances of me making a comeback were.

"Not great," I answered again. There was no need to be unrealistic. My contract with Telekom was due to run out at the end of the year, and Godefroot needed to know how things were looking. He knew that I didn't want to tell him anything other than the truth, and equally I knew that he would never abandon me now that time was running out and my career was almost over.

"Just take it easy, Bjarne," he said. "Just take your time and try to find out whether you'll be able to ride your bike again. If you're able to ride at a good level again next year, then you know there'll be a place for you on the team."

The pain of the injury, however, was making it impossible to sit on my bike for the number of hours I needed to train to mount a comeback, and one evening Anne Dorthe and I decided that we needed to discuss the situation. "What if this really is it?" I asked her. "I've always been a bike rider. What else could I possibly do?"

In my mind, it had always been clear why I was a cyclist. Someone could have tapped me on the shoulder at any time of the night or day and asked me why I was a bike rider and I would have been able to answer without a moment's hesitation. I would tell them that it was my life, and that my life made sense on a bike. I could constantly set myself new goals and continuously improve.

No one should be a bike rider because they don't know what else to do. A rider always has to be conscious of what they're doing, and I was convinced that it was important for everyone – no matter who they were – to have a goal, and to know why they were doing what they were doing. But I was far from certain that I still had that same level of awareness that made me want to continue in cycling. The truth was that I had increasingly closed myself off from the sport – that the need to expand my horizons and discover other sides of myself had begun to take over. "In a lot of ways, living as a sportsman or sportswoman is a very blinkered existence," said Anne Dorthe. "You don't ever have to make any decisions yourself.

You can't just easily visit your family or friends, or take part in every family occasion because you're either training or competing. Yet despite all that, you can convince yourself that you're not missing out. But that's not actually true."

Anne Dorthe had gone through all these thoughts and feelings when she'd stopped her career, and was now able to help me as a result. "I'd compare my life as a handball player to a motorway," she told me. "I was always going full bore, and then when I got injured it was like pulling in to a rest area. I'd never take an exit off the motorway – just get going again as quickly as possible and get back into the overtaking lane. But that kind of life makes you restless."

Throughout my career, I'd always been meticulous about insuring myself. I'd taken out a policy early on and, as I'd started to earn more, I'd been careful to keep my insurance up to date. In the past year I'd paid 240,000 kroner (£21,000) in insurance contributions to cover myself in case I had an accident. My insurance covered my salary for as long as I was injured, and in the case of involuntarily having to stop my career, I'd be paid compensation. Earlier on in my career, it had been terrifying to think about the day when I'd no longer be able to call myself a professional cyclist any more. It was scary to think about having to find something different to do with my life – to try to find a job that I could be just as passionate about. But I wasn't scared any more, and that was thanks in a big part to Anne Dorthe.

Meanwhile, my injury was proving very difficult to shake off. The consensus amongst the doctors was that I might never be able to train properly again, so I began to mentally prepare myself for the end. In December, Telekom organised a team get-together in Germany, and I went along, too – although not to train or to work out my programme for the new season. Rather, I went to say goodbye to both my colleagues and the sport. It felt strange to stand face to face with Jan, Godefroot and the others on the team. Together we'd achieved some fantastic results during the four years that we'd ridden together. There had been the big Tour victories in 1996 and 1997, and then there'd been the nightmare that was the 1998 Tour, which we'd nevertheless got through together. It was especially sad to say goodbye to Jan, who had developed so much during the time we'd been together on the team, both as a rider and as a person. He'd become a good team-mate, who was also a good friend.

As recently as the past summer he'd come with his girlfriend to visit Anne Dorthe and me in Italy. Like me, Jan hadn't ridden the Tour, either, and while the other riders sweated their way around France, we enjoyed ourselves drinking red wine on our terrace at the house in Italy. I remembered one afternoon at the house in particular, when Jan had wandered out to the terrace where my dad, who was also visiting, was sitting. My father spoke neither German nor English, so they didn't have a common language to communicate with each other, but with a combination of sign language and the odd word in English, German or Danish, they could enjoy the nice view together. My dad thought that Jan was a fantastic bike rider, and was proud to know him. From the living room door, I stood and watched the two of them together out on the terrace. It was a magical moment, and one which my dad and I would always remember. And it was one of the moments I remembered when I said goodbye to Jan and wished him all the best for the future. If he could continue to improve and stay disciplined, he had a good chance of dominating the sport for a number of years. Without each other, perhaps neither of us would have won our Tours de France. The question now was whether he was mature enough to lead the team on his own. As I hugged him goodbye, I wasn't afraid to say it to him: "You're now the leader of this team, Jan. It's your responsibility now."

While the other riders looked forward to the coming season, planned their training and racing schedules, and prepared themselves for a winter of watching what they ate and training four to five hours a day, I could leave them to it with a mixture of sadness and relief. For the first time in my adult life, I was going to be able to spend Christmas and New Year with a clear conscience when it came to enjoying all the festive food and drink, and wouldn't have to constantly be checking the weather to see what it meant for my training.

Even though it wasn't yet official, the decision had been made. My career as a professional cyclist was over. There was now no need to prolong the agony any longer or dream about some kind of miracle happening. My body had simply had enough, and so it was best that I stopped. Together with my lawyer, I scrutinised the insurance agreement, and worked out what stopping my career due to injury meant in terms of a compensation payout from the insurance company. It was a lot of money – well over 10 million kroner (£900,000), it turned out. That was a good reason why the insurance company wanted me to go through all sorts of medical examinations to be certain that I wasn't able to continue with my career.

In the previous few years, cycling had turned into a big commercial business in my eyes, and it was for that reason that I'd taken out an insurance policy that required such large contributions on my part. With a family and the responsibility that comes with that, it was important to me to be covered financially so that they wouldn't be left vulnerable if I got injured or was unable to race.

At the start of March 2000, I had the final medical examination that would definitively decide whether my injuries were going to prevent me from riding again, meaning that I'd be able to announce the end of my career to the public. The examination would also determine whether I'd be paid by the insurance company. If it was all over, then I felt that it was simply fate. Mentally, I was ready to stop, so it wasn't going to be any great shock. The doctor examining me was in little doubt. "There is no prospect of your injury getting much better," he said.

"Okay," I answered. Case closed. That was it – I'd ridden my last race, and it was over, like I'd expected. I filled out all the necessary paperwork, and then went to tell Anne Dorthe.

She understood better than most what it felt like. The difference between her situation and mine was that I'd had the best years behind me, whereas she had to stop while she was still at the top of her game. Had I been 28 and among the world's top three riders, with my biggest contract still ahead of me, and with no one linking me to doping, then no doubt I would have been crushed to have to end my career. But I was in my mid-30s, I'd been having trouble motivating myself during the past couple of years and had also obtained more good results than I ever could have dared dream of. A press release about my retirement was prepared and sent out, and I began to wonder how people would take the news. The plan had been to announce my retirement a day later, but through Telekom the German media had managed to get hold of the story anyway.

On the Friday morning we were going to appear on the TV show *Good Morning Denmark* to talk about my decision and then hold a small press conference afterwards. In the taxi on the way to the studio, the driver asked me whether I still rode for Telekom. "No – I've retired," I told him, giving myself a bit of a shock by having talked about my sports career in the past tense. It suddenly hit me that it was the end of an era for me – and it was a relief. I'd recently worked out that I must have ridden about 650,000km on a bike in my life.

After the show, a number of journalists asked me how I'd like to be remembered. "I hope that people will remember me as an ambitious sportsman," I told them. "One who went after the prize, and got it."

They also wanted to know how what my feelings were about Denmark after all the accusations of doping, and the debate about whether the stone in Herning commemorating my Tour win should be taken away. "I know that the Danish public supported me when I rode the Tour de France, and I'll always be extremely thankful for that," I said. "But then I went from being a hero to almost being exiled from my own country, and that really hurt.

"I'm a sensitive man, and people didn't know just how much it hurt," I continued. "It has been really awful, and I must admit that there have been moments when I really haven't wanted to be in Denmark."

Back home in Italy, I collected together all my cycling kit and packed it into boxes, just as I'd done already with my trophies, cups and other bits and pieces from my career. The only memories I needed were already safely stored away in my own head. But what I had to do next was convince both myself and everyone else that there was more to me than just having been a cyclist. Things didn't exactly count in my favour, though. There weren't many cyclists who had any kind of academic qualifications to fall back on. A lot of ex-pros ended up opening a bike shop or getting work as a bike mechanic. But that wasn't the direction I wanted to go in. I had thoughts and ideas that I hoped would take me elsewhere.

I wanted to expand my horizons by meeting new people with skills and abilities outside cycling. I wanted to meet people who had a different way of looking at the world compared to me, who could give me unexpected input, new inspiration and who had a different outlook on life and the possibilities that were out there. "You're the only one who can prove that you're more than just that rider with foam around his mouth," Anne Dorthe told me one day. "You're the only one who can change how people see you." And I wasn't going to be able to change people's perceptions just by talking about it. Anne Dorthe's dad put me in touch with a business coach, and we travelled to Århus to meet him. The meeting lasted several hours, but during that time he really opened my eyes to the possibilities that existed outside of cycling, and made me realise that there was a whole world just waiting to be discovered. I just needed to take off the blinkers I'd been wearing until that point. I knew that if I ever was going to go back into cycling I would have to be taking something completely different to the table – something that would change the sport. Perhaps that could be a new team with a completely different way of operating compared to what already existed. I thought that perhaps there was something in really professionalising everything – creating a real business and an organisation through which there were other opportunities to make money. It could be a business that concentrated not only on the racing, but which also endeavoured to create an economic foundation that wasn't reliant on the race results. But I wouldn't want to just be the directeur sportif, sitting in the team car during races, giving out orders and handing out water bottles. I'd want to be the director of the whole organisation.

For the time being, though, that thought needed to be pushed to the back of my mind, as I'd started to study for a business degree over the internet. Luckily, our own finances meant that neither of us needed to go out and find work immediately to pay the bills, so it meant that neither of us needed to rush in to making any decisions about our futures. It gave us a bit of room to travel together, enjoy being with each other and let our ideas slowly mature. In the meantime, there were a number of offers that came our way. One came from the Conservative People's Party, who contacted me to ask whether I wanted to represent them as a politician. I was interested in politics, but I hate the power struggles that go on behind the scenes, so I politely declined.

15 TEAM OWNER

T he wind rushed over my crash helmet, the throttle was all the way down and the idyllic, mountainous landscape went flying past. The scooter fought its way up the climbs, and I looked back to check that Bo was able to keep up behind. I was on a training ride with Bo Hamburger around Lucca. While Bo stamped on the pedals, I had a much easier ride on the scooter. Anne Dorthe and I had given ourselves a year to try to find out what we wanted to do with our lives, but it was okay to use a bit of that time to have some fun out on the open road.

Training Bo up for the Danish national championships was one of the little projects I'd taken on in the summer of 2000. He lived quite nearby to us in Tuscany and had asked whether I could help him with his training. Bo was the star rider on the Danish MemoryCard Jack & Jones team and was keen to demonstrate that he wasn't finished as a rider, which was the reason that he contacted me to help him.

"I'd like to try training more systematically," he told me. We increased the amount of training he did, and I filmed him while he cycled. Afterwards, we studied the tape, and I gave him pointers as to how he could improve his pedal stroke, for example. The training sessions went amazingly well, and I found myself really enjoying it, even though I was only on a scooter. We also used an SRM power meter – a training tool which I had been one of the first to try out as a rider. Attached to the bike, the small computer system measured all sorts of data about the rider, helping to optimise training.

It was harder to let go of the sport than I thought it would be. In June, Bo went to the Danish national champs in Vejle. Anne Dorthe and I went along to watch, too, and the training sessions I'd done together with Bo appeared to have paid off. He rode a good race, keen to finally win the title that he'd come so close to winning so many times before. On the last lap, Bo got away on his own and won the race ahead of Nicolaj Bo Larsen and Rolf Sørensen. Afterwards, he thanked me for my help with his training, and sang my praises to the journalists in his post-race interviews.

Bo and I stayed in contact, and he rode a good Tour de France for his team, finishing 36th overall. After the race, businessman John Trolle, who was the owner of main sponsor MemoryCard, apparently asked Bo what I was like, and whether it would be a good idea to get me involved in the team. Bo had some kind words to say about me, and Trolle asked him to get me to call him. He wanted to ask me whether I might be interested in being the team manager. It was a tempting offer.

I talked to Anne Dorthe about it, and she asked whether it would be wise to go back to the sport that, less than a year earlier, I had had enough of. "Would you be ready to talk about doping and the suspicion that comes with it?" she asked me. She'd hit the nail on the head, there – that was exactly what I was worried about. The TV programme, the accusations and my "never-tested-positive" answer hadn't exactly been forgotten by the press or the public. The interest in me, and the interest in my relationship with Anne Dorthe, was bound to blow up in the press again, and I had to take that into consideration when making my decision. John Trolle was waiting for an answer. "So, are you in?" he asked.

After thinking about it myself, and after talking to Anne Dorthe about it, I'd reached the point where I knew that, if I didn't give running a cycling team a go, I might regret it for the rest of my life. I'd be annoyed with myself if I didn't take all the thoughts and ideas that I'd had about running a cycling team and create something from it. I would regret not taking the chance while I could.

And it was that which helped make up my mind, compensating for my lack of desire to once again be under the media spotlight, although when it came to that side of things I'd also made a plan. I travelled to Denmark to meet up with John. "Okay – I'm in as the manager," I told him, then added: "But the team and the organisation has to be run on my terms."

My terms were accepted remarkably quickly, and he seemed keen to get me into the team and put me to work immediately.

On 20 August I was appointed as the new director of Team MemoryCard Jack & Jones, with John Trolle as the main shareholder and owner. Trolle's IT firm, MemoryCard, remained the main sponsor, and he was an exciting person to work with because of his charisma, initiative and confidence that he could do anything. But the next couple of months became an uphill battle. The company, Bestseller, who owned Jack & Jones, decided to pull out from their role as one of the main sponsors. I called a meeting with the team's administrative director and shareholder, Torben Kølbaek, who I had known since I was little. I told him my thoughts on the situation, and made it clear that I wanted to be in a position to make the decisions regarding the team, which meant him reducing some of his influence. My demands weren't well received, and during our conversation it became clear that we had completely different ideas and plans for the team and the organisation. It was a tough situation, especially because I'd known Torben for so many years. It was resolved by me buying out Kølbaek and taking over his share of the team.

Gradually, I realised just how much of a mess the team was in. There were rumours about the state of Trolle's IT company, too – that he was having trouble paying the bills, and was in fact close to bankruptcy. The team's financial situation was at breaking point before I'd even had a chance to make my presence felt.

The situation soon proved itself to be even worse than I first thought. Clearly, I hadn't been told the full story about the team's economic situation. At the start of October, Trolle informed me that he was pulling out of all the sports sponsorship deals that he was involved in, which included both the cycling team and Århus football club, AGF. It was true that he was at the point of going bankrupt.

By the end of November, the possibility was very real that we were going to have to pull the plug on the whole project. Another IT firm, CSC, was waiting in the wings with a large sponsorship deal, but only on the condition that their financial input wouldn't be used to plug the gaps left by our terrible finances. While this had all been going on, we'd signed a contract with one of the sport's biggest names – Laurent Jalabert – and had agreed to pay him over 10 million kroner (£800,000). Trolle, who had helped make the deal happen, had at the time agreed to put up a large part of the Frenchman's salary himself. To make things even more expensive, we had to deposit a four million kroner (£320,000) bank guarantee with the UCI to cover the team for the season.

I talked with CSC's Asger Jensby about what it would take to save the team. He reiterated that the company wanted to invest in the team, but repeated that they didn't want to throw money into what had become a black hole during the past year of the team's existence. The situation was critical, and at a board meeting we gave ourselves a limit of 10 days to try to find an economic solution before we would be forced to close the team.

One suggestion was to close the team and start a new company, but that wasn't really the way we wanted to run our business. The solution, in the end, was for me to buy John Trolle out and rebuild the team from the bottom up, hiring a core of people that I could trust to build the organisation up the way I wanted it. My investment in the company now stood at several million kroner, and I found myself as the owner of a cycling team. But there was a lot to do to try to get everything back on track. The money that Trolle had supposedly invested turned out not to exist. He'd never paid it in. Together with Alex Pedersen, who had been part of the team all along, having helped to start it, and our new board chairman Henrik Schlüter, I went through the team's finances with a fine-tooth comb. The positive side of the process was that I got to see right down into the deepest corners of the company, and had a real overview of the financial side of running a team and, indeed, a business. It soon became clear to me how I wanted to run the team: with common sense and responsible financial management. We certainly weren't going to get ourselves into the same difficulties as before.

Both CSC and internet service provider World Online invested large amounts of sponsorship, and we were looking ready to go for the 2001 season, led by Jalabert. We wanted to be an international team, made up of both foreign and Danish riders. To that end, Jalabert was very important. He might have been expensive, but he was the talisman who could lead the way and take us up to the next level. My gut feeling was that he still had that spark and still had a couple of good seasons and some top results left in him. It was him who could be our ticket to the Tour de France. I didn't know Jalabert personally, but I had certainly had my run-ins with him during my career as a rider – and most notably during the scandal of the 1998 Tour.

But when we saw each other for our first meeting after he'd joined the team we were able to let bygones be bygones, and it was obvious that he was still ambitious and was looking forward to new challenges. He was also ready to get his hands dirty and show that he was worth what we were paying him, and was prepared to be a role model for the younger riders on the squad. He could tell that me signing him was a big deal in every respect. What if – unlikely though I thought it was – he'd begun to have enough of cycling, and the only training he did was to ride down to the bank to draw some more money out of his very healthy looking account? As we put pen to paper, he looked at me with that relaxed look he always had. "Don't worry, Bjarne," he said. "I'll be giving this absolutely everything." His signature was a real boon, and showed the outside world that I really meant business with this team – that we had big ambitions and were ready to fight all the way.

As a rider, I'd made it to the top, but as a team boss I now had to learn how to deal with my star riders. My method was to build a mutual respect between us. I wasn't going to be some father figure for someone like Jalabert, but would instead show him respect for the results he'd obtained and his character. It was how I'd always wanted to be treated when I was a rider. He needed a change from the intense responsibility he'd had as leader of the Spanish ONCE team under Manolo Saiz, who was known for keeping his riders on a short leash.

At the start of December, we were ready to call a press conference in Herning to present our new-look team with its new riders and two new main sponsors. It was all part of my strategy; I wanted to change my relationship with the press for the better. I also helped my cause by employing former TV2 reporter and *BT* sports editor Anders Bay as the team's press officer – or the sport's first spin doctor, if you like. With his network of press contacts, one of Anders's jobs was to try to re-establish good relations with the media, whom I hadn't had the best rapport with since 1997. His job was to help me express myself better to the press, and get across what I was trying to say more clearly and concisely, which I certainly hadn't been so good at so far.

There were days when I'd dreamt of having someone around to give me advice when I'd been a rider. So many things might have been different if there had been someone to help, and things perhaps wouldn't have got so bad. Anders gave me confidence, and taught me to understand the mechanics of the press. He spent a lot of his time explaining to me why newspapers often wrote what they wrote, and why they reacted in certain ways, and I began to understand more and more how it worked, even though it wasn't always that easy. He had to both help me try to understand the press, and help the press to try to understand me. There were still days when I saw red over something I read in the paper, or over a headline that made me angry, and all my bad habits would come racing back again, and I'd be defensive and angry towards the journalists. "Is that the good old Bjarne Riis trying to come out again?" Bay would joke. It was the kind of thing that I'd need to hear to calm me down again, but it did take a bit of time to change my way of thinking and rebuild some bridges.

Absolutely everything seemed to go wrong in my first few months as a new team boss. On Tuesday 13 February 2001, I received a call from Geneva, where Laurent Jalabert lived. "Laurent's fallen off a ladder and broken his back," I was told. The news made me feel faint, and I had to sit down. Laurent was in hospital, and doctors didn't know whether he'd be able to walk again. He'd been at home in his garage, and went up a ladder to get something from a shelf. He'd lost his balance and fallen to the ground, where he was lying in agony for 20 minutes before his daughter came home from school and found him, and then called for help.

At the hospital, they ascertained that he'd fractured his backbone and seriously damaged three of his lumbar vertebrae – which was enough for doctors to fear that he could be facing the rest of his life in a wheelchair. It was little short of a catastrophe – for both Laurent and the team. Laurent had been an expensive acquisition for the team and was our star rider. In addition, our place at the 2001 Tour de France depended on him, as we hadn't received automatic entry to the race. Our only chance otherwise would be to impress the Tour organisers with the rest of the team during the spring, and then hope to still be invited. But with our top rider out of action, our chances of going to France hung by the finest of threads. No Jalabert probably meant no Tour for us. It was a crippling blow.

Luckily, though, Laurent was no softy. After a week-and-a-half in hospital, he was sent home, but under strict instructions to just take it easy. Ole Kåre and I discussed the situation. "Should I go down there and work on him?" Ole asked me.

"Is there anything anyone can do about a broken back, though?" I replied. I knew that Ole was capable of things that were beyond most people, but even he couldn't perform miracles. Jalabert, however, was one of the riders on the team who had already taken well to Ole's methods, so Ole headed to Geneva to see the Frenchman.

That evening, Ole called to update me on how things looked. "He looks like the hunchback of Notre Dame," he told me. Laurent was shuffling about like an old man in an attempt to minimise the pain. It was taking him five minutes just to put a sock on. Nevertheless, Ole was confident that he could help, and got to work. It didn't take very long to take effect: Laurent was quickly able to walk properly. Ole also worked on the psychological side of things and, even though he didn't speak French and Laurent only knew a few words of English, they were able to communicate.

The daily reports I received from Ole in Geneva began to sound more and more positive. Laurent was soon able to do a small amount of work on his home trainer, which gave us a glimmer of hope that he might still be able to be ready for the Tour de France, unrealistic though it seemed. The Tour organisers were set to dish out their wild-card invites to the race on 2 May, so with time running out, and with none of my other riders having shown much in the way of results so far, I decided that I'd just have to put my faith in Laurent being able to make some kind of miraculous comeback after all. Only Rolf Sørensen – who I had signed to the team for quite a bit of money in the hope of his experience rubbing off on the younger riders – had managed to show himself at some of the races.

Ole's treatment of Laurent, however, combined with the Frenchman's extreme willpower, paved the way for an extraordinary comeback. Jalabert felt well enough to start the semi-Classic Flèche Wallonne in mid-April – in plenty of time before the Tour organisers made their decision. He rode the first 120km before calling it a day, but it was a good sign that it was just a lack of fitness, rather than any back pain, that was hindering him. Laurent's return gave us the morale boost that we so badly needed, and made people believe in us again. Other riders on the team started winning as well, and it was clearly enough to convince the Tour organisers that it was worth giving us a chance as they picked us for one of their wild-card spots.

For me, personally, it was the fulfilment of a dream to go back to the Tour de France, and this time with my own team. It was a race I knew better than any other, and which had been such an important part of my life. One of our main sponsors, World Online, had changed its name to Tiscali, so we turned up in brand new jerseys as CSC-Tiscali. Laurent Jalabert was back in form, and everyone – not least Jalabert himself – had big expectations of him. Many were hoping that he might even be able to challenge Lance Armstrong, who had dominated the race for the previous two years and was looking for a third Tour title. But I had to be a little more realistic than that. Jalabert was definitely riding well, but he wasn't really at the right level to challenge for the overall classification. Instead, he would go after stage wins, plus we had a secret plan that he should go after the polka-dot "King of the Mountains" jersey in a serious effort to wear it all the way to Paris.

As early as stage four, between Huy and Verdun, Jalabert wanted to show the world that he was far from finished as one of the world's best riders. His broken back seemed like a distant memory as he crossed the line as the day's winner after 210km. It was redemption for everyone, and for the team it was as though a great weight had been lifted from our shoulders. We'd made our mark on the world's toughest bike race and the big investment in Jalabert had been worth every penny. But there was even more to come. Jalabert had completely changed, both as a rider and a person. We couldn't be sure that it was Ole's treatment that had made the difference, but earlier in his career Laurent had been a shy, quiet man. This year, though, he had become outgoing and smiley, which was great for us.

True to form, the French riders were like wild lions on 14 July – Bastille Day. The best way to celebrate their national day in front of their home crowds at the Tour de France is with a stage win, although the foreign riders are always out to spoil the party. That morning, Laurent was focused on it being his day. He wanted to end the day on top of the podium after the 162km between Strasbourg and Colmar.

At that morning's team meeting I told the riders that we had to go on the offensive. "We need to attack right from the beginning, and then later Laurent will take over," I said, and the riders nodded in agreement. However, patience wasn't Laurent's strong point, and he slipped away as part of a 16-man breakaway on the second of the stage's five climbs. The group stayed together until the descent off the final climb, where Laurent forced the pace. He was one of the sport's absolute best descenders, and only very few riders had the same exceptional skill and balance as he did. The others tried their best to follow him, but the Italian, Ivan Basso, crashed and broke his collarbone, while Laurent just rode away from them all. He held on over the last 10km of the stage and crossed the line, ecstatic as winner of the stage, 11 seconds ahead of the German Jens Voigt. It was the perfect victory. The French public went crazy, and race director Jean-Marie Leblanc looked over at me and nodded, as if to say that he was glad that he had invited us to the race and that I'd dared to put my faith in Jalabert.

Once the Tour hit the serious mountains, it was time for Lance Armstrong and my old team-mate Jan Ullrich to take over. The new focus on their duel was the cue to put our plan to target the mountains jersey into action. To make it work, we needed a bold strategy, although one which wasn't going to get in the way of the teams riding for the overall classification. We chose stage 13 – the race's "queen stage" between Foix and Saint-Lary-Soulan in the Pyrenees, which was the longest of the whole race at 222km. Armstrong, Ullrich and their respective teams would be watching each other, and would only react to attacks that could threaten their hopes for the overall classification. Laurent hadn't ridden too well during the previous couple of stages, though, so when it came to it I decided to postpone our planned offensive. But once the stage was under way, Laurent rode alongside me in the team car. "I actually feel okay today," he told me. "My legs feel pretty good." We were back on.

After 73km, and once we were on the day's first climb, nine riders went clear, and Laurent was among them. The Kazakh Alexandre Vinokourov was also there, as was Laurent Roux, irritatingly enough, who had the mountains jersey already. At this stage of the race, it was all about being patient, and this time Laurent showed that he could be. He needed to wait for the right time to surprise his breakaway companions with an attack. That moment came on the descent and, thanks to his fearless technique, he quickly got a gap over the others. The idea was for him to get away on his own and hoover up as many of the points available towards the mountains jersey at the top of each climb as he could, before Ullrich and Armstrong took over at the head of affairs.

Jalabert was flying, and was putting even more time into the chasers. He went over both the second and third climbs in first place, banking maximum points towards the jersey. In the team car, we kept on top of the maths and did all we could to encourage him. On the fourth climb, the "category one" Col du Peyresourde, Laurent seemed particularly strong, despite having been out there on his own for so long. Behind him, Ullrich and Armstrong started to wind things up. If Laurent could get over the next climb, the Col de Val Louron-Azet, in first place, he'd have enough points to take the polka-dot jersey. When he did it, we celebrated in the team car, but we quickly stopped when he crashed on the descent. His tiredness had taken over, and just a second's inattention was all it took. The crash gave him a few cuts and bruises, but he was quickly back on his bike and on his way again. He wasn't the only one to crash, either, as Ullrich missed a corner on the descent off the Peyresourde and went into a ditch. Again, there was no real damage, and Armstrong waited for him to get back to him.

The speed had gone out of Jalabert as he started the day's final climb up to Pla d'Adet. He battled on bravely, and we shouted encouragement at him from the car. But Armstrong, Ullrich and Joseba Beloki were closing in on him, and 5km from the finish Armstrong came flying past him, with Ullrich and the other favourites in hot pursuit.

It was a case of mission accomplished for us, though. After 150km out on his own, Jalabert had secured the King of the Mountains jersey and maximum exposure for our team. He came onto the podium to be awarded the jersey to the cheers from his home crowd. I had to pinch myself on the arm to prove to myself that it was true.

That evening, we celebrated at the hotel, even though Laurent was tired and all he really wanted to do was get treated by Ole Kåre's healing hands. The two of them had really hit it off over the spring, and Ole knew exactly what he needed to do to get the most out of the Frenchman. "I'm enjoying the relaxed atmosphere you've created in the team," Jalabert told me during a quiet moment. "I feel free and calm here."

On Sunday 29 July, the bunch rode the final stage to Paris. Laurent had had red polka-dots painted on to his white bike frame, and the team mechanics were all wearing polka-dot jerseys and caps. While Lance Armstrong took the applause as overall winner, Laurent delighted the crowd by accepting the mountains jersey. Those polka-dots were the proof that we were a team to be taken seriously, and I was thrilled with our two stage wins, the climbers' jersey and a team that had ridden a really great race. When I joined the team to ride a lap of honour up the Champs-Elysées towards the Arc de Triomphe, and then down again the other side to the Place de la Concorde, it felt as though the circle was complete: five years before I'd been here as the race winner, and this time it was as the boss of my own team. In the team bus we found a bottle of champagne to celebrate our results, and also to celebrate the fact that we'd managed to sign a contract with American rider Tyler Hamilton. He was one of Armstrong's strongest team-mates at their US Postal squad and had potential as a podium finisher at the Tour de France. It was definitely time to celebrate.

16 IN DOPING'S SHADOW

The phone woke us up around midnight at home in Italy. Such a late-night call could only mean bad news, and I was still a bit dazed and confused when I answered. All sorts of thoughts went through my head, and Anne Dorthe had sat up in bed. "It's Worre," came the voice from the other end. When Jesper Worre from the Danish cycling federation was calling you in the middle of the night, there was clearly something wrong.

"Bo Hamburger's tested positive," he said. "For EPO."

It was the night of Thursday 8 May 2001, and time seemed to stop still, while my brain went from 5km/h to 100km/h in the space of just a few seconds. "You're joking," I managed to say, with a sinking feeling in my stomach. It was like being woken from a deep sleep by having a bucket of cold water thrown in your face. We agreed that nothing would be officially announced until we knew more, and I put the phone down feeling terrible and confused about the situation.

Anne Dorthe tried to calm me down. "Just try to sleep for a couple more hours, as there's nothing you can do right now," she said, although she knew I'd barely be able to close even one eye having received such news. My thoughts had already run away from me as I wondered just what the consequences could be. I started thinking about the worst possible scenarios, knowing that there was a real chance of everything being ruined.

"Everything" meant the team and the organisation behind it, which I'd built up myself with my own money, and which very much had my name attached to it. And if my name was going to again be linked with doping, then the team was going to be at risk – especially if all the old skeletons were let out of the closet again. I was beset by one worry after the next, and spent the rest of the night bouncing from disappointment to anger to concern. I was disappointed that Bo had apparently been willing to break that trust between us, angry that he was prepared to gamble with the team and all his colleagues' futures, and concerned as to whether it would be linked to the doping rumours about me.

Early the next morning, I called Anders Bay. I told him that Bo had tested positive at Flèche Wallonne, and told him about my own concerns and worries that I'd spent all night thinking about.

Bay, who was actually on holiday, spending a couple of days visiting his parents, suggested that I should come to Denmark immediately in order for us to work out a strategy and prepare ourselves for the news coming out. At best, we could announce the news ourselves at a press conference and therefore have some control over it. Bay also told me that it was important to contact CSC's Asger Jensby, Tiscali boss Svend Erik Jensen and Tour director Jean-Marie Leblanc before anyone else did. Their reactions could be crucial to the team's continued existence, so I needed to be upfront with them. If CSC or Tiscali decided to pull their sponsorship from the team, we'd be in real trouble. And if Leblanc decided that he didn't want to invite us to the Tour because of a doped rider, it would be a real crisis. Everything hinged on Tour de France participation and the exposure it got our sponsors during those three weeks in France. "Get on the first flight you can and we can go and talk to Bo," said Bay. "We need to try to convince him to take part in a press conference with us. There's a good tradition in Denmark of forgiving people who admit that they've done something wrong."

I then spoke to Leblanc, who told me that we'd have to wait and see, but that it probably wouldn't affect us taking part in the Tour. Jensby asked whether the team's doctor could have been involved, and wanted assurance that there wasn't organised doping going on in the team.

"There is absolutely no chance," I told him. "Every rider knows that they will be fired if they get caught doping."

The reason he asked was that CSC had a clause whereby they

could pull out of sponsoring the team if there was organised doping. In the case of it just being one rider who had been foolish, then it shouldn't affect the team quite as badly, but we arranged to meet when I arrived in Denmark.

In mid-April, the International Cycling Union (UCI) had introduced a new urine test that made it easier to identify riders who were taking EPO. The day it was introduced, Bo was tested in Liège in Belgium and at the same time became the first rider to test positive through the new test. I also called our team doctor. "You need to find all the tests and information we have on Bo around the time he was tested by the UCI to see if there were any indications at all that he could have been doping," I told him.

Anders met me when I arrived in Denmark. We talked through what the likely reaction would be from the press, and our strategy to best deal with the fallout.

"It's actually pretty predictable," he explained. He said that first they'd be angry at Bo, followed by the difficult question of whether we'd fire him. If we fired him, they'd blame us. If we didn't fire him, they'd blame us, and be angry at us. Lastly, they'd go after the sponsors and ask them whether they still wanted to be associated with us. Perhaps predictably, I was keen for the press conference not to become a personal thing with me in the middle of it all. "There are two ways we can approach this," said Bay. "Either we stand behind Bo as a team and defend him, or Bo stands up and admits that he's made a mistake and takes his punishment." Either way, we were in pretty bad situation.

Bo was supposed to be our big Danish name for the Tour, and was the reigning Danish champion. Anders and I went to Gentofte, where he lived with his wife, Sanne, and their newborn twins. The atmosphere wasn't great when we met them. Bo was unhappy, quiet and concerned about what was going to happen next, while Sanne was in tears. If Bo was found guilty of doping, then it could badly affect their economic situation. It was an uneasy conversation, as Bo and I knew each other well. I'd worked a lot with him in his training recently, and he'd helped me a lot with the team. Bo had only been told the news of the positive test the day before our visit, but had clearly expected me to be sympathetic and take his side. But I'd spent all my time since the call from Worre thinking about how best to handle the situation. I'd come to the conclusion that the most important thing was the team, and I therefore had a responsibility towards my employees whose wages put food on the table for their families. Which was more important? Them or him? He needed to take responsibility for his actions, and I needed to take responsibility for my decisions. I'd decided that the 60 people employed by my company and their families were my priority, and that I had to ensure that they still had a job to go to each day. "We're going to have to suspend you," I told Bo, which clearly shook him. "You knew the rules."

His wife became angry, and started shouting at me. "After everything he's done for you."

I could completely understand her frustration, but everyone on the team knew the rules. If I wanted to be taken seriously as the boss, I had to stick to the guidelines, which I'd helped to devise. There was no way of checking whether the riders stuck to our rules 24 hours a day, but we had to act if it turned out that a rider had broken them – even if personal relations were on the line.

Anders took over from me. "How about taking part in a press conference and saying that you're sorry about what you did?" he suggested to Bo. "Say that you made a mistake, that you're going to take your punishment, and that you will fight to come back."

Bo considered the suggestion, but felt like we were putting too much pressure on him. "I want to wait for the B test," he said. The function of the B test is to verify, or otherwise, the findings of an initial A test. "Can't you wait with announcing anything until I'm out of the country?" he asked.

We told him that we couldn't, as we had already called a press conference for the next day in a hotel in central Copenhagen, and every hour that went by was crucial for the future of the team. The sooner we could announce the failed test, the better our chance of limiting the damage it did. If the media got wind of it before we'd had a chance to announce it, our chances of trying to manage it would be very slim. But my reasoning wasn't something that Bo and his wife could understand, and maybe it was too much to think that they might. Our views on the case and our interests were a world apart.

In my opinion, though, it was the best solution for the team. The team doctor got back to me to tell me that Bo's haematocrit level had been high the day before the UCI's test, but not alarmingly high. Bo said that he was definitely going to wait for the results of the B test before commenting on the case himself. We had to respect his decision, but his wife, Sanne, remained angry with us and felt that I had betrayed Bo.

Before the press conference the next day, Anders and I met up with Professional Cycling Denmark's chairman, Henrik Schlüter, and the team's main sponsors, Svend Erik Jensen from Tiscali and Asger Jensby from CSC, as well as Jensby's press officer, Erik Ove. We agreed on what we would say, and that we would be open and honest, while at the same time ensuring that things didn't just become all about me and my past.

The press, however, were spoiling for a fight. The new doping case in combination with me was a real treat of a story for them, but we were well prepared and able to put on a united front.

Every time I wiped some sweat from my forehead or made any kind of movement that could be mistaken for looking like I was under pressure, the photographers clicked away. We had to be in as much control as we could. Any unclear answer or wrong move could end up on the front pages and possibly harm the team's future. "I'm extremely sad to be here under these circumstances," I said. "But Bo, of course, knew the rules, which all the riders signed up to, and it is for that reason that he has been suspended."

"Has the team's doctor been involved?" I was asked.

"I have complete confidence in our doctors, and they assure me that they have nothing to do with the case," I said. "But the issue is that we can't control what the riders do when they're at home. We measured Bo's haematocrit levels ourselves the day before he was tested by the UCI and, although it was high, it wasn't particularly high compared to Bo's normal levels."

"This couldn't come at a worse time for you, could it?" a journalist asked.

"It isn't good that it's happened now, no," I replied. "But I've spoken with Jean-Marie Leblanc, and this case won't affect our participation in the Tour. It's about an isolated case, and Jean-Marie supports our decision to suspend Bo."

"Are you disappointed in Bo?" another journalist asked.

"Above all, I'm trying to run a clean team," I said, "but at the end of the day the riders have to be responsible for their own actions. I thought that I knew Bo, but, well, what can I say? Now we must wait and see what happens."

"You've been his personal adviser, so shouldn't you have had some suspicions?" came the question.

"I haven't been his medical adviser. I only provided him with psychological support and support as a friend," I clarified. "I can only hope that people believe me when I say that I didn't know anything about what's happened."

It had been pretty tough at times, but on the whole the press conference had gone relatively well, and there was a bit of a collective sigh of relief afterwards. We hoped that we'd presented everything we knew about the case and made it clear that it was an isolated incident. The sponsors' presence also helped to keep everyone calm, as it had been difficult to put a wedge between us.

A month later, as we were putting the finishing touches to preparations for the Tour de France, there was a new development in Bo's doping case. He'd already called me before to tell me that there was uncertainty surrounding the equipment the laboratory was using to test the B sample. I'd simply said that we would have to "wait and see what happens".

But suddenly there was total confusion. The UCI's new EPO test stated that if a rider's sample demonstrated at least 80 per cent of the signs that indicated EPO use, he would face a ban. Bo's A sample had shown a value of 82.3 per cent – and so over the limit. But the UCI's laboratory in Lausanne, Switzerland, had made two B tests of his urine. One showed a value of 82.4 per cent, but the other one showed 78.6 per cent. The case was presided over by the Sports Confederation of Denmark (DIF), who would be the organisation to hand out a possible ban.

As a team, we kept abreast of the situation, but decided to uphold Bo's suspension until a definitive ruling was made. I travelled to France with the team for the Tour, but many of the questions from the Danish media attending our pre-race press conference were about the doping case. Anders Bay tried to steer the questions back in the direction of the race, but the journalists present – and *Berlingske Tidende*'s journalist in particular – focused in on the fact that Bo could be acquitted due to a procedural mistake. They wanted to know if we thought he was innocent.

"It's not up to us to answer the question as to whether Bo is innocent or not," I said. "We're waiting to see what happens and, if the case is dropped, we will then respond to it. If there was a mistake in the procedure, then it's very unfortunate, but I do believe that the test works and, either way, we're talking about some very high figures."

"But are you not pleased about the prospect of one of your riders being cleared of doping?" someone asked.

"However we react, we'll be criticised for it," I replied. "If we say that Bo's guilty, then some people will think that it's wrong for us to think that, and if we choose to believe in him, then people will criticise us for that, too. So right now we're caught a little in the middle, waiting to see what happens, and then we'll make a decision once we know more. The judicial ruling is one thing, but the moral decision is quite another. Has Bo doped? Or has he doped and been cleared on a technicality? It's those kinds of questions that are troubling me at the moment, but it's something we can't make a decision on just yet."

On 9 August, Bo's case went in front of the DIF. Bo had hired the well-known lawyer Merethe Stagetorn to defend him. The confederation's doping board acquitted him due to the uncertainty surrounding the two B tests, where one was over the allowed limit and one was under. It meant that Bo would not be banned and was free to continue his career. Now it was a question of whether it was a career which he would continue with us. We arranged a meeting for the start of September, but prior to that I had a meeting with our sponsors.

At the end of August, I met up with Tiscali's Danish director, Svend Erik Jensen, to talk about whether they wanted to continue sponsoring the team for the following season, giving us enough time to find a new sponsor for the following year if necessary. Tiscali did want to continue for another year, and that was mainly thanks to Laurent Jalabert's results at the Tour, which made the company feel as though they got the international exposure that they were after. However, they were after even more international exposure, and asked that we considered taking part in the other two major tours – the Giro d'Italia and the Vuelta a Espana – as well as the Tour de France. For an ambitious team like ours, it fitted in very well indeed with our plans.

At the start of September, I met with Bo Hamburger to talk about his future. I took along our chairman, Henrik Schlüter, who was a lawyer. My take on the situation was that, even though Bo had been acquitted because of a procedural error, he still didn't have a future on the team. Too much water had gone under the bridge, and too much had been said in the press by, among others, Bo's wife, Sanne, who had said some very disparaging things about me. It wasn't what Bo had expected to hear; he'd hoped that I might have changed my mind about things. "We're terminating your contract, but we'll pay you for the rest of the contract period – that is, until the end of this year," I told him, adding that he wouldn't actually ride any more for us, either. It was a reasonable solution for everyone, and it gave Bo the rest of the year to look for a new employer.

"If that's how it's going to be, then that's how it's going to be," he said, reluctantly, and said that he of course didn't want to stay with a team that didn't want him there. But he didn't hide the fact that he thought he'd been betrayed. He told us he thought we should have given him another chance, and that I'd become a cynical bastard who could now only think like a businessman rather than a human being, and that I owed him for having helped me get back into the sport.

It was perhaps too much to expect that he might be able to understand my decisions and the motives behind them, but my responsibilities as the owner of a team were now different to when I was a rider or to when I trained Bo.

Once Bo had left the office, Henrik and I just sat there for a while in silence. Neither of us liked the way the case had been resolved, but we felt that we had ended our relationship with Bo in the most humane way possible. And we knew that we now needed to make some changes off the back of the case. "We need to test the riders more often and follow our gut feeling a bit more," I said. "If there are any riders that we don't think we can trust, then we need to be much harder on them."

In January 2002, I contacted my old trainer from when I lived in Italy as a rider, Doctor Luigi Cecchini. I asked him whether he would be interested in working for the team as our trainer.

"I'll have to think about it," Luigi told me, having recently turned 58, and having grown tired of the attention he'd got from the Italian police in relation to doping rumours. He wasn't sure whether he wanted to again be in a position where he'd be asked questions about his work.

Before contacting him, I'd already considered how it would be received by the press, but decided that I was ready to take the flack if that was the case. The reason I wanted to have Luigi on the team was that there were only very few people in the sport who were able to work out physical training programmes like he could. We wanted him in a capacity as physical trainer, not a doctor. "Okay, I'm in," he said. "But if there's going to be any trouble, then I'm gone again."

Jalabert was one of the first riders to be tested by Cecchini. "He's not in great form," came back the assessment.

The goal was for Cecchini to get the riders to train in the right way, including more in the way of power training.

A number of Danish journalists asked whether they might be able to attend one of Cecchini's sessions. "I don't think I can do that, Bjarne," Luigi told me when I called him up to ask whether it might be possible.

"The journalists just want to get an insight into how you work. They want to see, too, that we have nothing to hide," I told him.

"No – I can't do that," he said.

The amount of suspicion surrounding him, as well as the sheer number of negative pieces written about him, had made Cecchini less accessible than ever. When we told the Danish press this, it made them even more suspicious about what went on behind his closed door, even though we assured them that there was nothing suspect about his training methods whatsoever.

In May, we finally managed to persuade Doctor Cecchini to be interviewed by *Ekstra Bladet*. The newspaper's journalist, Niels Christian Jung, was the one who in his earlier job at DR had made the TV programme about doping, which also featured me, and now we were allowing him to ask Cecchini some difficult questions. Cecchini told the story about the investigations he'd undergone as part of the Italian police's fight against doping. "I felt like a criminal when the police suddenly turned up one day and went through everything in the house and in the clinic," he explained. "They went through every drawer, every rider journal and all my personal belongings. It was a horrible experience, and felt as though the police had also rummaged through my soul."

"Have you ever helped anyone dope?" Cecchini was asked.

"No, and these days I work only in a physical training capacity, and have nothing to do with medicines at all," he said.

But the shadow of doping never really went away. Anders Bay was no longer our press officer, but his replacement, Brian Nygaard, was kept busy fending off the Danish media each time they were after a doping story. In May 2002 Brian was contacted by various newspapers, all looking for a comment on the rubbish containing doping waste products that had been found in a ditch after the one-day CSC Classic in Åarhus, in which several of our riders had taken part. Numerous other foreign teams, of all sizes, had taken part, too, yet we were the ones the press went after. According to *Jyllands-Posten*, who had had the the rubbish analysed, there were traces of EPO. "Is it your rubbish?" the journalists asked Brian.

"I can guarantee that the rubbish containing the doping products does not belong to us," he affirmed. "We are alarmed by the discovery, and would like to point out that the team management is prepared for any of the riders to be drug tested at any time."

Two months later, the Lithuanian rider Raimondas Rumsas stood on the podium in Paris having finished third overall at the Tour de France. I was as surprised as anyone else to see him there, as he was one of the heavier riders in the sport. It hadn't been many months since his agent had almost given him to us for free. We'd tried to find out more about him at the time, and he didn't exactly have the best reputation. There were a lot of rumours about him, but nothing really concrete. However, my gut feeling was that it was best to listen to the rumours on this occasion, and I said "no thanks" to taking him. Instead, it was the Italian Lampre team who took him on.

I was particularly glad to have said no to the Lithuanian rider when the news came in the day after the end of the Tour that his wife had been arrested at the French–Italian border with a car filled with doping products. There were no fewer than 40 different kinds of medicines and drugs, including EPO and testosterone. Rumsas told the media that none of the drugs were for him, but were intended for his mother-in-law. He was fired by Lampre shortly afterwards, and had his third place at the Tour taken away from him.

That autumn, I was at home in Lucca when the phone rang. "Hi Bjarne – it's Marco Pantani."

The little Italian climber had had a tough time since having been caught doping at the 1999 Giro d'Italia. But his climbing ability couldn't be taken away from him – an ability that had won him both the 1998 Giro and the Tour de France the same year. "I've been thinking a lot about it lately, Bjarne," he said, "and I was thinking that you might be able to help me." His request came as somewhat of a surprise. Everyone inside cycling knew that Pantani had various problems. The doping case had affected him badly, and the rumours were that he was now fighting cocaine addiction. But on the other end of the phone he sounded very sure of himself and in no way desperate. "I need to switch teams, and I think you're the right person to try to get me back on track," he said. "Are you interested?"

It was very tempting. Maybe I was someone who could get him back on the straight and narrow. But I was in two minds: on the one hand, I would have very much relished working with such a good rider, and especially one who was so hungry to get back to the top of his game. But on the other, he now had a bad reput-ation, and I wasn't sure whether there was some truth in the rumours about his cocaine addiction. "I'll certainly think about it," I told him.

"Thank you," he said.

Before we would be able to even consider signing him, I'd need to find the budget to pay for him. I had discussions with various sponsors, including some Italian ones who were keen to get back into sponsoring a team. However, negotiations ran aground when Pantani wanted to bring a number of riders with him to the team, and that didn't interest me.

In February 2004, during the Tour of the Mediterranean, I switched on the hotel television. There were pictures of an ambulance leaving a hotel in Rimini in Italy. Marco Pantani had died after an overdose of cocaine. It was tragic news, and it immediately made me think back to our conversation about him joining the team in 2002. What if joining us would have changed his life? Would I have been able to have got him back on the right path and prevented it from ending like this?

17 A DIFFERENT TEAM

Freezing in a wigwam in a Swedish forest, Laurent Jalabert, Carlos Sastre and the rest of the team listened intently to former soldier BS Christiansen, who was busy explaining how important it was to work together as a team. "A bike race is a bit like being in a war – you have to be able to trust each other," BS told them.

For the past three days, BS had had the riders and the other employees on the team taking part in various tasks and exercises designed to put them in situations where they would have to be honest with each other, work together and communicate with each other.

The trip, and BS's presence, was all part of my plan to turn my team into one of the best in the world, and the most modern in terms of teamwork. I'd put the plan together through a combination of my vision for it and the sum of my experiences as a pro rider, which, looking back, were characterised by far too many unnecessary lows, too many things just happening by chance and too many instances when, internally in the teams, people were working against each other. They were all things I wanted to change. My team would be different. I wanted us to be innovative, cooperative and driven – just like any company in the business world. I had a number of thoughts, ideas and philosophies, but I wasn't so good at formulating them so that other people on the team could understand where I was coming from. It was for that reason that I'd brought in BS. He understood my philosophy and ideas, and could help make them a reality. He knew how to convey those ideas to make the team function that bit better. And it was the reason he was on our team training and survival camp in Sweden in December 2001. He was to help work out a set of values that would be fundamental to the team, and which we would follow when running the company.

With his personality and his methods, BS was able to inspire the riders, the team employees and me to think differently and to see everyday problems from a different angle. Making the training camp a survival camp gave the riders a different kind of experience to what they were used to, and forced them to think outside the box. "We're now going to divide you into smaller groups, and ask you to come up with a set of values that you think are important for you and the team," BS told the group.

Armed with paper and pens, the different groups, made up of a mix of riders and staff, set to work. It was a completely different way of working, for the riders in particular. They had all come from traditional cycling teams, where things had been done in exactly the same way since the 1970s. The teams, with a boss more akin to a dictator, had always been run in the same way, and things were done the way they were for that reason alone: because that was how it had always been done.

While other teams simply concentrated on trying to make their riders faster, we were busy trying to teach them about themselves. And most of the riders were ready to try out this new method of having a more social and technical element to the team.

Laurent Jalabert was one of them. "I find it strange that, as one of the team leaders, I always get to go to massage after training and racing before everyone else. It's wrong," he said. "Massage should be given first to whoever needs it most." As one of the more cultured members of the team, Jalabert helped to influence the mood and the attitude towards the new way of doing things that I was trying to introduce.

"They're beginning to see each other not just as riders or members of staff any more, but as human beings," said BS.

It was my goal to create a climate where people trusted one another, and where individuals were encouraged to contribute with their own ideas. We needed to work out how to make individuals' performances become collaborative performances.

BS was able to draw on a lot of experience from the military. "Bike riders, like soldiers, are individuals," he pointed out after his first meeting with the team. He thought that there existed a kind of "something for something" attitude – that is, that riders would say, "If I help you, then you also need to help me." Their goal was personal success, whereas our goal was to create team successes.

BS had become a much-needed breath of fresh air in the team, and I began to use him more and more as my mentor. He was disciplined, loyal and honest, and he brought real organisation to everything he did. He was also able to spot where there were problems in the company – people bad-mouthing or working against each other, and was able to reduce the friction by getting people to talk openly: "What's the problem here? And what can we do to resolve it?" It was always constructive and forward-looking.

My dream was to build the organisation up so that it functioned like a professional business, which – in theory, at least – could produce anything. It should be a business that didn't rely solely on sporting performances, and where the employees were left in no doubt as to what was expected of them and by which values they should work.

Concepts such as leadership, teamwork, manpower, personal development and coaching should be integrated into the team. The concept of structured coaching, in particular, had never really played a big role in bike racing. The antiquated opinion was that a directeur sportif was someone who sat behind the steering wheel and gave out orders. We wanted to move away from directeurs sportifs simply functioning as glorified tour guides. Their decision-making powers should instead be used through daily contact with the riders and they should have the ability to influence them and motivate them to train properly. In short, the directeur sportif's role should be to get the best out of the riders.

The new way of doing things would take a while to take real effect, though, I had to admit in the spring of 2002. The team's results had been disappointing, especially in the Classics, and only Jalabert lived up to our expectations with a stage win at Paris-Nice. I asked

BS to dig a little deeper, and he went with the team to races in Spain and Belgium to observe how the team was progressing. "The expectations have been too high," he told me. "There has been too much fire-fighting and too much hole-plugging to have been able to reach such high expectations.

"But like in military operations, it's important to adapt your strategy in accordance with the situation," he continued. "We need to develop a new plan with new goals."

He encouraged me to restructure things both at the management and rider levels. I also wanted to step back from the sporting side of things a little and work more within the company, which meant the directeurs sportifs taking on more responsibility. To that end, we decided to send them on a coaching course in Ålborg, where they would learn to become better leaders. The riders needed to be coached more than they had been so far, and we needed to engage with them more as people if we wanted them to improve, and if they were to really take the team's values to heart.

For example, Tyler Hamilton was our team leader for the 2002 season, and he was a rider who wanted to be coached and to develop and improve himself. He had been a talented ski racer until he broke his back in a crash, which put an end to that career. He used cycling as rehabilitation, and then became a professional cyclist almost by accident.

As part of his preparations for the season, I'd asked him to pull his ski boots on again to train on the pistes at home in the US. "Have you drunk too much wine, Bjarne?" he asked me when I suggested it.

"It'll give you power in your legs," I told him. "When I was a pro, I would have loved to have trained like that, but it wasn't really deemed acceptable back then."

So for the first time in five years, Tyler got back on his skis as part of his winter training. One week skiing, two weeks cycling, then one week skiing again, and so on through the winter at his home in New England.

The training paid dividends at the Giro, where Tyler finished the race in Milan second overall, despite a crash earlier in the race. When he had some X-rays done the day after the finish, it was found that Tyler had ridden for 16 days with a fractured shoulder.

★　★　★

Before we left for the 2002 Tour de France, BS and I discussed how the implementation of our team values was going. It felt like a never-ending battle with and against the riders to get them to take my ideas about how they should do things on board. Clearly it wasn't that easy for some of them to think the same way I did. I wasn't really sure how much pressure I should put on them as their boss. Different people needed to be treated in different ways. Some preferred the direct approach, while others needed to be treated with kid gloves.

Ekstra Bladet had written that I was "too hard" as a boss, and one person in particular said that I made tough demands on how the riders lived their lives, and that riders with a sweet tooth needed to be careful. Brian Holm, my former team-mate at Telekom, also told the paper: "Bjarne has a reputation as a very hard sports director who doesn't allow riders to eat sweets or drink cola. He has his principles, especially when it comes to training, and the young Danish riders find the extreme discipline especially hard." Brian had no doubt heard about my "forceps" technique, which was my own little way of measuring whether a rider was approaching form and keeping his weight down. My forceps were actually just my thumb and forefinger, which I'd use to measure the riders' fat on their stomach or tricep by giving them a little pinch. It was part of the job that you turned up to a race with good form and at the right weight.

The team's morale was also on the agenda before the start of the Tour, and in that respect BS had found a problem. "The riders are saying that they haven't really had a leader for much of the spring," he said. Laurent Jalabert was the squad's natural leader and normally took the initiative, but an injury had kept him out for most of the spring. It had also taken time for Laurent to feel comfortable in a leadership role. He'd come to us from ONCE, where the manager, Manolo Saiz, dictated how things worked, so Laurent and I had talked a lot about him taking on more respon-sibility. "We need you to do it," I'd told him. "Every time you say something, everyone listens to you with real respect."

"But it's still not really me," he'd said.

"But we really need you to do it on this team," I insisted. "It's your role."

And eventually he did take on that role and was able to learn to take important decisions on behalf of the team. As one of our three leaders for the Tour, he was about to put those leadership qualities to the test. During a race, you sometimes needed to make decisions in a hundredth of a second, and in those stressful circumstances, your qualities could be pushed to the limit.

That's exactly what happened during the Tour's team time trial. Jalabert was in a position to try to take the yellow jersey after the 67.5km stage, and time-trial specialist Michael Sandstød was the main man to help drive the team home in a good position. The team was like a well-oiled machine, cutting through the air like a hot knife through butter. We led through the intermediate checkpoints at 21.5km and 40.5km, and things were looking good for Laurent and yellow – until disaster struck. Sandstød punctured and had to stop to change his wheel. Should the team wait for him, as he was one of our strongest riders, or should they go on without him?

"Wait for him!" I shouted into the radio from the car.

Jalabert decided that the team should carry on. "Keep going! Keep going!" he shouted to the others, and on they went while the mechanics changed Sandstød's wheel as quickly as possible. Jalabert had shown decisiveness and had taken responsibility for the situation, and that was good. But it was the wrong decision.

"Damn!" I shouted angrily in the car. The rhythm had been lost, and the riders tried unsuccessfully to find it again. Behind them, Sandstød gave it everything, battling to get back up to the others. At one point, he almost made contact again, but as just one man against a speeding locomotive it was an impossible task. With a couple of other riders also dropping off the pace towards the end, the team could only manage fourth place on the line. It wasn't enough to get Jalabert the yellow jersey.

Jalabert stormed off to the bus, with me following close behind. I was just as angry. "What happened?" I asked him inside.

"We did the only thing we could do in the situation," he replied.

We argued back and forth about what the best thing to have done would have been, without agreeing with each other.

"You said before the stage that we should only wait if Carlos or Tyler punctured, so we didn't wait," snapped Laurent. "It's not good that it worked out like this, especially when half the team wanted to wait and half the team wanted to ride."

It seemed that there had also been trouble with the radio system, and it was unclear whether my command had even been heard properly by the riders. Because I'd encouraged someone to take on a leadership role, I also had to take responsibility for when things didn't go right. Later that evening we all talked through what had happened, and then moved on.

On the rest day, Laurent informed me that he had decided to retire at the end of the season. I'd hoped that he might ride one more season, but I also had a lot of respect for the fact that he wanted to stop while he was still at the top. Jalabert ended up winning the polka-dot climbers' jersey for the second year in a row. Carlos finished 10th overall in Paris, while Tyler was 15th, 28 minutes down on his former team leader, Lance Armstrong, who won his fourth Tour in a row.

At the start of September, Anne Dorthe gave birth to our first child together in Vejle hospital. The birth lasted seven hours, but I was there every step of the way. With little Cristian, I now had three beautiful boys.

For the 2003 season, everything was geared towards us having a good Tour de France. Tyler Hamilton had worked hard to be ready and was prepared to give it everything he had. But as early as the first week of the race our new team spirit was put to the test. On one of the early stages there was a huge crash, which took down a number of our riders. "What's happened?" I yelled into the radio. It seemed that everyone had got up okay, but as the peloton came into the finish we could see that Tyler was hurt.

I began to worry as we drove him to hospital for X-rays, and it gave me time to think about what it might mean if he had to drop out of the Tour. The squad had been built up of riders capable of supporting Tyler's goal of making the Tour podium, and our race tactics were all geared towards him as a result.

The X-rays showed that Tyler's collarbone was fractured in two places, in a "V" formation. Back at the hotel, we stared at the X-ray pictures, considering our next move, while Tyler stared into space.

"Are you in pain?" I asked.

"Yes," he answered, unhappily. We all knew that it was unlikely that he'd be able to continue in the race.

"Do you think you can carry on?" I asked, hopefully.

"I don't know," he replied. "I think that's going to be determined by the pain."

"It's your decision," I said. "No one's going to force you into anything. You're the only one who can feel how much it hurts."

We had trained for this kind of situation at our pre-season camps when our resolve would be tested and we would see how we'd react in a crisis. I called a team meeting and explained everything to the other riders and team staff, telling them that we had to make the best of the situation. With all the energy I could conjure up, I tried to get them pumped up again. "We can't do anything about what's happened," I told them, "but we can still fight on with everything we have."

Tyler fought on through the next few stages in immense pain, his collarbone strapped up, his body dosed up on painkillers and his team-mates supporting him every step of the way. Within the peloton, they created almost a protective ring around him to ensure that no one could bump into him and make his injury any worse, while at the end of the stage BS would act as his bodyguard and escort him safely back to the bus.

Stage after stage, though, he battled his way through, gritting his teeth in an effort to overcome the pain. He was able to stay with the bunch on the flat, but when the road headed upwards, he really struggled. When the pace went up, he had to stay seated, as he wasn't able to get out of the saddle and pull on the handlebars. It had been clear a long time ago that a podium place was out of the question. But his daily battle to stay in the Tour and to try to ignore the pain was fascinating in its own way, and deserved huge respect. Here was a man with extreme willpower and dedication who was capable of hiding his disappointment to carry on regardless. There weren't many other riders who would have been able to bring forth that fighting spirit having come to the race as one of the favourites and then seen their role become reduced to that of a rider just trying to get through each day. People were extremely sympathetic, and we were able to show them that we were a team that stood together, supporting our injured star and never giving up.

While Tyler fought his own battle, one of our Danish riders, Jakob Piil, won the 10th stage, giving the team a real boost. By stage 13 we were into the mountains, and on the road to Plateau de Bonascre Tyler was suffering, while Carlos, on the other hand, was riding brilliantly. In the team car, I was trying to keep an eye on both of them, but then Carlos attacked and got a gap, which, if he could hold on to it, could result in a stage victory. I needed to follow Carlos, even though, further down the climb, Tyler probably needed me more than the Spaniard. For a moment, I paused, but then made the decision to go with Carlos, in case he needed us. No one could follow him, and he rode to the finish alone. In the last few metres before crossing the line he took out his newborn daughter's dummy from his pocket and put it in his mouth as a celebration.

Back at the hotel, everyone was thrilled – apart from Tyler. He got out of the team bus and walked straight past me and up to his room without saying anything. He was clearly disappointed about what he thought my priorities were and felt abandoned. Later, we got the chance to talk, but he felt like I was just making excuses. "We have to fix this, Bjarne," he told me.

A camera crew from DR followed our discussion, so neither of us wanted to make a scene, but he felt that I really hadn't followed the team's values through my decision in the team car. Maybe I owed him an apology as I had deserted him when he needed me most. Later that evening, as I thought it all through, I came to the conclusion that it was a dilemma that had no real right or wrong solution. It was impossible to please everyone.

On stage 16 between Pau and Bayonne, Tyler really showed just how much willpower and character he had. With 90km of the stage still to go, he broke away on his own. He gritted his teeth and fought his way through the stage, holding the chasing group at bay. It was the sort of achievement that would go down in history, and the press, the team and the people watching at home went crazy when he crossed the line as the day's winner. The whole way I'd sat in the team car shouting encouragement at him. "Come on, Tyler! You can do it!" It was my chance to redeem myself in his eyes. He could tell that I supported him and had such respect for his fighting spirit. After the stage, I gave him a big hug. "I'm so proud of you," I told him, and he thanked me.

Tyler finished the Tour with a fantastic fourth place overall in Paris, Carlos was ninth and we won the team prize. But sadly Tyler then informed me that he was leaving the team and had signed a contract with the Phonak squad for the following year. BS had already had his suspicions, and so it didn't come as a huge surprise to me. "But is there no chance of me giving you a better offer to keep you here?" I asked Tyler.

"I've already signed, I'm afraid," he told me.

"It's disappointing not to even have had the chance to talk about it," I said.

THE MAN WITH THE FIRE EXTINGUISHER

18

Ivan Basso, our new Italian star, looked petrified as he stood at the top of the cliff preparing to jump down into the sea as part of our 36-hour survival camp. BS, who had organised the exercise, tried to calm him down. "Just trust us," he told Basso.

But the Italian was genuinely worried. "It's just that I can't swim," he said.

At first, we thought that maybe we'd misunderstood Ivan's English, but no, he couldn't swim. It took courage for our new captain to reveal one of his weaknesses. Despite the risk of losing face with his new team-mates, who he barely knew, he admitted that he'd never learnt to swim and that he was terrified of water. And then he jumped.

At that point, I could tell that we'd found ourselves a true star and a real leader. He was clearly a man who dared to be who he was, who was honest, and who wanted to communicate in order for the team to function properly. Even though he didn't speak very good English, he insisted on speaking it at his personal development meeting with the management team.

"What's your goal?" we asked him.

"To win the Tour de France," he answered.

"And after that?"

"I don't know," he said. "I'll think about it then."

The Italian knew what he wanted, and that was to knock Lance Armstrong off his throne. Ivan's combination of ambition and humility impressed us.

A few days after he'd had to jump off the cliff into the sea, he set himself the goal of learning to swim. He splashed around in the hotel pool while his team-mates tried their best to move him along from doggy paddle to something approaching a front crawl. But his tenacity paid off, and soon he was able to swim further and further without having to cling on to the edge. He was a young, talented rider who had dedicated his whole life to being a professional cyclist. He lived almost like a monk and planned his whole day around when he should should train, rest and eat. Every hour was planned and timetabled. He occasionally came to stay with Anne Dorthe and me, often for three or four days, so that we could train together. The rest of the time we had almost daily contact by phone and quickly built up a close relationship with each other.

I had learned that if I was going to coach a rider in the best way possible, then I also had to get to know them as a person – how they thought and how they would react under pressure. I had to invest a lot of time and effort in them, but I knew that I could make a big difference to their career with my advice and guidance.

Since Tyler had left the team, I'd thought long and hard about whether I actually wanted to invest so much time and emotion in another rider. I'd invited Tyler into my home, got to know him as a person and gave a lot of myself, too. It's why I'd been so disappointed when he didn't even tell me that he was in contract talks with another team. Maybe inviting my employees to my house was going too far, as there was a danger that we'd then become friends, which wasn't a great idea if I then later had to sack them because of cutbacks or because they'd breached their contract or something. But despite all of that, I'd decided I was going to continue doing it, even though there was a risk of it ending badly. I didn't want to run my company like a dictatorship. There should be room for feelings and closeness, and we should treat each other like people.

Ivan was our leader for the 2004 Tour de France, but in the lead-up to the race we worked specifically on improving his leadership skills. He wasn't what you would call a natural leader, lacking the authority and cold-bloodedness he needed for his colleagues to respect him. If he was going to lead the team, we needed to find some way of getting him to the top of the team's hierarchy. Ivan needed to know, and show, what it was he wanted. He needed to take charge out on the road, take the initiative and make a difference, with the same kind of authority of Laurent Fignon, Moreno Argentin, Laurent Jalabert or me.

"Respect is something you earn," I told him. It's healthy to have a hierarchy on a team, as long as it's based on respect. If not, then it's simply a dictatorship, and dictators always get toppled eventually. But Ivan needed a bit of a helping hand if he was going to take on the role of team leader. There were always going to be power struggles in any business, and ours was no exception. Even the values instilled into the team couldn't stop it – it was just human nature. The team's hierarchy manifested itself in a number of ways: who spoke the loudest at the dinner table, who sat where on the team bus, who the directeurs sportifs spent the most time with, and who was listened to when they opened their mouths.

The first week of the 2004 Tour was stressful for the team. A number of our riders had crashed during the first few stages and were battling on with a combination of battered limbs and raw skin. I felt as if I was constantly fighting fires. Our Norwegian rider, Kurt Asle Arvesen, had crashed during a sprint finish, while in the team time trial everything seemed to have gone wrong. In the wet weather, the riders had gone down one after the other, and we'd lost a lot of time. On one of the mountain stages, Bobby Julich had ridden too close to our team car when I was giving him a water bottle. He panicked a bit, lost his balance, crashed and broke his wrist. He finished the stage, was treated by Ole and taped up in order to be able to carry on in the race.

On the Tour's first rest day, I went out on a training ride with Ivan. At one point, his phone rang, and it was sad news. "My mum has been told she's got cancer and needs to have chemotherapy immediately," he told me. We cut the ride short and headed back to the hotel. Ivan was very close to his mother, so it would have been no surprise if he hadn't wanted to have carried on in the race.

"I do want to carry on," he told me, and asked me to explain the situation to the rest of the team.

Of his own accord, Ivan contacted Lance Armstrong, who had

beaten cancer and had become active in the fight against the disease, to get some advice and guidance. They talked to each other a lot about it, and met up one day to discuss it further, but when I heard about that I couldn't help but be concerned. I didn't want Ivan to build up a kind of dependence on Lance, so it wasn't good to hear Ivan say that he'd told Lance that if there was anything he could do to say thanks for his help and advice, then the American only needed to ask. I could, of course, understand that Ivan was sad, frustrated and wanted some advice about how he could best help his mum, but while we were still part of a bike race I thought it was a particularly bad idea to be in Armstrong's pocket.

"Ivan, if you need to talk, or if you need any other kind of help, then I'm here for you," I told him, and explained that I was worried that Armstrong might find a way of using the situation to his own advantage. Ivan was, after all, his biggest rival.

Ivan's mum was due to have her first chemotherapy session on Friday 16 July, and he was keen to give her the best support he could by winning the stage that day. He wrote her name on a piece of tape, which he stuck to his handlebars so that he'd be reminded constantly who it was he was riding for. The stage to La Mongie was one of the toughest Pyrenean stages. But Ivan was focused, and Carlos showed that he was ready to ride for him. The Spaniard attacked on the final climb and split the group of favourites, and only Ivan and Lance could follow him.

I followed the stage on the small TV screen in the team car, and each picture was dominated by three men: my two CSC boys and the defending Tour champion. At that moment, I was an incredibly proud team boss. Unfortunately, Carlos had to drop off the pace, but Ivan was riding fantastically. Next to me, in the passenger seat, BS was ready to explode with excitement.

In the last 50m, Ivan upped the pace yet further, and Lance couldn't react. Ivan won the stage and dedicated it to his mum, while in the car BS and I celebrated like mad. In the finish area, despite his exhaustion and the press attention, Ivan asked our press officer, Brian Nygaard, to ring his mum and tell her that he'd won. The win bumped Ivan up in the general classification, and he was now a serious contender.

That evening, I was sitting with Ivan in his room, talking through the stage and how he was feeling, when Brian came in. He had a telephone number for Ivan from Lance. He'd apparently found a cancer specialist who he was recommending Ivan's mother visited.

The next day was another mountain stage, finishing at Plateau de Beille, and again it came down to just Ivan and Lance on the last climb. "He's going to let him win," I said out loud in the team car. I had the feeling that Ivan was going to let Lance take the stage win to say thank you for all his help and for the stage win the previous day. Sure enough, Lance won the stage ahead of Ivan, while I filled the car with swear words. This wasn't the way races should be won – especially as I still thought that Ivan had a chance to threaten Lance in the mountain time trial up Alpe d'Huez a few days later.

Lance, in yellow, led second-placed Ivan by a minute and 25 seconds in the general classification. It meant that the Italian would start just before the race leader in the time trial, and I knew that Ivan was capable of doing something special. From the team car, I encouraged him in Italian to give him as much support as possible on the 16km route up to the top of the mountain. But I could see that things weren't going well. Ivan's pedal stroke looked far from easy, and he rocked from side to side in the saddle, clearly working hard to find some kind of rhythm. The word from the race radio was that Armstrong was flying, and was about to catch Ivan. The motorbikes that had been just ahead of Lance overtook our car, and I looked into the rear-view mirror and could see his team car and the cheering spectators. I shouted to Ivan that he should just concentrate on his own race and not look over his shoulder. But it was too late. As I spoke on the radio, the American came past the car. He slowed a little, and deliberately looked in through the window to make eye contact with me, as if to demonstrate who was in charge. "You understand now? I'm the one who's going to win," he seemed to be saying. Even though it was just for a split second, it was a real demonstration of power. I gave him a sideways smile. It was a kind of "marking of territory" that reminded me of me when I was a rider. He then accelerated again and overtook Ivan. It wasn't exactly what we'd hoped would happen, but I had to admit that it was a spectacular sight watching the yellow jersey showing us who was the strongest. Ivan finished the race third overall, and it was a proud moment to see him cheered by the crowds in Paris in our team jersey.

In the meantime, my family was growing. In January 2004, Anne Dorthe had given birth to our second child, Matias, while we'd been on holiday in Lanzarote, and then on 13 May 2005 we had our third child together, another little boy who we called Andreas. Shortly after the birth, I received the news that my grandma had sadly passed away. Even though my relationship with her had been less close in the later years, her death still hit me very hard. She was the one who'd been there for me when I was a child. She'd found it difficult to forgive me for having divorced Mette, but thankfully we'd managed to rebuild our relationship later on.

At the 2005 Tour de France, the plan was for Ivan to take on Lance Armstrong for overall victory. Key to this was a good team time trial, and we'd brought in time-trial specialist David Zabriskie to help us. He was a shy and curious lad, with huge talent. As early on as the opening time trial on stage one, Zabriskie took the yellow jersey. He beat Armstrong by two seconds and recorded the fastest-ever Tour time trial in the process, with an average speed of 54.6km/h. He defended the yellow jersey well, and still had it going into the team time trial on stage four.

The team were having an outstanding day out on the road, flying through the checkpoints along the way of the 67.5km stage. After 25km, the team – made up of David, Jens Voigt, Bobby Julich, Ivan Basso, Luke Roberts, Kurt Asle Arvesen, Giovanni Lombardi, Nicki Sørensen and Carlos Sastre – led Armstrong's Discovery Channel team by 25 seconds. At the 45km mark, we were still ahead by six seconds, but our advantage had then dropped to just two seconds with 61km covered. We were still in control, but just as we approached the finish, disaster struck. David's bike slipped away from underneath him, and he crashed. The team couldn't wait, and carried on to the finish. But those few seconds of chaos proved costly: we lost the stage to Discovery Channel by two seconds and, while David limped home, battered and broken, Armstrong took over his race leader's jersey.

Jens Voigt was then third on stage nine, and it was enough for him to take the leader's jersey. But we only had it for another day, as Armstrong, Ivan, Ullrich, Alejandro Valverde and Cadel Evans battled it out for the overall classification in the Alps.

In the end, Ivan finished second overall behind winner Armstrong, with Ullrich taking third. It was Armstrong's seventh Tour victory in a row, and he'd already announced earlier in the season that it was to be his last. This left an empty throne, which both Ivan and Jan wanted to occupy in 2006.

Our main sponsor, CSC, had decided to extend their sponsorship for another three years, putting us in a good financial position to try to help Ivan win both the 2006 Giro d'Italia and the Tour de France. By that point, I had put together a team capable of winning both stage races and the spring Classics. Frank Schleck, from Luxembourg, had started at our team as a stagiaire – a kind of work experience or apprentice role – back in 2002 at the age of 22. Together with his younger brother, Andy, Frank was one of our big hopes for success. Frank made his breakthrough at the 2006 Amstel Gold Race, dominating the race and winning it in style. Our Swiss time-trial specialist, Fabian Cancellara, had been a new signing for the season and quickly met expectations by winning the cobbled one-day Classic, Paris-Roubaix. But Ivan was our stage-racing sensation, and was one of the favourites for May's Giro d'Italia. He, too, lived up to all expectations by dominating the race, but following the mountain stage to Trento Monte Bondone on 23 May, I heard some disturbing news when I visited the press centre. In Spain, the police had arrested the former ONCE team manager Manolo Saiz, who had become manager of the Liberty Seguros team. They had also arrested a sports doctor, Eufemiano Fuentes, and raided two Spanish laboratories.

According to the media, the police had found a large amount of doping products, from EPO to anabolic steroids, and 100 bags of stored blood and equipment for blood doping. The rumour was that they had also found a list of 200 sportsmen, which included a number of pro riders, who were clients of the doctor. Apparently the list included big names from football and tennis as well as cycling.

While Ivan defended his pink leader's jersey, various riders' names started to come out in connection with Fuentes. "Have you heard that Ullrich's name's on the list?" someone asked towards the end of the Giro. Jan was also taking part in the race, and denied any involvement with the Spanish doctor, while his T-Mobile team forced all their riders to sign a declaration that they had nothing to do with Fuentes. It was the worst possible scenario with the Tour de France fast approaching.

Ivan won another mountain stage at the Giro, and went on to win overall thanks to some fantastic riding. It was a huge triumph for the team. But during June, the full extent of Operacion Puerto – as the case was being called in Spain – started to be seen. The French minister for sport asked the Spanish authorities to reveal the names of the riders who were suspected of having been doped by the doctor in order to prevent them taking part in the Tour de France.

A few days before everyone taking part in the Tour was due to meet at the start in Strasbourg, Spanish newspaper *El Pais* revealed that there were apparently 58 riders who appeared on the sports doctor's list of customers, under different code names. They apparently included Ullrich and Tyler Hamilton. When our team arrived in Strasbourg, the Spanish doping scandal overshadowed everything. We decided to ensure that none of our riders were involved, and all our riders assured us that they had had nothing to do with the Spanish doctor. But on Thursday 29 June, two days before the start of the race, it all kicked off. The media reported that Ivan was among the 58 names allegedly on the Fuentes list, along with others such as Oscar Sevilla and Santiago Botero. The news left us feeling shell-shocked. Ivan assured us once more that he had nothing to do with the case, and that there must have been some kind of mistake. The pressure on us began to increase, but I didn't know how I should react. If Ivan was saying he had nothing to do with it, then I could do little else than believe him. He stood up on the team bus in front of his team-mates and the staff and said, "I have nothing to do with this case."

The next morning, the riders went out on a training ride, while Brian Nygaard and I had a meeting about the case. The next thing we heard was that T-Mobile had decided to suspend Jan Ullrich and Oscar Sevilla until they could prove their innocence. They were out of the race. One of the two big favourites for the Tour was out, and the decision meant that all eyes were now on us. How were we going to react?

Brian and I discussed the situation at length. My thoughts were that we shouldn't do anything off the back of some rumours in the newspaper. We needed to see the documents to prove that Ivan was involved, otherwise it was going to be hard to convince us. The team managers all met with the Tour organisation, who passed on the evidence they'd been sent from Spain. The papers were extremely confusing, but we recognised Ivan's name. "We need more proof than this, though," we said. But the papers were all we were getting access to, and the Tour organisers had made up their mind.

"All the riders that appear on the list will be thrown off the Tour," they announced. It meant that we needed to get hold of Ivan and tell him that he was out.

As we left the managers' meeting, all hell broke loose. Hundreds of journalists flocked around us, aggressively trying to find out what was going on. I was trying desperately just to try to get to the exit from the building while replying to the questions with short answers. It seemed unreal. Just a few hours ago we had the race's big favourite, and now we were having to deal with these rumours.

"As long as the case hasn't been resolved, I can't be disappointed," I said. "Ivan and his lawyer need to prove that he is innocent, but until then I believe in Ivan. But I'm taking the necessary steps, as I have no choice."

Back at the hotel, I went to see Ivan, who was deeply upset. "What's happening, Bjarne?" he asked.

"I'm going to have to send you home," I told him. "That's what the organisers have decided."

Ivan began to cry, and it broke my heart. "I'm sorry, Ivan," I said, with tears in my eyes. At that moment, we both knew that nothing would be the same again after this. I could understand his thoughts and reaction, so it really hurt to have to send him home, especially as the evidence so far didn't seem particularly convincing. All our riders had accepted that they were to use only our team doctors when they signed their contracts. If Ivan had worked with Fuentes, then he had broken his contract and breached the UCI's code of ethics.

I gathered BS, Brian and the directeurs sportifs for a meeting. We were going to have to come up with a plan B. "Carlos and Frank are our best bets for the overall," I said. I was trying to be decisive, but inside I felt anything but. The thought that Ivan could be an innocent pawn in some kind of doping hunt was unbearable. Carlos had talent, as did Frank, although neither of them were really quite at the stage where they could be right up there with the very best. But they were the best cards we had to play. The riders and the team staff were brought up to speed as to why I had had to make the decision to send Ivan home, and that we were now turning to plan B. "Now we're going to ride for Carlos," I said. Looking around as I told them, their sad faces betrayed just how well-liked Ivan was on the team.

During the next few days there were more revelations, which made it almost impossible to concentrate on the race. The press were ready to confront me about every rumour and every suspicion. One newspaper said that Ivan was accused of having blood doped during the Giro, and that he had allegedly gone under the code name "Birillo". According to the paper, "Birillo" had had their blood harvested on 30 April and 1 May ready to be transfused on 12 May.

The story gave rise to all sorts of speculation, as some Danish journalists were saying that Ivan's dog back home in Italy was called Birillo. I was asked various questions about my role and what I knew. "Surely you had some suspicions seeing as you worked so closely with Ivan, didn't you?"

"Shouldn't you have more control over what your riders are getting up to?"

"With the close relationship you had with Ivan, were you not suspicious of the progress he was making?"

But if Ivan was telling me he was innocent, then I decided that I needed to support him until I had any reason to do otherwise. The same people who had criticised how I turned my back on Bo Hamburger were now criticising me for supporting Ivan, which I continued to do despite the rumours and leaked documents that were coming out, which we had no guarantee were real.

The UCI had followed Ivan all year and held him up as the perfect example of how a rider's haematocrit level should look. He had a maximum value of 43 per cent, which hardly ever changed. If the UCI themselves hadn't even noticed anything suspicious, then how on earth were we supposed to?

The general atmosphere reminded me too much of 1998, which was still so painful to remember. I could feel my emotions from back then – feelings I'd tried to forget – coming back more and more often these days. But despite all the talk of doping, there was still a race going on, and on Saturday 15 July, the riders took on that year's longest stage, between Beziers and Montelimar.

With just 30km covered, our 34-year-old German rider Jens Voigt got into a breakaway with four other riders, including the Spaniard Oscar Pereiro. The little group quickly built up a big lead, and to our surprise, it looked like they were going to be able to hold their advantage all the way to the finish. Jens was clearly the strongest of the five of them, and so it suited him when, approaching the finish, Pereiro decided that it was time to try to leave the rest of them behind, and he and Jens took off. With around a kilometre to go, Jens attacked the Spaniard to try to get free, but it didn't work. But in the sprint, Jens opened it up and was able to hold off Pereiro as he tried to come around him. Jens won the stage, and I was thrilled for him – a loyal team player who was always ready to sacrifice himself for the team.

Three days later was the stage to Alpe d'Huez and, with Carlos and Frank as our best bets in the overall classification, it was a stage that could be key. Early on – after just 30km – a group of 25 riders got clear of the bunch, with Carlos helping Frank to be a part of it. "This is the one if you want to come," he'd shouted to Frank. Frank took the invitation, as did Voigt and Zabriskie, and at one point the lead group had a four-minute lead over the peloton.

By the foot of the final climb – Alpe d'Huez – Frank, Jens and Dave were still there, which meant that, as our best chance on the climb, Frank had been delivered perfectly. The Italian, Damiano Cunego, attacked, and Frank was the only one who was able to follow. With 2km left to go, Frank attacked, and this time Cunego was unable to react. Frank was able to solo to the finish line to win what had become a tradition-rich stage, and our joy was complete when Carlos came home just 25 seconds down on the main podium contenders.

American Floyd Landis was crowned the Tour winner ahead of Oscar Pereiro and Andreas Klöden, while Carlos finished in a fine fourth place overall, which was a far better result than I could have ever hoped for when he took on the captain's role from Ivan. Just a few days after the race had finished came yet another shock from the race organisers: Landis had tested positive for testosterone after his epic win on stage 17. When his B sample was confirmed as positive, the title was handed to Pereiro, and Carlos was bumped up to third place.

Ivan's case was a wake-up call. We needed to play an active role in fighting doping and keep a better watch on our own riders. Our former captain Tyler Hamilton had tested positive for having blood doped during the 2004 Olympics, and documents obtained by *Politiken* also revealed that he had apparently doped while he was riding for us in 2003. The documents allegedly showed that Tyler was systematically doping himself with EPO, growth hormone and testosterone, and that he was blood doping. These revelations meant that there were now some serious questions being asked about what was going on on our team, and they couldn't have come at a more frustrating time, as we were actually in the process of setting up our own anti-doping programme. We had asked one of Denmark's leading doping experts, Doctor Rasmus Damsgaard, if he would head up our new programme, which would be the first of its kind in cycling, for which I'd allocated over two million kroner (£185,000). Danmarks Radio asked me whether I wanted to take part in a programme about the fight against doping, which I eventually agreed to do. The camera crew, with presenter Tine Gøtszche, flew to our house in Lugano, Switzerland, where we had recently moved, to do the interview. A question came up along the way during the interview, which was critical right from the start:

"Did you know that Tyler was taking all these products?"
"No, of course not."
"How could you fail to notice?"
"They're not prisons we're staying in when we travel – they're

hotels. And the riders have free time, of course. If you read through the evidence, he didn't take all of it during the Tour de France. But an injection doesn't take long to do."

"We hear that you're very close to your riders – as though they're almost your sons – and that during training you follow their every pedal stroke. How could you not know what was going on when you were so close to them?"

"It's a good question. If I'm with them over a period of, say, three-five days when we're training together, I am close to them. But then a fortnight might go by when I don't see them, and so then I don't have full control over what they're doing."

"Doping expert Rasmus Damsgaard said in Politiken: 'There must have been someone who knew what was happening. And I would say that with the way a cycling team works, you'd have to almost go out of your way not to know about such extensive doping.' Did you go out of your way not to know?"

"No, of course not. It was part of our philosophy right from the beginning that we should know what was going on at all times. We didn't want to have anyone hiding anything. So no, that's total rubbish. We wanted to know everything that was going on."

"And yet now you're about to hire Rasmus Damsgaard as an expert on your team. Why is that, when you don't believe what he says?"

"I've got to the point where it's become extremely stressful to hear that we're being accused of things that we're not a part of. But my mission all along has been to create the world's best cycling team following the proper means. I want us to be the pioneers for the future of cycling."

They then showed a clip of "that" documentary, during which it was suggested that I had doped during my racing career.

"There has never been any concrete evidence against you. You have never tested positive. But there was circumstantial evidence and suggestions that you had been involved. Could we not say that you're now doubting Ivan Basso on the same basis as people doubted you?"

"For me, that's not what the point is here. The point is, what have we got today, and how are we going to deal with things going forward?"

"But if we're going to deal with things, then surely we also need to deal with the accusations."

"I'm here to address what I think is important today in cycling. That's why I'm here, and why I haven't hidden myself away. I want to prove that we can have a clean team. I want to prove that we're trying to do the right thing to make that happen."

"But you say that Ivan Basso needs to be cleared not just technically but that it must be beyond any reasonable doubt that he was involved. Should you not be cleared beyond any reasonable doubt? Shouldn't you say to everyone that you have never doped?"

"I have no problem with saying that. But at the same time I want to say that I am still here, and that I want to fight for this sport. That's my goal, and I have never hidden myself away."

"So can I get you to say that you have never doped?"

"You can."

"May I hear you say it?"

"I have never doped."

"Thank you – and I think that there will be a number of people out there who have been waiting to hear you say that for many years."

When the interview was over, the room was very tense. I was annoyed that I'd been forced into a trap again. And I was annoyed that we hadn't covered all the questions and the themes that we were supposed to cover. If I'd known I was going to be asked whether I'd doped again, I would never have agreed to the interview.

Ivan attended a hearing with the Italian Olympic Committee at the end of August. He responded to questions about Fuentes but denied any involvement with the Spanish doctor. The committee deferred the decision as to whether there would be a disciplinary case against Ivan until an unspecified date.

We had various conversations with Ivan about what should happen next. "Armstrong's team has offered me a contract," he revealed one day. As a result, we came to a mutual agreement to break Ivan's contract so that he could leave our team and join the Discovery Channel squad. My assessment of the situation was that if we wanted to maintain our sponsors' confidence and hopefully have a future as a credible team, then we needed to almost start again with our anti-doping programme, which would be trustworthy and transparent.

We had no choice but to say goodbye to Ivan, but on a personal level it hurt to have to let such an ambitious and nice guy go – someone I'd spent some great times with, and someone I'd invested a lot of my own time and feelings in. But I knew that a rider of Ivan's ability would be able to come back to the highest level again.

In May 2007, Ivan admitted to the Italian Olympic Committee that he had been involved in Operacion Puerto, but said in a press conference that he had never doped. He said that he had approached the Spanish doctor with the intention of doping. His confession meant that he was handed the standard two-year ban for a doping offence.

Rasmus Damsgaard agreed to head up our internal anti-doping programme, which we set up in December 2006. The programme covered all 28 of our riders on the team, and was recognised by the International Cycling Union (UCI) as well as the World Anti-doping Agency (WADA) anti-doping code. The riders would be tested for all forms of doping, including EPO, blood transfusions and growth hormone. All urine tests would be analysed by the UCI and WADA before going on to Bispebjerg Hospital in Copenhagen where they would be analysed further by Damsgaard. The programme had three goals: to catch possible cheaters, to set a new standard in the fight against doping and to protect the riders' health and integrity.

During the 2007 season, altogether the riders were tested 941 times. Each rider was tested an average of 28 times, and also had their blood screened 13 times. It made our riders some of the most tested athletes in the world. Each rider had a biological passport, in which all the tests, information and statistics to do with blood values and figures were recorded. It meant that any changes to their blood profiles, haematocrit levels or any other biological values, which could indicate doping, would be detected. At the same time, the results from the programme were put into a report and made public so that anyone could see whether our riders were clean or not. New riders to the team had to agree to sign up to be part of the programme as part of their contract, and a number of other ProTour teams also introduced their own internal anti-doping programmes. All that was left to do was for me to clear up the rumours about my own past.

19 THE CONFESSION

From the garden at our house in Vejle there was a fantastic view over the forest and the fjord. A number of ideas and strategies for the team had been conjured up while sitting in the garden.

But I had other things on my mind that afternoon in May 2007. I sat on the lawn alone other than for our dog, Oscar. My past was catching up with me – namely, my doping in the 1990s and the lies that had come with it.

A former soigneur at Telekom had written a book in which he'd revealed that systematic doping had gone on at the team in the mid-90s. An extract from the book had been given to the big German magazine *Der Spiegel*, and it had featured on the front cover with the title "Thick Blood", with a picture of me and Jan Ullrich. In recent days, a number of my German colleagues from the team, including Christian Henn, Bert Dietz and Udo Bölts, had admitted doping. Telekom had now called a press conference, during which it was expected that both Erik Zabel and Rolf Aldag would also admit to having doped. Perhaps it was also time for me to do the same.

In the years since 1999, when the TV programme *The Price of Silence* had accused me of doping, it had acted has a hindrance to virtually everything I did. It was like having a rock in a rucksack, which just got heavier and heavier. Even though it had happened so many years ago, I was finding myself thinking about it more and more. It should have been the other way around, of course, but I wasn't going to be allowed to forget about it. I needed to take the heavy rock out of the rucksack to lighten the load and avoid sinking into the ground – for my own sake, but also for that of my family and the team. It would perhaps give the freedom I so badly needed.

I wandered into the house and through to the living room, where I turned on the TV. On teletext I saw the headline "Zabel admits doping". He was one of Germany's biggest cycling stars who had won 12 stages of the Tour de France and the Tour's green jersey as best sprinter six times. Later, I saw a clip of Zabel at the press conference. "I'm sorry that I lied for 11 years. When I read the article in *Der Spiegel*, I knew that it was over," he said, and began to cry. It seemed to me that Zabel and the others were almost suggesting that they were forced to dope against their will. But that wasn't the case at all. They were the ones who had taken the decision to dope, so I thought that they should act like grown men and take responsibility themselves for what they'd done. That applied to me, too. And now it was my turn.

Back sitting on the lawn, I thought through my decision again. I was never going to be able to escape the shadow of doping unless I was prepared to step up and admit what I'd done. I called Anne Dorthe. "I've decided to hold a press conference," I told her.

"Okay," she said. "You're definitely sure that's what you want to do?"

"Yeah – it's the right time," I said. "We're ready for it. It's time to let everyone know."

"I support you," she told me. "It's the right thing to do, as it's been tearing you apart. It's time to let it out."

Next, I called Brian Nygaard. "Are you ready?" I asked him. "It's time. I'd like you to call a press conference, please."

Brian knew what it was about, and set to work. The sponsors, the board, the riders and other important team contacts would need to be informed before I stood up to say my piece.

Brian and I arranged that he would call the press conference at the team's offices in Lyngby, just outside Copenhagen, but that he'd wait to send out invitations until the evening before. "I've begun to prepare our strategy, but in the meantime you need to prepare what you want to say," he told me.

It was strange to suddenly be opening up about something that had been so private but also so painful. It was a chapter of my life that I'd done everything I could to forget, and I'd tried to hide it away in a corner in order to carry on with my life. On the other hand, it was my chance to draw a line under something I really wasn't proud of and start afresh. I felt ready to take responsibility for my actions. The accusations had followed me since the TV programme in 1999, and were a constant reminder of my past. Until then, I'd not seen any reason, or felt the need, to stand up and admit what had happened during the 1990s. I wouldn't have been able to handle the consequences that would have affected everyone around me: my family, my friends, the team and the staff – all people who had had nothing to do with what I'd done back then. Was it right that, so many years later, they should pay for what I'd done? But after a while, it had started to affect me. Living with the secrets and lies was holding me back. During my career, Mette had often warned me against what I was doing, and so I decided to ring her to tell her what I was about to do.

"But why now?" she asked. "Why do it so many years afterwards? And do you really think that it will change anything?"

"It's just the right time," I told her. "Would you tell the boys for me?"

Throughout their childhood, Jesper and Thomas had known about the rumours. They had even once had someone shout "EPO pigs!" at them. Luckily, though, they'd been good at making friends who didn't care who they were. They had grown up used to the outside world's interest in me, and had discovered for themselves what should and shouldn't be taken seriously. I'd never told either the boys or my dad about what I'd taken as a pro rider, as I'd never felt that I should load them or the rest of my family with such a burden.

Mentally, I'd begun to prepare myself for the kinds of questions I was going to be asked. I knew, for example, that I was going to be asked whether I regretted what I'd done. And yes, today I do regret what I did, and wish that I'd handled things differently to the way I did. But when I was in the situation at the time, and needed to decide whether to dope or not, I felt as though it was the right thing to do. It was for that reason that the press conference wasn't going to descend into an emotional, tearful show. I was going to explain what I did, explain why I did it, and apologise for having done it. I didn't want any sympathy from anyone.

Back then, doping had been part of the job, and the way to reach your ambitions. The choice to dope was mine. No one had made me do it. Everyone who injected themselves with EPO knew that they were doping, and doping was against the rules, so I couldn't see why people were revealing what they did and then breaking down in tears 10 years later as though they hadn't been master of their own lives and decisions. That just gave mixed messages.

Before the press conference, I went through the accusations made against me by the Telekom soigneur Jef D'Hont, who'd published his book earlier in the year. According to the book, Jef was known in the peloton as "Jef Waterbottle" because he had created an energy drink containing doping products. The drink apparently made riders stronger, but couldn't be detected by any tests. In the book, Jef said that during the 1996 Tour I'd once had a haematocrit level of 64 per cent, but that wasn't true, and I'd decided that I was going to say as much in the press conference. He had also written:

> Riis could be a nice guy sometimes, but he would never give up his
> EPO. It's true that the product was already popular in the bunch,
> but he really pushed it on. Thanks to Riis, its use escalated quickly
> and frighteningly.

> During the Tour, Riis took 4,000 units of EPO every second day
> and two units of growth hormone, which was double the normal dose.
> There was no risk of him being caught by the drugs tests, as it simply
> wasn't possible to detect those products at that time.

I'd never had any respect for Jef, and that was unlikely to ever change with the revelations he'd come out with. He doped riders himself, mixing all sorts of things together to give to young riders and injecting others with God knows what, and yet here he was acting as though he was the sport's big saviour. That wasn't how it was going to be with me. My confession was enough in itself – I wasn't going to try to take anyone down with me. No one else should have to suffer the consequences of what I'd done. They'd have to make up their own mind whether they were ready or needed to say anything. It had taken me the eight years since the TV programme to get to this point and be ready to put the past behind me, and so I didn't want my confession to force anyone to have to come forward if they themselves weren't ready to do so.

I rang Brian and told him my thoughts. "I don't want to sit there and say which riders did what, which directeurs sportifs knew what or which doctors took care of what," I told him. It wasn't my responsibility, nor my desire, to point out others and say, "They did it, too," or, "He was the one who got hold of it for me." It needed to be their own decision to talk about what they'd done.

I also rang the chairman of our team's board, Henrik Schlüter, to inform him of my decision.

"That's fine, Bjarne," he said. "I'll support you all the way."

But there was someone who needed to know before anyone else. Someone who it was going to really hurt. Someone who had supported me all along, and who had hoped that it was the people accusing me of things who were wrong. My biggest fan. I wandered up to the annex where my father was busy fixing something or other. He had seen the confessions made by my German team-mates and could no doubt tell by my expression what I was about to tell him. "I'm going to go on television in the next few days and tell the truth," I said.

He nodded, silently.

"I wanted you to know before anyone else."

"Yes."

"Could you look after the house for us while we're in Copenhagen, please?"

"Yes, of course. I'd love to."

There was no reason for either of us to say any more. He knew that I knew that this was painful for him, but that he supported me whatever I did. He didn't say so, but I could tell that he didn't think I should do it.

The next morning, Henrik and I drove to Copenhagen to meet Brian at one of his friend's apartments. We went through our plan, and tried to guess the kinds of questions I'd be asked at the press conference, and tried to decide what kind of answers I'd give. We told our sponsors what was going to happen and, as far as we could tell, it didn't say anything in the contracts with them about me standing up and talking about my past, so we had to hope that there wouldn't be any problems in that respect. We rang Carlos and the Schleck brothers, Frank and Andy, and told them what was going to happen at the press conference, and then talked through all the different scenarios that could present themselves at the press conference, down to the last detail.

"You can expect the journalists to go really hard on you," Brian said.

"I'm ready for that," I said. I genuinely felt confident, resolved and mentally ready.

"They'll also see it as a victory," Brian continued. "It'll be a case of, 'We won and you lied.' That's how they're going to think."

His phone was going off constantly. The invitations to the press conference had been sent out, and a number of journalists had got an inkling of what was going to happen. Both DR and TV2 were going to broadcast the press conference live.

"That's perfect," said Brian. "If it's on live television, then you'll get to deliver your message and tell it like it was yourself. There won't be any room for any commentators to give their interpretation; the viewers will be able to form their own opinion."

"What's the worst that can happen?" I said.

"That no one comes," Brian laughed.

Henrik, Brian and I all agreed that I should be completely honest when confessing what I'd done.

"You'll need to say exactly what you took," said Brian.

"Does it matter?" I asked.

"Yes – as there shouldn't be any more questions when the press conference is over," Brian answered.

Both the team and I needed to be able to move on after the confession. We could decide what I was going to say, and how I was going to say it, but how other people were going to receive it was out of our control. None of us there in that apartment were in any doubt that the press conference was crucial to the team's future. The worst-case scenario was that I'd have to step down as the owner.

In the hours leading up to the press conference, I relaxed in one of the rooms at our HQ in Lyngby, trying to prepare myself mentally.

It seemed like a bit of a relief already – relief that my secret would soon be out in the open and I'd be able to move on with my life. The newspapers were full of speculation as to what it was I was going to announce, and a lot of them had printed reminders of the times over the years that I'd denied having used banned substances. The press had completely taken over our offices in Lyngby, with TV vans and trucks outside, and a huge number of photographers and journalists, many of whom had come early to secure themselves places in the front few rows.

Anne Dorthe was smuggled in through the back door and came to find me. "How are you doing?" she asked.

"I'm nervous about how it's going to be received," I admitted.

"You have nothing to be ashamed of," she reassured me. "No matter what, there's no one who can take your career away from you. Remember, that was how things were back then."

Her support gave me a real lift.

"What you do and say in the future is going to have a lot more clout once you have said what you need to say," she said.

I couldn't help the tears welling up in my eyes as my feelings began to overwhelm me in the last few minutes before the start of the press conference.

"Go in there and be strong," Anne Dorthe told me. "You don't need to be unhappy about anything. It's a very brave thing you're doing, going in there and saying how things were."

BS, Brian Holm and a number of other familiar faces were there to support me and to be available for the media. Anne Dorthe gave me a hug before I went into the conference room. "Be strong," she said.

I had a few notes written down on a piece of paper and had gone through it a couple of times. Now I needed to show that strength that Anne Dorthe said I was in possession of when faced with adversity.

"Are you ready?" asked Brian.

I nodded.

The photographers clicked away as we went into the room and sat down in front of everyone.

Brian kicked things off. "Welcome, everyone. I hope you find this exciting, interesting and useful."

As arranged, I then took over. "Good to see everyone. I have a statement that I'd like to read out. It will take a little while, but I'm sure you've got time to wait," I said, and looked out over the sea of sweating journalists.

Apart from the sound of the photographers' cameras, it was completely silent. "The time has come to lay my cards on the table," I said. "I rode as a pro during the time that the sport was the way it was. I did things that I now regret, and which I wouldn't have done today. I'm now ready to acknowledge my mistakes."

My feelings started to bubble up inside, but I stayed focused and retained my façade of composure.

"I doped," I said, and paused.

"I took EPO," I continued, as the photographers clicked away.

I'd said it – my secret was out, and I went on to explain that I had doped between 1993 and 1998.

"It was part of my daily routine," I explained. "But I take full responsibility for my actions. I bought the drugs myself and it was my choice to take them. I'm sorry for the doctors that have been embroiled in this, but at the end of the day I am the only one who can be held responsible for saying yes or no to actually doping."

The general atmosphere in the room was respectful, and I was asked the kind of questions we'd expected and that I was prepared for. I began to feel more relaxed, even though I was laying my feelings on the line.

"I thought that the past could be the past, but that isn't the case. So I want to say that I'm sorry."

Someone asked how I now felt about my 1996 Tour victory, and the huge homecoming held for me at Tivoli Gardens in central Copenhagen when I returned home to Denmark.

"I feel okay about it. I'm proud of my results, even if they weren't earned in an entirely honest way."

"So you still think you're a worthy winner of the Tour de France?" someone else asked.

"No – I'm probably not," I answered. "But I'll leave it up to you to be the judge of that."

The press continued to be fair with their questions, with a German journalist the only one to turn nasty. Maybe he had expected the same kind of show that he'd seen in Germany, but he wasn't going to get that from me. The tears were only close to coming when I was asked how it felt to tell those close to me that I had doped – and I thought of my father, who I knew was at home watching on TV.

But I kept my composure, and replied that it had been hard.

"My only comfort is that the people who know me best are there to support me," I said. "I made mistakes, and did things that were and are banned. I take full responsibility for that. I'm part of a sport that is, I feel, now changing for the better. If that development hadn't happened, then I'm pretty sure that I wouldn't have been here revealing what I am today."

I was asked whether I intended to remain in cycling.

"I've chosen to be part of this sport, and I believe that I have a reasonably influential role within it," I said. "At least, it's my ambition to be influential, in which case it's probably appropriate for me to have resolved things when it came to my past so that I can move forward.

"I have so much to give to my team and to the sport," I continued, "yet lately I haven't been in the best position to do that because I've just not had the energy. But I'm faced with two choices. Either I can give it all up, and disappear from the sport, away from the spotlight, and just live a quiet life with no media attention. Or I can stay and do what I need to do for the team to stay on track and for me to get my energy back to work on the project, which I think is the world's best cycling project, and in itself deserves recognition and respect."

"But have you not considered that you might not be able to continue on the team after this?" I was asked.

"If everyone thinks that I should pack up and leave, then I'll do that – that's fine," I said. "I just don't think that that's any kind of solution, though. I just hope that people can recognise that cycling needs people like me – someone who dares to do things differently, and who has the courage and the willingness to fight for something that everybody wants."

"Is what happened in Germany the reason for you to be sitting here today, or has this been something that you've been planning for a while?" a journalist asked.

"Sitting here today is something I've imagined many times,"

I answered. "But it was also a question of timing – of doing it at the right time."

Brian had decided that the press conference should be "open ended" in that the journalists could keep asking questions until they didn't have any more to ask. A lot of them focused on who had provided me with the products, what role the team doctors had played and who else had been involved. Each time, though, I repeated that I was the only one responsible for what I'd done. Some journalists were after my adviser and coach, Luigi Cecchini, who had been the subject of a number of stories. The truth was, in his time as my personal trainer he had never given me any banned products nor written me out any prescriptions for any. And since it was me who had decided to hold the press conference, Cecchini shouldn't be involved in any respect. He'd been through enough already.

"Yes, I have cheated and lied about what I did," I said, "and that was wrong – I know that now. But that's not how it was back then. Doping was part of the scene that I was part of."

Someone asked how high my haematocrit had been when I won the Tour.

"I don't remember exactly, but it was high enough to win," I said.

"Do you think your Tour win might be taken away from you after this?" I was asked.

"I've not thought about that at all," I replied. "My yellow jersey is lying in a cardboard box at home in my garage, and can be collected if anyone thinks I shouldn't have it any more."

"What do you think about your own credibility?" I was asked.

"I can't force you to believe that I'm telling the truth, but I'll just have to live with that," I said.

The questions had begun to dry up, but the TV crews were trying to draw it out so that I'd appear live on their news programmes. Before we finished, though, I had one last message for the Danes watching at home. "I want to say sorry, but despite everything, I still hope you enjoyed watching me ride. I did my best," I said.

That was how I saw it. I did what I had to do to compete with the world's best riders at that time. That was the truth, whether people liked it or not. As one of my former colleagues from the cycling world back then once said to me: "You had to choose between being at one end of the ladder or the other. You chose to be at the top end – and I would have done the same, of course."

After the press conference, Anne Dorthe kissed me, with tears in her eyes. "It's over now, and you did brilliantly," she told me.

Once the media had all left, I sat and drank a beer in the canteen with the team staff, who had helped set everything out for the press conference. The text messages started to come ticking in, but one in particular gave me a lump in my throat. It was from Jesper and Thomas:

"Well done, Dad – we're proud to be your sons."

Their response meant everything to me. How the public, press and those within the sport reacted was out of my hands; the most important thing was that those closest to me understood the reasons why I did what I did. I didn't need them to approve of it, but just wanted them to accept that I stood by what I did, and that I assumed full responsibility for it.

In the car on the way home to Vejle, I was even quieter than normal. In my head, I was going through every single minute of the press conference, but I felt relieved. It was as though I'd had a heavy burden lifted from my shoulders.

Plenty of experts and commentators didn't think that I'd shown much repentance at the press conference. It irritated me that they had to show off with their oh-so-wise opinions at my expense. What did they know about how I was feeling inside? I had spent almost 10 years of my life wondering how people would react if I admitted what had happened. I'd thought long and hard about how people would see me afterwards, so don't say that I didn't care when I said "sorry".

When we arrived back home in Vejle, my dad told me that a load of photographers and journalists had turned up on the driveway while the press conference was going on on the TV, and he'd had to tell them to go away.

On the Saturday morning after the press conference, I quietly took myself off into the forest to chop down some trees and split some logs, and Dad came and joined me with a quiet "hello". We didn't say much to each other, but I was lost in my own thoughts anyway, going through what had happened in the past couple of days. Dad didn't say anything directly about my confession, but I could tell that it had been painful for him – and some of the reactions in the papers, which he'd gone out and bought, had hit him hard. "I want you to know that I'm always here for you, no matter what," he told me.

Whilst we chopped wood, I just wanted him to tell me how he really felt about what I'd done. But he didn't. He was just so loyal. Brian called me. He'd read all the papers – both the Danish ones and the international ones. "It all looks okay," he said. "It's pretty much what we expected."

Dad and I stopped our work in the garden and I headed inside to check my emails. There were hundreds of them, and I read as many as I could. By far the majority of them were positive, with only four negative ones among the 500 or so mails I'd received. My next task was to take a look at the papers. They made for some tough reading. The reaction was aggressive, and it was clear that some journalists had waited 10 years or more for my confession. I'm not sure what I had expected, but I must admit that the reactions really hurt. Beneath the headline "You Cheated Us, Bjarne," *Ekstra Bladet*'s cycling correspondent, Lars Werge, had written:

> *What you must understand is that it's not so terrible for Bjarne Riis. He made his own choice – like he said himself – and that was to trick us all. Admitting what he did this late means nothing – the time for forgiveness has long since passed.*

In *Jyllands Posten*, Christian Thye-Petersen wrote:

> *Listening from the sidelines, it sounded as though Bjarne Riis just wanted to get this over with, as there was no way back for him if he wanted to be left in peace to run his team.*
>
> *So he gave what one could call a major confession with a minimal apology, triggered by events in Germany which left Riis, metaphorically speaking, with a gun against his head. But it was good that he did it.*

The international press also commented on my confession. In the German newspaper *Bild*, their commentator had written:

> *Bjarne Riis proved to be the biggest doping cheat of them all. His confession will have shocked his many Danish fans.*

And the *New York Times*, too, wrote about the press conference:

> *He was a national hero in the small Nordic nation of Denmark, with its proud cycling tradition. Now Bjarne Riis has revealed that he was a doper.*

After reading what the papers had to say about me, I just wanted to hide myself away and lick my wounds. It had been a relief to say my piece, but it was also a psychologically stressful confession. It was a huge confession to make in front of a whole nation, and it had been such a painful thing to have had to hide for so many years. But no matter what the reaction had been, Brian and I had agreed that it would be best for me to keep a low profile – both for the team's and my sake.

For the following few weeks, I barely went out of the house – at most taking a little walk in the area around the house. A number of journalists tried to get hold of me via the intercom at the front door, but I politely got rid of them each time. I had nothing to add to what I'd already said at the press conference.

The new Tour de France race director, Christian Prudhomme, reacted strongly to my confession. He said that I wasn't a worthy winner of the race in 1996, and that he was considering removing my name from the list of winners. The Frenchman's condemnation hit me hard, but it was what he said about my role as a team owner that hurt me even more.

"He's cheated, and so I ask myself whether he deserves to run a big cycling team today," he said.

Brian and I discussed what the Tour boss's reaction meant for our team. "Maybe I should stay away from the Tour this year," I suggested. That would be the worst punishment I could imagine – deserting the team for the world's biggest race of the year.

"Let's just wait and see what happens," said Brian. "Let's not make any hasty decisions."

I travelled back to Switzerland to our house in Lugano and turned my phone off for a while. All attempts to contact me were ignored, and Brian took care of all communications. On a ride around the area near our house, I thought a lot about whether my confession had changed anything. Had I found peace with myself when it came to my past? Had the sport become cleaner? Were the critics, the teams and the sport willing to move on from here?

In truth, there probably wasn't too much that had changed. There were still going to be riders who cheated – just like there were no doubt cheats in other sports. But you could change the past in a number of ways. My way was to introduce the anti-doping programme to the team, run by Rasmus. It showed that there was a willingness to create a cleaner sport. Maybe revealing what I'd done would help young athletes who faced the same choices as I had. Maybe they'd think that doping wasn't the right way for them to reach their goals. It's when faced with that choice of whether to step over that line the first time that an athlete has to be strong. Stronger than I was. Once you'd said yes to doping, like I did at the start of the 1990s, there was no way back.

My confession was hopefully the start of a process whereby I'd start looking at my life in a different way. A new beginning. My life had become easier because I didn't need to hide anything any more. That heavy stone had been taken out of my rucksack.

At least, those were my thoughts on a good day. I also experienced a number of bad days in the aftermath of what I'd done. There would be days when I'd just sit in the office feeling completely drained of energy. I'd imagined that there was going to be a real moment of forgiveness – an understanding of why I did what I did. But it didn't happen.

The Tour de France organisers still hadn't announced whether I was welcome at the 2007 race. I hadn't expected them to react the way they did, and it was as though they didn't recognise the anti-doping measures I'd implemented within my team.

Brian and I met to talk about how we should handle the

situation. Even though he tried to hide it, he was clearly surprised at just how unhappy I looked. "Are you ready to go to the Tour?" he asked me.

"I really don't know," I answered, honestly.

Brian knew me better than most, and it would only take him a few seconds to read my mood. I had no desire to abandon my big project, but at the same time I couldn't subject the team, the riders and the sponsors to the negative publicity that me being there with them at the Tour could bring. The riders had prepared themselves for the event for months, so I didn't want anything to take away from their efforts. Neither did I want to go to the race if I wasn't welcome.

"How are you feeling?" Brian asked. "Be honest."

There were tears in my eyes. I probably wasn't in the right frame of mind ahead of such an important task. I was more ready for a holiday far away from the Tour de France than I was to be a leader and an inspiration.

"Are you ready to talk about doping every single day for three weeks?" Brian asked.

The year before we'd had to send Ivan home before the race had even started because of Operacion Puerto. Now, after my confession, it was very likely that I would be constantly asked about doping.

"No, I don't really fancy that," I replied.

Emotionally, I was feeling completely run down and really not ready to field more questions from journalists.

"If that's how you're feeling, then I don't think you should go to the Tour," he said.

"No," I said, holding back the tears. It was the right decision, but it gave me a horrible feeling in my stomach.

Anne Dorthe and I travelled to London for the start of the 2007 Tour, where we checked in to a different hotel to the team. We went to a reception held by CSC, where I informed them that I wasn't going to be with the team during the race. The worst part of it was still to come, though: telling the riders and the staff that I wasn't going to be there with them in the team car. I gathered them all together after the reception for what was an emotional moment for me. "Guys," I began, looking around at them all, with tears in my eyes. "I don't feel up to the task of being able to lead you here on the race, and don't want to remove the focus on the team with my presence."

The riders respected my decision but said that they were going to miss me. For the prologue time trial, I sat in the grandstand with the sponsors. But I wanted to be with the riders to see them off, so I wandered down to where they were warming up. The photographers were all there ready to get a picture of me with my riders, and they got it. No one was going to stop me waving them off properly.

Our Swiss time trial specialist, Fabian Cancellara, won the prologue so would start the first stage from London in the yellow jersey. I then left England with my family for a holiday in the Seychelles. Anne Dorthe and the kids were pleased to be able to spend July with me for once, as it was a month that I normally spent travelling around France.

During the race I was in regular contact with Brian and directeur sportif Kim Andersen who kept me up to date with the race, how the team was getting on and to get my opinion on tactics if need be.

Fabian also won the third stage, and held on to the yellow jersey all the way until stage seven.

I should have been pleased, but I didn't really feel that way. I couldn't help thinking about one thing: next year I was going to be back at the Tour with my team, and we were going to make a real impact.

20 A CLEAN TOUR WINNER

The hotel room was small and smelled of sweaty cycling clothes, and we were tired after a day of training in the mountains. As cyclists, we were used to living in cramped conditions like this, and were quick to find something positive in the small space that we, two grown men, had to fit into. "At least we each have our own bed," we laughed to each other.

Carlos Sastre and I were sharing a room for a night in a hotel in the French Alps. We were on a combined training-camp-meets-reconnaissance-trip ahead of the 2008 Tour de France. Carlos was one of two captains for the race, along with Frank Schleck. Frank's little brother, Andy, had potential as a future podium finisher but was still a bit too young and inexperienced. The Schleck brothers were good fun, approachable and well-liked on the team, as well as being extremely talented bike riders. Both were excellent climbers but still lacked a little physical power to really be considered at the top of their game yet. They had grown up on our team. They knew the team's values and were exactly the kind of riders that I'd been trying to create on the team.

The purpose of the few days in the Alps with Carlos was for me to help fine tune his form for the mountains, where the race's key stages would take place. But it was also important to get the team's top riders to work well together, to be able to communicate with each other and to be committed to doing what was best for the team. The Schleck brothers and Carlos had been at odds with each other on multiple occasions. Small power games, jibes and disagreements, which, if left unresolved, could grow into something bigger and more damaging to the team. They needed to understand that they needed each other if they wanted to get the best out of the race.

In April I'd already asked Kim Andersen to do something about the situation, as it was his responsibility to handle any friction. The three of them each had their quirks, and each of them was convinced that their way of doing things was the best and only way. Carlos was particularly headstrong, and could argue for hours about the smallest things, and it was almost impossible to change his mind and convince him that there were alternative choices when it came to equipment, training routes or race tactics. "Yes, Bjarne, but . . ." he'd often say in his charming, Spanish-accented English before he put forth his argument.

Sometimes we'd had to talk things through. Carlos had often tried to run the show on his own. He didn't want to race in the same events as the others and didn't want to go on training camps with the other riders. They were some of the problems we talked about that evening in the hotel room. We talked about the episode that spring, when Carlos, Andy and Frank had been at loggerheads. And we talked about the results of Rasmus Damsgaard's anti-doping work with our team, and about how widespread the doping problem still was within the peloton. "How widespread do you think it still is, Bjarne?" Carlos asked me.

"No doubt there are still some riders in the peloton who are doping," I said.

"Yes, but don't you think they'll get caught?"

"According to Rasmus Damsgaard, it is very hard to dope and not get caught these days, yes," I replied.

For the past couple of years, I'd been very wary when it came to talking to my riders about the subject of doping, as there was always a risk of being misunderstood or misinterpreted. All the more so when one of my former riders, the German Jörg Jaksche, told the press about a conversation we'd had in 2006 during his time with the team. Jörg had asked me a lot about what the doping situation had been like "back then in the 1990s". I told him a few stories about how things were. And we discussed a particular cortisone product that I had used when I was riding. He later completely twisted our conversation in an interview he did with *Der Spiegel*, who had paid him to tell them the story about his own doping during his career.

Since then, I hadn't wanted to talk to my riders too much about it, and so I quickly changed the topic of conversation with Carlos in the hotel room. We talked instead about our families, our dreams and our plans for the future. When it came to the Tour de France, we had the same dream: Carlos wanted to win it as a rider, while I wanted to win it as a team manager. "With the route as it is this year, it'll be the most consistent rider who wins it," I told Carlos. "If you can get a good gap on your rivals by winning a stage in the mountains, then you've got a good chance of taking yellow all the way to Paris." He listened to me with a look in his eye that suggested that he knew that this year was the year that he had the greatest chance of finishing on the podium. It would perhaps be the biggest and only chance of his career, as there weren't that many really tough competitors that he'd be up against, our team was strong and he'd put in the required amount of training on the right kind of terrain. "You have the opportunity to go right to the top," I told him, honestly.

"Thanks, Bjarne," he replied. "I'll do my best."

The only problem was that you never really knew where you were with Carlos – at least, that was my experience after the six years he'd ridden for me on the team.

"Good night, Bjarne," he mumbled, tired from the tough day in the mountains and our conversation, which had got both of us thinking about a number of things.

As he fell asleep, I stayed awake thinking about the time back in 2001 when Laurent Jalabert had introduced me to Carlos. "Here's the guy you need on your team, Bjarne," Laurent had told me, pushing forward the small, slender climber who rode for ONCE at that point. With dark circles under his eyes, and with almost grey, withered skin, Carlos introduced himself to me with a "hallo". He didn't speak any English. Immediately, it was hard to imagine the little Spanish mountain goat as a future star on my team. But Jalabert had highly recommended him having ridden with him at ONCE, and their team manager, Manolo Saiz, tended to be pretty good at spotting potential in riders.

While with the Spanish outfit, Carlos had only been used as a domestique, but with us he'd also been given his own chance to ride. But could we get the team to ride as a unit, and get him to really believe in himself?

On the training camp in the Alps, Carlos was focused and went about riding himself into form. On his best days, he rode with an easy pedal stroke, an elegant climber's style. He was a real talent, and someone you didn't really have to help much to make him really good and release his potential. Occasionally we had to talk to Carlos to remind him to ride enough kilometres in training, but he always had an explanation or excuse ready. "Listen, Bjarne – I live in the mountains. High up. The air's thinner, and there are lots of mountains, and that's why I don't need to train as much as the others," he told me one day.

"What about your speed, though, Carlos? You're not training at a high enough average speed," I replied.

"That'll come on its own, Bjarne. The roads around here are a lot rougher, and so it's not possible to ride at such a high speed as on the other roads," he said, by way of explanation.

Our conversations were a kind of battle. If I recommended a certain type of training, he'd argue that he should do the opposite. If I thought he should raise his saddle a couple of millimetres, we'd have a long conversation that would end with him keeping it the way it was. In my opinion, all his excuses were down to him not wanting any kind of structure or system to his training; that he just wanted to ride on feel alone. I also thought that he was perhaps worried about not living up to expectations – both his own and everyone else's. And so he dismissed what might be best for him in order to reduce the amount of expectation. But if we really thought that we had the chance to get Carlos into yellow, then we needed to stop with the bad excuses. Every time we'd worked out a plan for a stage which put some form of expectation on his shoulders, he'd always try to talk his way out of doing it. In our morning meetings just before a stage or a race when we'd work out our tactics, he'd always doubt that we were in a good enough position to actually pull off what was planned, and would try to find the problem with our tactics. He'd finish things off with a "Let's wait and see tomorrow" rather than "Yes – let's give it a go."

So this time I'd decided to treat him a little differently in the build-up to, and during, the Tour. I was going to push him and provoke him to take chances, even though there was that risk that he could fail or lose everything. I'd decided to take a leaf out of my old directeur sportif at Ariostea Giancarlo Ferretti's book who used to provoke me in order to make me dare to take chances.

Carlos and I cut short our training camp in the mountains because of bad weather, and I persuaded him to come to stay at my house in Switzerland in order to train a bit more.

The first half of the year had been a great success for us, with Fabian Cancellara winning Milan-San Remo, Tirenno-Adriatico and two stages of the Tour of Switzerland. Jens Voigt had got us a stage win at the Giro d'Italia, Chris Anker Sørensen got his first professional stage win at the Dauphiné Libéré and Frank Schleck had finished second at Amstel Gold. Results like those gave us good international coverage, and it was much needed. Our main sponsor, CSC, had decided to pull out at the end of the year, and so we were on the hunt for a replacement. But there was a lot of competition. Other teams like Crédit Agricole, Gerolsteiner, High Road and Slipstream were also looking for main sponsors, and ideally we all wanted a big, international company to come in. We'd been in negotiations with the Danish investment bank, Saxo Bank, for some time. They were officially a European bank, with offices in London, Geneva, Zurich, Singapore and Marbella. Its head offices were in Copenhagen, and it was owned by Kim Fournais and Lars Seier Christensen. Already in some of our earlier meetings, I could tell that we were a good match. They were ambitious when it came to sponsorship, and were keen for international exposure. If we could agree terms, they wanted to try to get onto our jerseys in time for the Tour de France, rather than wait until the new season. We agreed on a two-and-a-half year contract, which gave us the security we needed for the team.

At the press conference in Copenhagen to announce the new agreement at the start of June, there were big smiles all round. We knew that there were going to be questions about my doping confession, and about what conditions they had had written into the contract in case of there being a doping case on the team.

"Bjarne is part of the front line in the fight against doping, and were we not confident that that was the case, then we wouldn't be sitting here today," Lars Seier Christensen told the media.

"It's not in our nature to look back," the bank director continued, "but I think that we're well equipped to deal with anything that might come along."

When I arrived at the start of the 2008 Tour de France in Brest, it was with butterflies in my stomach. The last time I'd led my team at the Tour was the horrific 2006 edition, when we'd had to send Ivan home before the race had even started. Since my doping confession, there were a number of people who thought that I didn't deserve to come back to the race, and that I should stay away forever. Among them was the seven-time Tour winner Lance Armstrong, who told *Procycling* magazine that CSC-Saxo Bank and I should be sent home. The background for this was that the organisers hadn't invited the Kazakh team Astana to the race after their star rider, Alexandre Vinokourov, had tested positive on the race the year before. Armstrong thought that if the organisers were going to kick Astana out, then they ought to also kick us out, too. No doubt his thoughts were fuelled by the fact that his former team manager, Johan Bruyneel, was now the boss at Astana. But that was their problem. I'd decided that the best way for me to come back to the race was to provide the organisers with a clean winner. Carlos was our candidate for the podium, while Frank and Andy would try for the top 10. Fabian Cancellara was our card to play for the prologue and the time trials, while Jens Voigt, Kurt Asle Arvesen, Nicki Sørensen and Stuart O'Grady would look after Carlos, Frank and Andy. We did our best to have a quiet, relatively easy first half of the race, and then my plan was to really go for it from around the halfway mark.

During the briefing ahead of the Hautacam stage, I went through our tactics for the day. "Here's what we're going to do . . ." I said, with a confidence that I hoped would rub off on the riders.

And it did. The team delivered the goods. We showed what we could accomplish when we worked together. We controlled the bunch, and put riders in all the right breakaways. Fabian got into the day's main break, which got a big lead, just as I'd said would happen in the meeting. The goal was to make the other teams work in order to tire them out before we really put our plan into action once we got to the Hautacam.

Jens set a vicious tempo up the Col du Tourmalet, which dropped Alejandro Valverde and a number of the other big names, and then on the flatter section in the lead-up to the final climb, Jens and Fabian – who had dropped back from the break in order to help – again gave it absolutely everything in order to soften everyone up before delivering Carlos and Frank to the foot of the Hautacam. Those two then took it in turns to attack on the climb, putting pressure on race favourites such as Cadel Evans and Denis Menchov. Frank went off the front with the two Saunier Duval riders, Cobo and Piepoli, but wasn't able to follow them in the last couple of kilometres, and he finished third, just a single second away from taking the yellow jersey. Sastre came home seventh, and Evans took over the overall race lead. What we needed next was a stage victory, and Kurt Asle was the man for that on stage 11 to Foix. The Norwegian did what he did best and got himself into a break, and fought it out with the remnants of the group on the line, just beating Martin Elmiger and Alessandro Ballan to take the stage victory by a whisker. The stage win gave us a real confidence boost and thrilled our sponsors, who got the publicity they were after.

By that point, the Italian Saunier Duval rider, Riccardo Ricco, had won two stages, but the talk was that he'd won them a little too easily. The reason for that became apparent halfway through the race: Ricco was caught out in a dope test, just as Liquigas's Manuel Beltran and Moises Duenas of Barloworld had been already in the race so far. Ricco's Saunier Duval squad chose to pull out of the race, while the papers were filled with talk of doping. At Duenas's hotel, the police had found various banned products and medical equipment, including syringes, needles and blood bags.

On our team the conflict between the Schleck brothers on one side and Carlos on the other began to boil over. Things were tense between them, and none of them knew where they stood with each other. Carlos had the feeling that the brothers were only riding for each other and not to help him win. The brothers told him that he was imagining it. Carlos sent a few taunts their way, but was then touchy when the two boys from Luxembourg gave as good as they got. The press had got wind of the unrest, and wanted to know more. They asked who the leader was – Carlos or Frank? – and I talked a good game. "We'll have to see what happens, and see how each of them is riding," I said. "We've got a plan, but plans can change. You need to have more than just one. We'll just go with my gut feeling."

Jens Voigt was a little more honest than me when he was asked who decided whether the team should ride for Carlos or Frank. "That's up to the man who pays the bills," the German smiled.

The situation actually threatened to split the team if it got out of hand. There was a risk that the other riders would get involved, and it would ruin everything if people started choosing sides or forming little cliques. I decided, therefore, that I needed to call a meeting between Frank and Carlos. "Guys, we're riding to win," I reminded them at our hotel. Frustration had built up on both sides, and so we tried to talk through what the problems were.

"I just feel like they're not riding enough for me," said one of them.

"That's not true," said the other.

It played out like that for a while until after few minutes I'd had enough. "Listen, boys," I said. "If you're not able to work it out yourselves, then I'll have to give you some clear orders."

During a stage race, it's quite easy for a rider to go into their own little world, making it difficult to sometimes see the bigger picture. And that means that silly, unimportant little things can sometimes grow completely out of proportion. If that became the case, then it was my job to give the riders some perspective. "Together, we're stronger than anyone else, so let's work together," I said, putting an end to the 20-minute meeting. Frank and Carlos promised that they'd concentrate on working together instead of fighting against each other.

The mountain stage on Sunday 20 July was the stage I'd decided we were going to use to try to get the yellow jersey. On the 183km stage to Prato Nevoso, we took charge of the bunch with 40km to go. Fabian, Stuart, Jens and Nicki went to the front and upped the pace. Once on the climb, Andy took over and split the group up. Carlos, Denis Menchov and Bernhard Kohl jumped away from the other favourites with 4km to go. Frank also attacked Cadel Evans in the yellow jersey and managed to steal nine seconds from the Australian, which was enough to take the jersey. Carlos ended the day in sixth place overall, just 49 seconds down on Frank. It had become a really dramatic race, with six riders still in the hunt for victory, with just a few seconds separating them all. It meant that we needed to focus if we wanted to stand on the top step in Paris. At the hotel that evening we could be rightly pleased with the situation as it was: Frank had the yellow jersey, and both of our captains were in strong positions.

Three days later came the stage to the legendary Alpe d'Huez. It was the race's "queen stage" with three *hors catégorie* – "beyond category" – climbs, which made it a day that would definitely go a long way to deciding the Tour. If anyone could get a big enough gap over the others to take the yellow jersey on Alpe d'Huez, then they'd have a good chance of holding it all the way to Paris.

At the morning meeting, I pressed Frank and Carlos to show some initiative and leadership. The others on the team would give that much more if their leaders took responsibility. "Anyone got any ideas about how we can win today?" I asked. "What do you think, Frank?"

His reply was defensive both in attitude and tactically.

"What about you, Carlos? What should we do today?" I asked.

"Win the stage on Alpe d'Huez," he said, without hesitation. It was that kind of willingness to take a risk that I wanted to see from him.

We left the team in the capable hands of Fabian, who came to the front and smashed the race apart on the penultimate climb and on towards the final ascent of Alpe d'Huez. Once on the lower slopes of the last climb, it was up to Nicki, Kurt and Fabian, still, to lead the race at breakneck speed, making it too difficult for any of our nearest rivals to get away off the front. Then, while Menchov, Evans and the others concentrated on Frank in the yellow jersey, Carlos went on the attack and gave them something else to think about. No one could follow his easy climber's pedal stroke. At that point, I had to make a decision in the team car: was I going to stay with Frank because I thought he could keep hold of the yellow jersey, or was it more likely that Carlos would be able to get such a big gap that he'd be able to secure the overall classification now? I decided to leave Frank in his yellow jersey behind and drove up to Carlos to support him. "Come on, Carlos!" I shouted at him from the car. "You can win the Tour today!" He increased the time gap back to the chasers, which was important when it came to the overall classification, and rode home alone as the winner of the stage.

Carlos had been the most consistent rider in the race, and it was a real triumph for the team, as Andy also came across the line in third place. Carlos now led overall, with Frank second. As Carlos was cheered up on the podium, with over a minute-and-a-half's advantage over his closest rival, I thought back to our talk at the hotel in the Alps. What had happened at the race had proved that, as a team owner, I needed to believe in my employees, even those who weren't always the most obvious winners. I needed to motivate them and convince them that they could do it if they dared to set themselves goals. And Carlos dared on Alpe d'Huez.

Carlos's win also meant that the team hierarchy had fallen into place. He was the one we'd be riding for, and the Schleck brothers would have to help to secure him the overall victory. But it didn't mean that peace had broken out. The rumours were that Carlos was about to sign with another team for the following year. As the possible Tour winner, he'd be able to push for a much bigger salary and be the team's undisputed leader. On our team, even if he won the Tour he'd still have to share the captain's role with the Schleck brothers. But the task there and then was to fill Carlos with as much self-confidence as possible ahead of the final time trial, and I decided that would be best achieved by delaying the chat about whether he was negotiating with other teams until another time.

But on the evening before the time trial, a story in the German newspaper the *Süddeutsche Zeitung* threatened to ruin everything ahead of the stage. The newspaper wrote that I had supposedly contacted Fuentes – the sports doctor accused of systematic doping in the Operacion Puerto case – on Frank Schleck's behalf. The Danish newspapers were asking for a reaction from me, but I didn't particularly want to have to come forward every time there was some kind of rumour. This accusation, however, was so serious that

I didn't really have much choice. "These are some very serious allegations, which we flatly deny," I said. "I have never had any kind of contact and I would never be able to send any of my riders to a man like that."

"But can you not understand that would put question marks next to your defence when you lied so many times yourself about doping past?" asked the journalist.

"I do understand it, yes, but I have put my own past behind me now and have other responsibilities," I replied.

The story would hopefully go away on its own but was bound to turn up again one of these days.

The next day, I was there with Carlos every step of the way as he got ready and warmed up on the turbo trainer ahead of his time trial. "Just tell me what I need to do," he said to me when we discussed how he should approach riding the route.

As the wearer of the yellow jersey, Carlos was the last man to roll out on the 53km time trial. He led Cadel Evans overall by one minute 34 seconds. Carlos set out perfectly, with a smooth pedal stroke and no unnecessary upper-body movements. The yellow jersey appeared to be giving him wings. In the team car, we kept one eye on Evans's time, but it didn't look likely that the Australian was really going to claw much time back from Carlos. "Come on, Carlos!" we shouted into the microphone. We tried to whip him along, but we could tell by Evans's intermediate splits that the Australian really wasn't as much of a threat as we had first thought. Carlos flew across the line in 12th place on the stage, but in a really good time, losing only 29 seconds in all to Evans, which meant he had a lead of a minute and five seconds going into the final stage to Paris.

It was the culmination of our work together, and our many conversations and disputes. And our unwavering ability to challenge each other as people, rider and employer.

The other riders came running over to Carlos, having watched his ride on TV. "Carlito!" roared Fabian, thrilled. Jens Voigt and directeur sportif Scott Sunderland hopped and danced around with joy. Everyone had worked for each other during this Tour. Our philosophy had really paid off when it counted.

Back at the hotel, I found a moment's peace and quiet to think through the promises I'd made, and which were now going to be kept with victory in Paris. The main one was my promise to deliver a dope-free winner, but I had promised the press, the riders and the cycling world that we would become the world's best cycling team. And this year we'd won both the yellow jersey and the Tour's teams classification.

In Paris, Carlos was celebrated as the Tour winner, with Frank finishing sixth and Andy 12th. As a team, we then rode a flag-waving lap of honour on the Champs-Elysées. For me, it was like rewinding back to 1996. My feelings this time were a mix of pride, joy and a need to show the outside world that it had really happened. It felt like redemption having had to miss the race in 2007 but now coming back and delivering a winner. We ended our lap of honour near the Arc de Triomphe where we had some pictures taken. It was while we were there that I ran into the Tour race director Christian Prudhomme, who congratulated me. "Thanks," I said, and then added, "and here's your clean Tour winner."

"I know," he said, and smiled.

Victory at the Tour had raised Carlos's market value and, as his contract with us also ran out at the end of the year, there were a number of rumours doing the rounds. The day after the Tour, I sat down with Carlos to talk about the future. "If I can get the money, then we can extend your contract," I told him.

But a fortnight later, I received a call from him. "I've decided not to continue with the team," he told me. It was no huge surprise.

At the end of August, the Italian media reported that the Canadian bike manufacturer Cervélo were going to be the main sponsor of a new team, with Carlos supposedly as their leader. Around the same time, I went to the Tour of Spain, where again Carlos was our main man for the title. But I was told that the atmosphere hadn't been good. There were rumours within the team that Carlos was already trying to recruit some of our riders, directeurs sportifs and staff members to take with him to Cervélo.

On a training ride with the team just before the start of the Vuelta a España, we rode along next to each other and talked about the course route. I then said that I'd heard that he was trying to recruit some of my staff. He defended himself, and it descended into an argument. "Can you not just concentrate on the bike race instead of trying to play team manager?" I asked him.

That evening, I called a team meeting. I explained a bit about the situation and asked everyone to remain loyal. "I know that there's a lot going on behind my back at the moment," I said, "which I find hard to accept. If anyone has any problems, then they must come to me."

During the race itself, former Tour de France winner Alberto Contador annihilated everyone on stage 13, winning the stage and taking the gold leader's jersey, leaving Carlos down in third place.

There was more disappointment when the big Spanish newspaper *El Pais* published an interview with Carlos:

> *"There's someone who has damaged and split the team since the start of this race, and who clearly doesn't want anyone to achieve anything at this Vuelta."*
> Is that person Bjarne Riis?
> *"It's the team's leader . . . I am just mentally exhausted. I have experienced many challenges in my 25 years as a rider, and it is sometimes difficult to accept other people's decisions, and not least to have to live with them. You end up exhausting yourself . . . When you've won a race as big as the Tour and dedicated your life to the rest of the world, and when you don't feel that you've been valued enough, it destroys you physically."*

Reading what he said, I felt like I should have thrown him off the race and fired him on the spot. But I decided that such action would probably do the team more harm than good. He was leaving the team anyway, and thanks to his behaviour everyone would be able to see that we wouldn't be able to continue to work together. Brian talked to Carlos, who said he'd been misquoted. But it was a time of introspection for me. When you come up against someone saying things like that, then you have to ask yourself, "What am I doing wrong?" I'd got to know myself pretty well as a leader and felt well in control of both my strong and weak sides. My strengths were that I was decisive and could maintain my focus when things got tough. My weaknesses were that I took things too personally, that I expected people to always think the same way as me and that everyone wanted the same things as me. Sometimes I thought that I could also be a bit hard on people if I thought they weren't living up to the expectations I had of them. Carlos was one of those I'd given a long leash to since he'd arrived on the team. He paid that trust back by continuing with his accusations, this time to the Spanish paper *Marca*:

> *"Riis didn't like spending time with me, but couldn't do without me, either, because he knew that I was the one who helped achieve a balance on the team . . . Between us we came up with some clear ideas, but he's sabotaged all that."*

Even though it was tempting to respond to Carlos's claims, I decided not to say anything in public.

He finished the Vuelta in third place overall, which was won by Contador. Saying goodbye to Carlos was sad after seven years, and it really shouldn't have ended the way it did.

During the world championships in Italy at the end of September, the story about Frank Schleck and Doctor Fuentes reared its ugly head again. According to the document that the *Süddeutsche Zeitung* was in possession of, Frank had transferred 50,000 kroner (£4,500) to a Swiss bank account with the code names "Codes Holding" in March 2006. The bank account belonged to Eufemiano Fuentes. This led everyone to the conclusion that Frank must have paid Fuentes to help him dope, and Frank was called before the Luxembourg Anti-Doping Agency. It was time to have a serious talk with Frank. "What's going on?" I demanded.

"I just wanted to know what it was all about," he said, clearly upset. He knew that he'd been stupid and hadn't thought. "But I've never doped myself," he said.

I contacted the team's sponsors to fill them in on what was going on, and Frank flew to Denmark to explain himself to Kim Fournais and Lars Seier from Saxo Bank. Later, Frank asked to give an explanation to the UCI's legal department in order to clear up any possible misunderstandings. He explained that he had paid the money for a training programme, and didn't know that the bank account belonged to Fuentes. The money transfer had apparently triggered a huge argument when Frank told his dad about it, and his dad told him not to use the training programme. With my experience from the Bo Hamburger case and from having to dismiss Ivan Basso from the team, I decided to support Frank and believe his explanation. If he was convicted by the Luxembourg Anti-Doping Agency, then that would be different, and we'd have to deal with it.

A Belgian newspaper added more fuel to the fire by publishing a list of 30 riders who had apparently recorded abnormal blood values and were sent a letter by the head of the French Anti-Doping Agency saying that their samples would be further analysed for signs of new drug CERA, which several riders had tested positive for at the Tour de France.

According to the Belgian paper, the list included Carlos, Frank, Stuart O'Grady and Fabian Cancellara. I asked Rasmus Damsgaard, the head of our team's internal anti-doping programme, what he thought. "If one of your riders had used CERA, we would have found it in our EPO and urine tests – you can be absolutely sure of that," he told me.

In December, the Luxembourg Anti-Doping Committee announced that they weren't going to bring a case against Frank, and concluded that there was no proof of doping or any attempt to dope.

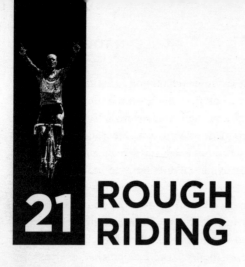

21 ROUGH RIDING

As the 2009 season got under way, we had to try our best to put Carlos's farewell to the team behind us. From a sporting point of view, everything now revolved around the Schleck brothers for the Tour and Fabian Cancellara for the Classics. Frank Schleck had already shown at Paris-Nice in March that it was going to be a big season for him and his brother, finishing second overall in the week-long stage race.

Frank was the kind of rider who you had to push to make him believe in himself but, at nearly 29, it was time for us to put more responsibility on his shoulders and for him to learn to feel comfortable with people's expectations of him. His little brother, Andy, was my big hope for the season. With his gung-ho attitude, he was a lot less risk-averse than Frank, and had real potential for the big stage races. At 22, he had plenty of time to develop yet, too. Andy's breakthrough had come at the 2007 Giro d'Italia, where he'd finished second, and my former directeur sportif, Cyrille Guimard, described him as "a young Laurent Fignon".

Monaco was the setting for the start of the 2009 Tour de France. We were setting all our hopes on the Schleck brothers for the overall, while Fabian was the man to try to get us the yellow jersey early on in the race. The Swiss rider was used to having responsibility heaped onto his shoulders and didn't mind the pressure at all. He was a Classics specialist whose wins included Paris-Roubaix and Milan-San Remo, and he was almost unbeatable when it came to time trials – a discipline in which he had won multiple world titles and was reigning Olympic champion. He did it again in Monaco, too, winning the 15km opening time trial and taking the race's first yellow jersey. From then on, it was all about us holding onto it for as long as possible without using up too much energy, which we did right up until the sixth stage.

Our team was made up of a number of humble and hard-working domestiques who were there to help our leaders in any way they could. It was a role I knew well from my time riding for Fignon.

Nicki Sørensen was one of them. He knew his role on the team and commanded a lot of respect from the other riders for the way he rode. It meant there wasn't a rider on the team who could begrudge Nicki taking his chance at the Tour, which he got on stage 12 to Vittel. All day, a number of riders had tried and failed to get away, but eventually one break stuck. Nicki, though, sat back in the peloton, alert and ready to try something unexpected. At the right moment, he attacked and bridged up to the breakaway group and, with 25km to go, attacked again, with only one other rider capable of following him. With 7km to go, he was in danger of being caught. "Now's the time, Nicki!" I yelled at him. He went again, this time on his own, and held off the chasers to take the biggest win of his career. We were all thrilled for him. It was one of the most well-deserved wins anyone had seen in a while, and a number of Nicki's team-mates had to fight back the tears.

Jens Voigt was another of our hard-working domestiques, but he also knew how to get into the right breakaways. He was a product of the former East Germany, always ready to work for others and always in a good mood. Jens got his chance on stage 16 and went away with the day's main break. However, on one of the descents he lost concentration for just a fraction of a second and his bike slipped away from beneath him. He hit his head hard on the road, and I was one of the first on the scene. It didn't look good: he had knocked himself unconscious, and there was a lot of blood. I supported his head in my hands, but he looked awful. The race doctor arrived and immediately called for an ambulance. Once I knew that he was in good hands, I went back to the team car and called BS, who was in the second car, further back. "Jens has crashed, and it's serious," I told him.

BS went to the hospital and stayed with the German, who was suffering with severe concussion, a fractured cheekbone and some nasty cuts and bruises all over. "There's a chance that they might have to operate on his brain," BS said.

Later, following the Tour, while Jens was still in hospital and facing yet another operation, I called him up. His contract was going to run out at the end of the season, and the day before the crash we'd been negotiating a new one but hadn't been able to come to an agreement. With serious injuries, and at nearly 38 years old, the prospects of him getting a new contract perhaps weren't that great. "Hey Bjarne! How are you?" he said, cheerfully, from his sick bed.

"Jens, I just wanted to say that you've got a contract for next year, no matter what," I said, and wished him a speedy recovery.

At that year's Tour, Lance Armstrong and Alberto Contador were team-mates at Astana. The team's hierarchy, though, hadn't exactly been worked out, which was obvious enough for those of us not even on the team. Lance had said that he was going to ride for Contador, but it was clear that the American was only interested in his own chances at the race he'd decided to make a comeback at. Having won it seven times before, he wasn't prepared to play second fiddle to the young Spaniard. We needed to use the unrest on the team to our advantage, but that required a willingness to take risks. Andy and Frank had begun to get a little tired of that phrase, which I was constantly using each time an opportunity presented itself.

"You need to be willing to take more risks," I told them yet again. "We need to play Lance and Contador off against each other more and take advantage of their rivalry."

But Frank always seemed to have a reason why we should wait until later on in the stage.

"But if we wait much longer, it'll be too late," I told him.

The mountain stage to Le Grand Bornand was the Tour's "queen stage" that year, and we had to do something. I told the team as much that morning, and we made a plan. We went on the offensive almost immediately, and set a high tempo to try to wear down Armstrong. Sastre, now riding for Cervélo, went on the attack, and Andy, Frank, Contador and Andreas Klöden went with him. Lance was unable to follow. Carlos later had to let the others go, and Klöden was the next to fall off the pace. The other three came to the finish together, with Frank winning the stage from Contador.

Things changed again with the 40km time trial, where Armstrong was stronger than both of the brothers. It put the American back on the podium, with Frank 34 seconds down on him. Yet again, I had a word with Frank about how he had to take more risks if he wanted to stand on the podium in Paris. If he wanted to beat Armstrong on Mont Ventoux, then he couldn't ride defensively or wait to see what the others did. "This is your last chance to do something," I told him ahead of the Ventoux stage.

But Frank hadn't changed. "Let's just wait and see what happens," he said.

Mont Ventoux – "the bald mountain", as it was known – was perfect for attacks. Juan Manuel Garate and Tony Martin had attacked and were up the road, while the Astana team set a high tempo on the lower slopes of the climb in an effort to stop Frank and Andy attacking. Andy was able to attack anyway, hoping to make things difficult for Armstrong so that Frank could attack the American. But Frank didn't have the legs, and while Andy went on ahead, with Contador sticking to his wheel, Armstrong pulled up alongside Frank to psyche him out. The American looked him straight in the eyes. "You can try to do whatever you like, but I'm going to be right here on your wheel," Lance told him.

I watched from the car. "The battle's over," I thought. And it was. Frank didn't try any more attacks.

In Paris, Alberto Contador stood on the top of the podium as the race winner, with Andy a step below him. It was a well-deserved second place; we'd dominated the race and had pushed for the victory all the way to the end.

On Saturday 1 August, while the Tour of Denmark was on, our garden at the house in Vejle had been decorated with flowers, the tables were positioned so as to be able to enjoy a view across the fjord, and everything was planned and in place. Our wedding day was to be a day we'd remember forever. Anne Dorthe looked amazing in her dress, and I could tell how happy she was. Even though we'd become a family, with three of our own children, it meant a lot to get married.

In September, Brian Nygaard asked me for a meeting. He'd been offered a job in the UK with the new British team, Sky. On the one hand I understood why he wanted to go, but on the other he was one of my closest and most trustworthy colleagues, and I'd miss him. I'd always be thankful for everything he'd done, but I'd really miss him as a person as we'd spent a lot of time together and had gone through some difficult times with the team, which had helped form a strong bond. We decided to announce that he was leaving at the start of October, and Brian promised that he would help find his replacement.

At the end of November, the team headed off for a survival camp on the Spanish island of Fuerteventura, and BS and I had a chat. "Maybe it's time I called it a day," BS told me. It was something that we'd both thought about. He'd been an important part of the team, and had really helped me grow as a person, but all good things come to an end, and 10 years of working together was a long time. During that time we'd had 10 very memorable training camps, and countless stressful and sometimes seemingly unresolvable tasks to face at the Tour de France, which we had nevertheless come away stronger from. A number of riders had also chosen to leave the team, but there were still more surprises to come before the year was out.

In December, Saxo Bank contacted me to let me know that the upcoming season would be their last sponsoring us. Their decision caused a lot of anxiety in the organisation. All the teams were having trouble attracting the big sponsors, and our staff had begun to notice how hard it was getting, too. They started to worry whether they'd still have a job in the future, or whether they should start considering other teams. I'd heard rumours about a new "super team", due to be based out of Luxembourg. The rumours also said that the Schleck brothers, whose contracts with us ran out after the 2010 season, were going to be the team's leaders. "What's going on?" I asked Frank and Andy.

"We don't know any more than you do," they replied.
It wasn't the end to 2009 that I'd hoped for.

At the start of March, Danish newspaper *BT* wrote:

> *According to Italian newspaper* Gazzetta dello Sport, *the Schleck brothers are considering starting their own team for next year. Furthermore, they could take Fabian Cancellara and directeur sportif Kim Andersen with them.*
>
> *Andersen says he understands why people might be surprised that the Schlecks are not categorically denying that there could be something in the rumours.*
>
> *"But at the same time, you have to remember that Frank and Andy are not married to Saxo Bank or Bjarne," says Andersen. "Their contracts run out after this year, so they could be open to offers. Not that I'm saying they don't want to stay. It's tough for them, because they want to be open to everyone."*
>
> *And is Andersen married to Riis?*
>
> *"No – it's a professional environment. I've also had other offers in the past, but I've always chosen to stay. We'll have to see what happens, though," says Andersen, denying that he knows any more than he's said.*

A few days later, on Saturday 13 March, I read more disturbing rumours in the media – this time on the website *Cyclingnews*:

> *Former Astana team manager Marc Biver has admitted he is in talks with a Luxembourg company about creating a team around Frank and Andy Schleck for 2011.*
>
> *It seems that Biver has been working on the idea of a Luxembourg team led by the Schlecks for some time, perhaps since as far back as November last year.*

Having read all the rumours, I took out my laptop on a flight to Paris and wrote in my diary:

> A crap day. One of those days when it isn't great to work in cycling.

The newspapers are saying that Andy, Frank and Kim are trying to build their own team. They've told me themselves that they don't know anything about it. But they're not telling me everything – or am I just being too sensitive? But I want to know, so they should just tell me if there's something going on.

I'm on a plane to Paris now, and Kim's picking me up at Orly airport. I'm going to have to talk to him and find out whether I can trust him. He's an important part of the team.

And if the rumours do turn out to be true, what will I do? It will be a catastrophe, and will no doubt cause a huge argument. What if I have to tell Kim to leave?

I hope that I can trust my employees, and that they stay loyal to me!

I hope that my gut feeling about it all is wrong. I really don't want to be disappointed, or to have to take drastic action. I don't want to have to face the consequences. Just how angry would I be? I'm not sure, but I know I'd be extremely disappointed.

When I talked to Kim, he told me that he'd been misquoted in *BT*. "That may be the case, but I don't want to have to read anything like this at the moment," I told him.

But I soon received more news about him and, needing to know what was going on, I spoke to him again. This time, he told me that he wanted to stay with the brothers. I then talked to Andy and Frank. "I just need to know what your first priority is," I told them.

"You're one of our options," they replied.

"One of your options?" I said. "Have I become an option?"

"Yes," they replied, but could tell it wasn't what I wanted to hear.

"This is not how I want things to be between us," I said, and asked again, "What is your first priority?"

"You are our first priority," they said.

It was a bit of honesty and commitment that I wanted from them, but my gut feeling was that I wasn't getting it.

One day, I received a call from someone I knew within cycling.

"Do you know what some of the people in your team are up to?" he asked, and filled me in on what he knew. The upshot of it was that I'd have to confront the brothers and Kim at the Tour of Switzerland.

But the Schleck boys beat me to it. "Now we've been contacted by the Luxembourg team," they told me, "but we haven't decided what we're going to do yet. The team's going ahead with or without us."

I wasn't so sure about that, but I asked them whether my former press officer, Brian Nygaard, was involved.

"He might be," was all they'd say.

That was no great surprise, as I'd heard rumours that he was. Next, I talked to Kim. I'd heard that he was in fact already deeply involved with the new team and was already in the process of hiring staff – and had been talking to mine. I decided that he needed to stop working for us, with immediate effect.

"Okay," he said, "I have to accept that."

"It's not even up for discussion," I told him.

Kim was the one who had had responsibility for the Schlecks and their training, but was also one of my most important directeurs sportifs. But I could see no other way. In my eyes, what he'd been doing was disloyal and unacceptable. In any other business environment, he would have been dismissed long before this.

Fabian won the first stage and Frank won overall at the Tour of Switzerland. I was pleased with their form but was still worried about what was going on behind my back. I needed to keep my future plans for the team very close to my chest, and not talk out loud about our search for a new sponsor, or about the team roster for next season. If Frank and Andy were going to leave the team, and if they were going to take other riders with them, then I needed to think about who to replace them with.

Secretly, I'd been talking to Alberto Contador, who was considering changing teams, and was interested in joining us. It made negotiations with a new main sponsor even more important. We were in touch with a big company who were interested in becoming the sole main sponsor. While I waited on an answer from them, I went home to Denmark to celebrate Jesper having finished his school exams and to attend the national championships a week before the Tour. The arrangement was that the potential sponsor would be in touch just before the start of the Tour. If we could agree a deal, I'd be in a position to announce that the team would be continuing, and that everything was in place, which would take some pressure off during the Tour. I waited to hear back from them, as there were just some details that they wanted to check.

Finally, the call I'd been waiting for came through, but it wasn't what we'd been hoping for. They weren't going to sponsor us. So we had no new sponsor, the big names were on their way out of the team, and time was running out.

During the national championships, I tried to pretend that everything was okay, but that really wasn't the case. The news that Kim had been fired had got out, and I was being asked what it all meant. The photographers circled me, waiting for a moment when I might look a bit down or make some kind of action that suggested "giving up". The Luxembourg team with Kim as a directeur sportif and the Schlecks as its stars was clearly well on the way to being established. And then I got confirmation that Brian Nygaard was going to be involved, too. He was going to be the team manager.

22 2010 TOUR DIARY

The new Luxembourg team was in the process of hoovering up my riders and staff. In just a few days' time, my staff and the press were expecting me to kick off the Tour de France by being able to announce a new sponsor. But it wasn't going to happen, and our managing director, Trey Greenwood, was already working on plan B and C. We were certainly not going to have anything in place before the Tour, though.

I felt tired, confused and lacking in energy, with less than a week to go before the start of the Tour.

I was contacted by a journalist from TV2, who apparently had something to tell me. "I've got hold of a secret email correspondence that shows that Frank Schleck was already in negotiations with the new Luxembourg team last year," the journalist told me. "Would you like to comment on this? We'd love to have you on live."

"I'll think about it," I said, and promised to get back to them.

If it was true, then the Schleck brothers had been taking me for a fool for a long time, and directly lying to me. I could feel the disappointment and anger rising up in me. The coup against me had been running for longer than I'd thought. I wondered how many of my riders and the staff had been plotting their escape while still working for me. Even now I didn't know how many might leave. I then had a horrible thought. Who was it that wanted things to go so badly for me during the Tour that they'd leak a confidential document that they knew would cause problems internally on my team? But there wasn't really anyone I could talk to about it as I really didn't know who I could trust any more. Really,

I should have fired Frank in the same way as I fired Kim. There weren't many work places that would accept disloyalty from an employee.

I rang a friend of mine in Denmark who had nothing to do with cycling. "How's it going?" he asked me.

"I've had better days," I said, and told him about the whole sorry mess. Our chat helped clear my head a little and give me a better picture of everything that was going on.

I got back to the TV2 journalist and told them that I didn't want to comment on the new revelations, but said that I was going to talk to Frank once we got to the Tour. TV2 ran their story that evening, which helped make up my mind. I didn't want to hear any more about what he'd been up to and instead wanted to hear him promise that there wouldn't be any more trouble during the race, otherwise I would have to send him straight home.

That evening, I received a call from Andy. "What's going on?" he asked. He was clearly worried that I might be about to send his brother home before the race had even started.

"What's going on? Clearly nothing that's helping me, that's for sure," I said. "When we meet tomorrow evening, we're going to have a talk – you, Frank and me."

Tuesday 29 June, Brussels
I arrived at the hotel late in the evening, and had Frank and Andy come to my room for our meeting. They were clearly uneasy about the situation. "I want complete loyalty from you both for the whole Tour," I told them. "That means there'll be no sitting there nego-tiating with my riders or staff members trying to get them to ride for your team next season.

"I know more than you think," I continued. "And I can act more drastically than I've done so far. For the next three weeks, we're going to try to win the Tour – we owe each other that much, don't we?"

The brothers nodded.

"Only you can decide what you do next year, but for the rest of this year you work for me," I reminded them. "I don't want to fight with you for the next three weeks. I don't want to hear any crap about your project. Just remember that the whole team has come here to ride for you, so no more bullshit. I really don't want to hear a word about your new project, and you're not to speak to the press about it, either. Are we agreed on all that?"

"Yes," they both said without hesitation.

After that, I gathered the rest of the team together to tell them that Frank, Andy and I had had a meeting. "We've agreed that there's not going to be any trouble during this Tour – that is, there'll be no talking about the new team in the evenings."

The riders seemed surprised that I was tackling this head on.

"And watch out for the press, too," I said. "Every day they're going to go after a story about an internal split. We're not going to go down that road – we owe each other and the team that much."

Thursday 1 July, press conference, Rotterdam
On the team bus on the way to the press conference, I talked to the riders about what we were going to do, and read them what I'd prepared to say to the press. Most of them were grateful to be told, as it meant that they were prepared for what was going to happen. I was going to run the press conference in a no-nonsense manner. I had a message that I wanted to get out. I wanted to put a lid on the internal problems and I wanted to announce the lack of a sponsor in a way that suggested that it wasn't a huge problem for us.

"There have been quite a few rumours that I was going to announce a new sponsor here at the Tour de France," I said. "Everyone who works in this industry knows that finding sponsors takes patience and hard work. I am patient, and we're working hard on a number of possible solutions. My team are up to speed on what's happening, and when we have something to announce, I will announce it, but I believe that we will have a team going forward."

Kim and Brian's team also needed to be neutralised.

"We have no comment to make about the new team that's being started. We're here to ride the Tour de France," I said. "With perhaps the strongest team here, we've got a good chance. Frank and Andy are feeling sharp and ready to fight, and the rest of the team is also ready."

Throughout the press conference I felt strong, full of fighting spirit and alert – all of that despite our situation.

Saturday 3 July, prologue: Rotterdam, 8.9km
In the last few hours before the start of the race, Trey and I had been negotiating with IT firm Sungard. They were already one of the team's smaller sponsors, but now they were showing interest in moving up a level. Cristobal Conde, Sungard's administrative director, told us that they did want to become a main sponsor and committed to increasing the amount of money they were putting into the team. Fabian won the prologue and could wear the race's first yellow jersey, while Andy seemed a bit disappointed with his own performance. Maybe he had too much on his mind.

Monday 5 July, stage two: Rotterdam – Brussels, 223.5km
Every day that we held the yellow jersey gave maximum exposure to our sponsors, and companies interested in coming on board could see that there was some good airtime to be had at the Tour. Fabian's yellow jersey gave him status and made life easier for him in the peloton, as it meant that other teams gave him more room. But there were responsibilities that came with wearing the jersey, too. The other riders expected leadership from whoever was in yellow and their team, and that's exactly what was required 30km from the end of the stage.

We had been riding up at the front of the bunch to reel in an earlier breakaway, but things went wrong for us on one of the descents. It was extremely slippery, and one of the motorbikes following the race crashed, causing panic in the peloton. Around half of the bunch hit the deck, including Frank and Andy. Both of them were quickly back on their bikes again, albeit battered and bruised, but then Andy crashed again. Even though Matti Breschel was smart enough to give his bike to Andy, his team-mate, whose bike had broken, Andy was still left three to four minutes behind the bunch due to the accident. Jens Voigt and Nicki Sørensen worked hard to try to pace both Frank and Andy back to the bunch, but up front Fabian took the initiative to tell everyone that they needed to wait for Andy, Frank and a number of other riders who'd crashed to catch up again. Most of the other riders were happy to do what Fabian suggested, although there were a few who were annoyed by the decision because it meant that the stage wouldn't end in a bunch sprint, as the go-slow meant that they couldn't catch Frenchman Sylvain Chavanel, who was out on his own. Chavanel won the stage, and a further consequence of Fabian's decision was that he lost his own yellow jersey. Frank and Andy, however, had made it back to the bunch thanks to their Swiss team-mate.

Tuesday 6 July, stage three: Brussels – Spa, 201km
The third stage included a number of tough cobbled sections, and all the riders were afraid of crashing. On one section, Andy led onto the cobbles, but the German rider Tony Martin tried to come through on the inside, crashing and bringing Frank down with him. He was lying on his side, completely still, when I got to him. He was clearly in pain, but when he saw me he reached out, and I took his hand and gave it a squeeze. Although neither of us said anything, we both knew that this was the end of his Tour. I rushed back to the team car, counted to 10, and then got on the radio. I told the riders that Frank was out of the race with a broken collarbone. "Guys, you need to focus now, so let's ride," I added. Fabian and Andy got the message and went on the attack. I wanted to motivate them to really focus, despite having lost such an important member of the team. We needed to win the yellow jersey back.

Frank was probably the only rider who was going to have been able to stay with Andy in the mountains, so now there was a risk that Andy would be isolated on the climbs, while Alberto Contador would have a number of team-mates capable of staying with him. On the other hand, it could be good for Andy to have to grow up a little more and get by without his big brother.

While Thor Hushovd won the stage, Fabian did enough to take back the yellow jersey, and Andy took some important time off his rivals, including Contador. That evening, Frank came to the hotel to say goodbye and collect his luggage before travelling home to Luxembourg for an operation. We were both as disappointed as each other that he had to leave the race.

Sunday 11 July, stage eight: Station des Rousses – Morzine Avoriaz, 189km

The 189km stage to Avoriaz was the race's first serious stage in the mountains, and it turned out to be a dramatic day. Lance Armstrong suffered a number of crashes and was unable to follow the leaders – including Andy and Contador – as a result. On the final climb, I saw signs of weakness in Contador. He was riding on the wheels of his team-mates, whereas normally the Spaniard would be attacking on a climb like this. It could mean that he was in trouble, and so, with 7km to go, I was keen for Andy to attack. "Andy, I think you need to ride now," I told him through his earpiece.

"No – I'll wait until we get to the Pyrenees," he said.

"But I'm convinced that Contador has a few problems," I said.

With 1km to go, and Contador now without any team-mates, I again urged Andy to go for it.

He attacked, got a good gap, and won the stage. If he had done that with 7km to go, he could have won the Tour. It would have given him a decisive advantage – I'm convinced. Armstrong came home 12 minutes down on Andy, who was now just 20 seconds away from the yellow jersey. Everyone was thrilled afterwards, except me.

Monday 12 July, rest day, Morzine

We were all set to announce Sungard as our new main sponsor at a press conference. "We only want you to announce it after the Tour," they told us. That was okay with me, though, as long as they were in.

I immediately called everyone together on the team bus to tell them the good news. "The team's existence is secured for the next two years," I told them, proudly. Most of them were thrilled, but I noticed a few people who looked less enthusiastic. Perhaps it was because they were already a long way down the road with their negotiations with other teams, having doubted that we'd get a new sponsor. The press seemed surprised, as I think some journalists had already written me off as a team boss. They were then all over Andy, asking whether it changed anything when it came to him potentially changing teams. "We're here to ride the Tour. We'll talk about everything else later," he said, brushing them off.

Tuesday 13 July, stage nine: Morzine Avoriaz – St. Jean de Maurienne, 204.5km

In the early hours of the morning, I came up with my plan for the day's stage, which would hopefully allow Andy to get the yellow jersey. Two category one climbs and the *hors catégorie* Col de la Madeleine made the stage perfect for our tactics.

The initial phase was to get someone in the day's break. When the opportunity arose, I got straight on the radio to Jens Voigt. "Now!" I yelled. Jens got away in the break, who built up a good advantage. The plan was under way.

The second part was to happen on the Col de la Madeleine. As we approached the climb, I got on the radio again: "Andy, tell me when you're ready."

"I'm ready!" came back his reply. Now it was time to really get things going.

"Start pushing when the road starts climbing," I told the team.

They were to ride hard when it was steep, but to stay off the front on the parts where it flattened out. On the next flatter section, Alexandre Vinokourov attacked, and my riders considered going with him. "No – let him go," I shouted. There was no point taking the lead when it was easy for everyone else to just follow. It cost too much energy for very little benefit. Chris Anker and Jakob Fuglsang came to the front again on the next tough section. They really put on the pressure, which caused all sorts of damage. Cadel Evans, in the yellow jersey, was suffering. It wasn't long before only Andy and Contador were left to battle it out on the mountain.

Now it was time for phase three, which was to get Jens back from the break. "Jens, save your energy and let yourself fall back. Andy's on the way," I told the German through the radio. Jens did as I said and waited for Andy to catch up with him.

I pulled up alongside Andy. "Jens is ready," I said, and looked at him and then at Contador. It was a strange feeling. Here I was trying to stop the Spaniard winning, while it was very possible that he was going to be my team leader for next year. They caught up with Jens, who immediately got to work at the front of the group, using the last of his energy to drag Andy a good way up the climb until he had no choice but to drop back, exhausted, just before the top.

Up ahead, Frenchman Sandy Casar held on to win the stage, while Andy crossed the line in seventh and took the yellow jersey, with Contador moving up to second overall.

That evening, we sent out a draft of the contract to Contador, who then rang me to talk it through. Shortly after that, I received a text message from him: "I'm looking forward to working together for many years to come. It's a big project we're starting together."

Thursday 15 July, stage 11: Sisteron – Bourg les Valence, 184.5km
Stuart O'Grady and Jens Voigt were our most experienced riders. Stuart was the road captain, steering the team out on the road. But I was unsure where they stood in terms of their futures with me. After the stage, I pulled Stuart aside first. "What are your plans for next year?" I asked him.

"I've had a good offer," he said. "A high salary. I'm going with the Schleck brothers."

Next it was Jens's turn. "I'm really happy here on the team with you, Bjarne, but I think I'm going to follow the brothers, as we always ride the same races," he told me. "And then Kim has always been my directeur sportif, so I want to continue working with him."

Did the people behind the Luxembourg project really want to start a new team, or did they just want to take half of my riders and my whole infrastructure and then go from there?

Later on, I talked with Torsten Schmidt, another of my directeurs sportifs. "What about you next year, Torsten? Are you on the team?"

"What do you mean?" he asked.

"Are you still going to be with us for next season?"

"Yeah, well . . . I just need to think about it," he said.

"Have you signed with someone else?" I asked.

"I'm just trying to see what's going on," he replied.

Torsten had also had an offer from the Luxembourg team – I was sure of it.

Saturday 17 July, stage 13: Rodez – Revel, 196km
It had been a hard past couple of days. The mass exodus from the team really hurt – and it hurt most of all because these were people I'd trusted who were now ready to tear the team apart. I was very disappointed.

After the stage, I decided to talk to Andy. "What's Kim's involvement in all this?" I asked.

"I don't really know," Andy replied.

We talked some more, and I told him that I felt that there was some loyalty lacking in the team.

"Can't you ring Kim and talk with him about the situation?" Andy asked. He clearly didn't want to be caught between Kim and me.

"I am sorry about all this, Bjarne." Andy said.

Sunday 18 July, stage 14: Revel – Ax 3 Domaines, 184.5km
The atmosphere in the team was a bit better again. We agreed that Andy would have to see how the stage developed, and that it was Contador who needed to go on the attack if he wanted to try to get our yellow jersey.

As expected, during the stage Contador was in an attacking mood every time the road went up. He tried to rid himself of Andy numerous times, but Andy easily kept him under control. At one point, it was like watching a track race as both riders almost came to a stop on the final climb, daring each other to take the lead. It allowed Samuel Sanchez and Denis Menchov to come back up to them and then go on ahead to try to get some vital seconds back on the two riders. But my tactics were going to come into play again the next day, when we would be facing two category two climbs and an *hors catégorie* climb up to the finish line, where we would be hoping that Andy could distance himself even more from Contador. Andy needed to have as big a lead over Contador as possible going into the final time trial on the penultimate day – a discipline in which the Spaniard was much stronger than Andy.

Monday 19 July, stage 15: Pamiers – Bagnères de Luchon, 187.5km
This was it – it was now or never. The team had given it everything, with Jakob and Chris Anker delivering Andy to the bottom of the day's final climb, just like we'd planned. Andy then attacked on the climb, surprising Contador and getting a gap. But then, disaster, and time seemed to stand still. Andy lost his chain, and had to stop, twice, to get it back on properly. Contador, meanwhile, took advantage

of the mechanical mishap and kept riding. Andy sprinted to the top of the climb, but wasn't able to catch up, so then proceeded to plunge down the descent on the other side in death-defying pursuit. Contador crossed the finish line 39 seconds ahead of Andy, and with it took the yellow jersey by eight seconds. Andy was furious, while the race's new leader, Contador, was booed by the crowd when he went up onto the podium to collect his yellow jersey. Everyone was on Andy's side.

I watched the footage again on the team bus after the stage, and in my opinion Contador did the wrong thing by not waiting. But what could I do? I couldn't very well criticise Contador for doing what he did when I was already in contract negotiations with him to get him on the team for next season.

Just before going to bed, my phone beeped. It was a text message from AC – Alberto Contador. "I'm sorry about what happened. I just attacked and went for it. Hope you understand."

It was a text message from our closest rival, yet at the same time this was someone who I was lining up to be my new star rider, so he wasn't sure where he stood.

"We all had a bit of bad luck today," I wrote back. "But you made a mistake today."

After that, we spoke on the phone. "What do you think I should do?" he asked me.

"It's probably best that you say sorry," I told him.

"You're right – I'll issue an apology," he said.

Around midnight, I got another text message. "I've apologised – take a look on my Twitter account."

I had a look at the video message he'd made.

"I'm glad to have made it onto the podium today, but I'm less happy about the way I got there," Contador told the camera. "I attacked Andy after he'd had a mechanical problem. The race was in full swing, and perhaps I made a mistake. I'm sorry. But during moments like that all you can think about is riding as fast as you can. I'm disappointed in myself because for me a spirit of fair play is so important."

I sent him a text message back, saying that everything would be okay, but that it might just take a bit of time.

Tuesday 20 July, stage 16: Bagnères de Luchon – Pau, 199.5km
A number of riders had seen Contador's apology. And now the talk
– including on our team – was that the Spaniard should be taught
a lesson. I appealed for calm, urging everyone to stop all thoughts
of a witch hunt and reminding them that earlier in the Tour we'd
been cut some slack when the Schleck brothers had crashed on
the slippery roads in the Ardennes and Fabian had made his contro-
versial decision. However, I was more worried about an article in
French sports paper *L'Equipe* in which it said that I had talked to
Contador about possibly working together. The article meant that
I would have to choose my words very carefully from now on.
When TV2 asked for my reaction to the story, I told them: "I've
seen and heard that there are a lot of rumours going around at the
moment."

"But is there anything in those rumours?" they asked.

"No, there's not at the moment," I replied. It was a reminder
that I needed to keep my cards very close to my chest.

On the stage, Andy stuck close to Contador, while Armstrong
tried to get something out of the race by going on the attack. He
got fourth on the stage, while Andy and Contador came home side
by side. This wasn't a good finish for attacking the yellow jersey,
but we still had one chance left, and that was Thursday's stage,
which finished on the Col du Tourmalet. Our directeur sportif,
Torsten Schmidt, came to find me after the stage. "I'm talking with
another team," he told me.

"I'd realised that, and okay – it's your choice," I said. "But promise
me one thing."

"What's that?" he asked.

"Just that there's no bullshit from you this last week," I said.
"That would be unacceptable."

"Okay – I promise," he said.

Wednesday 21 July, rest day, Pau
It was a great start to the second rest day: everything was in place
for us to sign Contador. Trey, Contador's brother Fran, his lawyer
and I had ironed everything out, and our sponsor situation was also
resolved, so now we could look forward. Contador sent me a text
message. "I'm really happy. I think we can do anything together,

and even think that winning the Giro, Tour and Vuelta in the same year's possible. And I'm not crazy," he said, ending his message with a smiley face.

But that afternoon, I had a meeting with Fabian and his manager. "We want to get out of the contract," the manager said, and tried to come up with a number of explanations for why.

"No chance," I said. I wasn't interested in talking with Fabian and his manager like this.

"Fabian, you know what's happening on the team with our sponsors, and you know about Contador," I said.

I was disappointed and immediately started to think about what the consequences could be for the team. In the space of just a few minutes, I'd really been brought down to earth.

Fabian was one of the few riders who I'd spoken to about the plans I had for the team. Already back in April, after Paris-Roubaix, I'd talked with him.

"I'm ready to build the team solely around you, if you want me to," I'd told him.

"Let's see," he'd replied.

Later, he was also the only rider I'd talked to about us potentially signing Contador, so I was even more disappointed.

Thursday 22 July, stage 17: Pau – Col du Tourmalet
I'd slept for two hours at the absolute most during the night. I'd tossed and turned thinking about Fabian's desire to leave the team.

Before the stage, the riders sat on the bus waiting for our team talk ahead of the Tourmalet stage. It was our last chance for Andy to take back the yellow jersey, and everyone was nervous. "So, no more poker today. Now we have to lay our cards on the table. It's all in," I said, looking around at the riders. Fabian and Andy sat in their tracksuits, concentrating hard.

"The plan is, as they say in Italian, *tappa maglia*. We're going after the stage win," I said.

"And the jersey," added Andy.

The stage win and the jersey – that was the goal. Everyone knew that it was on the Tourmalet, the last climb of the day, that Andy needed to beat Contador.

"We need all of you to work at the bottom of the climb. We

need to give Andy a good lead out on the lower slopes. You need to give it 'full gas'," I said.

Out on the road, the boys delivered the goods. When the race hit the bottom of the Tourmalet, they put their foot down. Soon it was going to being a straight duel, and then it would be up to Andy to try to finish things off.

With 10km left to go, Andy went on the attack in an attempt to get rid of Contador. The Spaniard was able to respond, but Andy kept the pace high to try to tire Contador out. Andy attacked again and again, but couldn't get free. Neither of them were showing any signs of weakness. Next, Andy tried a few psychological games – staring at him, challenging him and talking to him. "Don't you want to come past?" If the Spaniard had been having trouble, then this kind of pressure might have worked. But he just shrugged it off and instead attacked himself to show Andy that he should have kept his mouth shut.

So this was it. They both knew that they were as strong and equally matched as each other, and that neither of them could shake each other. It was a great race.

We'd played our cards and tried to do what we could. Now it was all about the stage victory, and Contador recognised that it was our team, and Andy, who had dominated the stage, and he let Andy go in the last few metres before the line. Andy won the stage but lost the battle for the yellow jersey. He was only eight seconds behind Contador overall, but it would mean that he would have to surpass himself in the final time trial if he was to beat Contador. Even though I was frustrated that our plan hadn't worked 100 per cent, I tried not to show it too much. When a journalist asked what we needed to do to stop Contador winning the race, I told him, with a smile: "We'll run him off the road."

Saturday 24 July, stage 19: Bordeaux – Paulliac, 52km time trial
In the morning, I went over the time trial route with Andy, with him doing some of it in the car and some on his bike. As we went, I tried to coach Andy – to guide him, support him and to make sure he stayed focused. Later on, he warmed up outside the bus on the trainer and looked concentrated and ready. He believed that he could beat Contador and take back the seconds he needed. "Don't

think. Shut yourself away inside yourself," I said to him, in short bursts. "Let nothing bother you. Push everything else to one side."

In the meantime, Fabian rode a perfect time trial, as only he knows how, and it looked likely to be good enough for the stage victory. He could always deliver when he had to. All the way to the start ramp, I spoke to Andy through his earpiece. "Stay in control of your breathing and breath deeply."

For the next 53km I was going to give everything I had left to support him in riding the time trial of his life.

"Come on, Andy!" I yelled and screamed from the car as we got the information through that he was actually beating Contador. He was just a couple of seconds off taking the yellow jersey, and I needed to let him know.

"Just two seconds off yellow!" I shouted. It would give him extra motivation. We were now talking about the tiniest of margins, where things could come down to fractions of a second: getting a gear shift wrong, taking a corner not quite right or just a moment of weakness. In my mind, I had a flashback to the 1989 Tour when Fignon lost everything in the time trial. I knew what could happen.

While Andy was riding the time trial of his life, the TV pictures showed Contador looking uncomfortable on his bike. If we could keep going as we were, it would be a sensation. I'd almost lost my voice as a result of screaming. But then the times started to go the wrong way. Contador appeared to have found his rhythm, and was getting better all the time, while Andy was running out of steam. By the last kilometre, I knew it was over. There was to be no miracle.

Andy hammered home in a great time, and slumped down, exhausted, onto the tarmac. Contador followed him in, 31 seconds faster. But nothing could change how proud I was of Andy. He had done himself proud, too, having taken risks and given it everything.

Contador knew that he'd done enough to win and was fighting to hold back the tears. But we'd been closer to beating him than many people thought. And despite missing out on the yellow jersey, we could celebrate Fabian's stage victory. While I was in the finish area in the team car, I received a phone call. It was Carlos. Sastre and I had only talked sporadically since he'd left the team after his

Tour win. He'd just finished 20th on the stage. "Bjarne, I've been thinking a lot about things lately," he said. "I've still got the energy and the desire to keep going, but I need a new team – one that really looks after you. And now that the brothers are leaving, could there be any chance of you taking me back?"

"I'm surprised that you've called," I told him. "But let me think about it."

Back at the hotel we celebrated yet another stage victory, but I was lost in thought about everything that was going on behind the scenes on the team. There was a new sponsor opportunity that had presented itself: Lars Seier from Saxo Bank had visited us on the race and wanted to talk about extending their sponsorship of the team after all. And when he was told about our contract with Contador, he was really keen to remain as a sponsor. "It sounds like it's too exciting for us to run off now," he said.

Sunday 25 July, stage 20: Longjumeau – Paris, 102km
The mood was relaxed and everyone was happy that we only had one stage left. But it was also a bit sad to call the riders together for our meeting on the bus, knowing that this would be the last time that we'd sit together like this as a team, and the last time that we'd go out of the door as one, as we'd been for these past three weeks. Even though we were all tired, we were all relieved. We'd managed to stick together despite all the negative attention on the team's internal problems. A lot of people on the team had got through the race despite keeping secrets and not knowing what they were doing next. Jakob Fuglsang was one of those who came up to me. Before the national championships I'd offered him a new contract for the following season, which he'd said he was going to think about. But now he'd reached a decision. "I've signed with another team," he told me. As long ago as November the previous year, we'd agreed on a three-year contract and had shaken hands. But he hadn't wanted to sign anything when it came down to it, which had puzzled me at the time.

"I knew all along," I told him.

The stage was like a parade all the way to Paris – a time when photographers get their opportunity to get pictures of smiling riders. Andy and Contador did their own little stunt, going on a pretend breakaway, which ended with them grinning and shaking each other's hand and thanking each other for a great race. Later, though, none of the sprinters' teams were going to miss the chance of taking a win on the Champs-Elysées. Mark Cavendish was like a missile, and no one could get close to him. It was another stage victory for Brian Holm, Rolf Aldag and the HTC team, who had had a great Tour. At the finish, Andy was cheered as the runner-up. There was champagne for everyone at the bus, and Frank turned up to join the party, too. Sandwiched between the two brothers, I rode up the Champs-Elysées as the photographers snapped away.

An hour after the finish, Trey came to me with a piece of paper. "Have you got a second, Bjarne?" We went inside the empty bus, with everyone else drinking champagne outside. "You just need to sign this," Trey said. It was Contador's contract. I signed it, and Trey left the bus again. At 7am the next morning, Contador was going to sign it at his hotel.

The new deal with Saxo Bank was confirmed, and we got confirmation from Sungard that they accepted that Saxo Bank were going to continue as the main sponsor instead of them.

That evening was the post-race party. The riders were all dressed up, as were their girlfriends and wives. Anne Dorthe was there with me, but I wasn't in the best mood. I knew that I should be happy, though: we had our sponsorship in place, Andy had finished second, the winner was going to ride on my team next season and we had dominated the race.

23 A NEW CHAPTER

At the beginning of August, I drove from Vejle to Copenhagen for a big press conference to announce the extension of our deal with Saxo Bank as our main sponsor and to announce the signing of Alberto Contador as the team's new star. On my way there, I thought through the past few months. Had I been too gullible? Too naïve? I realised that I'd made a series of mistakes, among them giving too much responsibility to some of my employees who I thought I could trust. I'd put trust in people who had then betrayed it. But trust was an important aspect of the way I wanted to run my company, and I didn't want my experiences of the last few months to cloud the fact that my company was built on trust and honesty.

There was a big media presence, and TV2 were broadcasting the press conference live. "Today we've signed a one-year contract with Saxo Bank," I announced, proudly. Lars Seier then explained why the bank had changed its mind and had decided to continue. We then waited to announce our new star signing to give the sponsorship story the time and attention it deserved, and to take questions from the press.

Contador was unable to attend the press conference, partly because he was racing and partly because it would have given the wrong message out to Astana, where he was still under contract until the end of 2010. "We have also signed a two-year contract with Alberto Contador," I went on. "The team's ambitions are obvious: we want to win the Tour de France. But Alberto and I have talked, and he told me that he wants to try to win all three grand tours in the same year. That's quite an ambition, but one that I'd happily be a part of."

A journalist asked whether I thought Contador would fit in with our team's philosophy.

"I think he'll fit in very well with our team," I answered. "But I'm convinced that we still haven't yet seen his full potential."

The next day, Trey and I went to meet Contador at his lawyer's house in Madrid. There were smiles all round the table, and Alberto said he looked forward to riding for us, and we said how much we were looking forward to having the world's best rider on our team. He wanted to bring three riders with him to our team, plus a mechanic and a soigneur, both of whom were extremely competent.

After a busy few days, I travelled home to Denmark and my family. Back at the house in Vejle, I enjoyed walking around the garden and looking out over the fjord. It was a good place to think. There on the lawn, I'd often think about my dad, and about how much I missed him. When he died, I promised myself that I would try to change my priorities in life, and try to be a more cheerful person. BS used to always say, "You need to be something for yourself before you can be anything for others," and I'd tried to take that on board. I'd made more time for myself, and that had really helped. I felt like I'd got better at prioritising my children and my family, as before I'd sometimes felt like I wasn't there enough for my kids – that I was travelling too much, and was always too busy with cycling and the business. So these days I tried to be a lot more open with my boys, and to have experiences that would bring us closer together. Around the dinner table we took more time to talk and mess around and have fun, and I tried to teach them that it was okay to talk about our feelings.

My relationship with Mette was good. We respected each other and the way each of us had chosen to live our lives. We had been through a lot together, but she had to take a lot of the credit for what I'd achieved as a rider. She had also managed to accept Anne Dorthe and allowed her to be a part of the boys' confirmation, and that had meant a lot to me.

At the start of September, I travelled to the Tour of Spain to talk through Fabian Cancellara's future with him. We had a good chat, and we agreed that we'd be able to negotiate a solution that was satisfactory to both of us. On the race's first rest day, I went out after dinner for a drink with a friend of mine. At around one o'clock in the morning, I saw Andy Schleck and Stuart O'Grady – who were both riding the race – come into the bar. Andy saw me when I got up to go to the toilet, but when I got back, they'd both gone. I went back to the hotel and went to bed.

During the night, others had heard noise in the corridor and had seen Stuart and Andy out there. The next morning, at about 9.30am, the other riders came down for breakfast, but there was no sign of Andy or Stuart. Our directeur sportif, Bradley McGee, and I went upstairs and banged on their hotel room door where they were lying in bed snoring. The night's excesses had taken their toll. "What the hell were you doing?" I asked them.

"Oh, it was only a couple of beers," they said.

"Rubbish," I told them. "Enough of your crap."

Their attitude and behaviour was completely unacceptable, and they were in no state to take part in any useful way in that day's stage. I had no choice but to send them home immediately.

In the next few days I heard from a number of people who thought that sending them home was the right thing to do, and that it sent an important message to the rest of the sport that such unprofessional conduct was really not acceptable.

During the race, Fabian and I managed to come to an agreement about how he could be released from his contract but, despite that, he decided to quit the race anyway, showing a complete lack of respect for his sponsors and team-mates. It was a real shame that, after four years working together, it ended like that. I would have expected more from a star of his calibre, and I was deeply disappointed.

But it was time to start a new chapter of my cycling team's story, this time with Alberto Contador as its main character. Everything had fallen into place, and I had new riders, directeurs sportifs and staff members on board. The organisation had been trimmed and optimised for the future. The last few details for the design of the new jerseys were being finalised, and I felt like we were ready for the new season.

On Wednesday 29 September, the phone rang at around midnight, just as I was on my way to bed. It was Alberto Contador, and he almost immediately gave his phone to his lawyer, who spoke better English than Alberto, and who explained what the late-night phone call was about. It was bad news. "Alberto tested positive at the Tour de France," he told me. The thoughts went round and round in my head. I was almost in shock.

The lawyer explained that Alberto had tested positive for clenbuterol, which had been found in very small quantities. "But Alberto is innocent," he added. The clenbuterol was thought to have come from some Spanish steak, which Alberto had eaten on one of the rest days.

That night, I didn't sleep well. Everything had been built around Contador, and it was supposed to be a new start. But if he was now going to be banned, then everything was going to be up in the air. For now, he was innocent, but all sorts of scenarios were played out in my mind. It was a catastrophe, and I wondered what the sponsors were going to say.

On Friday, I went to Madrid to see Contador myself and hear his explanation. I was especially keen to hear why he hadn't told me anything about the positive test when he'd known about it since 24 August. "The UCI asked me not to tell anyone," he said. "I hadn't even told my own family."

I believed him and his explanation, and that he was innocent. The worst thing that could happen next was that his case would become political.

The days that followed were difficult, as both Saxo Bank and our bike supplier, Specialized, had clauses in their contracts whereby they could pull out if Contador didn't ride for the team. We were extremely worried. I talked with both Saxo Bank and Specialized about the future, and what could happen if it didn't include Contador. The team's future, and the futures of 65 employees, hung in the balance. I visited Lars Seier, who also lived in Switzerland, to talk through the situation. It was important to know where we both stood. Saxo Bank decided that they were going to support the team and continue their sponsorship no matter what the outcome of Contador's case, and Specialized came to the same decision shortly afterwards.

EPILOGUE

Arriving at the hotel, we were met by at least 20 TV vans, their aerials extended, ready to transmit our press conference to the world. The hotel was swarming with journalists and photographers, while technicians were busy laying out cables.

"This is going to be crazy," someone said in the car I was sharing with team director Trey Greenwood, press officer Anders Damgaard, Alberto Contador's assistant, Jacinto Vidarte, and Alberto's brother and manager, Fran, who drove us safely down into the hotel's underground car park.

The press descended upon us as we stepped out of the lift into the hotel reception. "No comment," I told them, making it clear that this wasn't the right time to be asking questions.

We made our way to the office where we had arranged to meet Alberto and his lawyers, followed all the way by the photographers, and it was a real relief to close the door behind us. The office was not much bigger than a shoebox – perhaps 10 square metres, furnished with a small round table and a single chair. But it would do for us.

While we waited for Alberto to arrive, we needed to come up with a plan. It was Thursday afternoon on 7 February 2012, and we were at the Hotel Las Artes in Pinto – a suburb of Madrid. Before the press conference, we needed to discuss the ban that had been given to my star rider little more than 24 hours previously. Alberto had been handed a two-year ban for having tested positive for clenbuterol, and now the press and the fans were waiting for

Alberto's reaction, and to hear whether I was going to fire him
from the team.

Plenty of experts had already come out with their opinion and
analysis of what they thought I should do. Some said that I should
show Alberto the door as it wouldn't be right to have a rider
convicted of doping on the team, while others thought there was
no problem with him remaining on our squad.

It had been pretty hectic since we'd been given the verdict on
the Monday afternoon. We'd gone through what it all meant, and
had spoken extensively to our sponsors. We'd actually been quite
surprised by the verdict, in that it hadn't really fitted into any of
the scenarios we'd imagined. It was based on likelihood – a verdict
handed out on the basis of probability. All along, Alberto maintained
that the only way he could have tested positive was as a result of
having unwittingly ingested clenbuterol from eating a contaminated
steak during the 2010 Tour de France. It was an explanation that
CAS – the Court of Arbitration for Sport – had conceded was
indeed possible, albeit not that likely. They did believe, however,
that the clenbuterol could have come from contaminated dietary
supplements.

That meant that – according to the verdict – Alberto was
acquitted of having intentionally doped, but was punished for the
presence of a doping product in his body. And the reason we'd
supported Alberto all along was that – as the CAS verdict confirmed
– we, too, believed that he hadn't intentionally doped. We maintained the view that, unless anything could be proved otherwise,
Alberto had our full support in maintaining his innocence, and
the court's decision meant that we could happily continue
working with Alberto without having to compromise on our
principles or ethics, which was a view also happily shared by our
sponsors.

Alberto himself was both upset and frustrated by the verdict.

"Although I have to accept it, I don't understand it," he told me
on the phone immediately after his lawyer had received the court
papers.

Having had 24 hours to sleep on it, I was keen to see how he
would handle the questions that were soon to come his way. I knew
myself how difficult it was to stand up in front of everyone with

that feeling of having been unfairly treated whilst also being emotionally drained.

We had decided that he would write a statement that he would read out at the press conference. And, before the press conference got under way, we would go through it with him and try to prepare him for the kinds of questions that the press were likely to ask.

"I'm just going to go and check how things are looking out there," said Anders and, as he opened the door to our little office, we could hear the noise of the journalists and photographers, all falling over each other to get in the best possible position for when Alberto arrived at the hotel.

In the meantime, I took out my own notes and went through what I was going to say.

It had only been a couple of months before that I'd been on my first tour of Denmark doing motivational speaking, talking about my life and my experiences as a businessman.

I was naturally very shy, and wasn't exactly born to stand on a stage in front of a room of somewhere between 400 and 1,000 people and talk to them, but it was something I'd decided I was going to learn to do, so had said yes to doing the tour. The experience and techniques I'd learned from public speaking were things I'd used to help my development and build self-confidence.

"Here comes that tunnel vision of yours, then," Anders smiled when he came back.

He meant that I had tunnel vision because my nerves were completely unaffected by all the chaos outside our little room as I sat with my notes and a highlighter pen practising what I was going to say.

Tunnel vision or just plain old concentration – call it what you will. I needed to go in there to deliver a speech that would be absolutely crucial for my team's future.

"I've just spoken to some of the Spanish photographers," said Anders. He explained that there were between 40 and 50 TV cameras, kilos of cables and a load of journalists all crammed into the meeting room next door.

"The photographers told me that there are more people here than there were at the press conference ahead of 'El Classico'," he said.

That really showed how big a deal this was: that we were on a par with arguably the biggest football derby in Europe.

Anders also said that he'd made a deal with the photographers. "None of them will be crawling around behind us trying to take pictures," he explained. "They're going to give us some space and won't be trying to photograph our papers or the backs of our heads, or making us feel uncomfortable."

Suddenly, there was a lot of noise from outside – of all the photographers and journalists all shouting at once. It was 6pm, with an hour and a half to go before the start of the press conference.

The door opened and, in a blaze of camera flashes and TV camera lighting, Alberto hurried inside.

"Hello Bjarne," he said to me, and we gave each other a hug. While he said hello to the others, I tried to think what I could do to help support him.

"How are you feeling?" I asked him.

"I'm okay," he told me.

Alberto was still upset, but at the same time he seemed quite relieved that a decision had been made when it came to planning ahead with his career. Since the end of August 2010, he'd been riding around not knowing whether he even still had a future in cycling.

We talked more about the situation, and took a look at the statement he'd prepared for the press conference. What he wanted to say was naturally tinged with his own pride and passion, so together with Trey, Anders and Alberto's brother, Fran, we fine-tuned and polished what he'd written a little. Making a rash comment at a press conference like this could have terrible consequences.

At one point, Anders decided that he needed the bathroom, and the doorway was again lit up with camera flashes and lights when he left the room – quickly followed by the groans of the Spanish media that it was just a Danish press officer on the way to the toilet rather than their superstar rider.

But once Anders had returned, it was time to go through to the meeting room, and we had to make sure we stuck very close to Alberto so that the photographers weren't able to surround him and separate him from the rest of us. And it nearly worked. I was right behind Alberto, but left too big a gap at one point, and so he was quickly swamped by photographers, all swinging their cameras, and I had to push them out of the way to stop myself being hit by their equipment. But I got hit anyway; they really couldn't have cared less.

Once we made it to the stage, the camera flashes went crazy. A couple of photographers seemed to forget the deal we'd made about not getting behind us on the stage, and were shooed away, while we tried to adjust to the bright lights shining on us.

A number of Alberto's fans had also turned up, and they stood at the back of the room clapping their hero. I looked around, readying myself for what was about to happen. There must have been between 200 and 250 people crammed into what wasn't really that big a room. Anders welcomed everybody, and then I started things off with the statement I'd prepared.

"I think we'd all agree that this case has gone on for far too long. We'd hoped for a different outcome," I said, working towards the conclusion that everyone was waiting to hear, "but we have to respect the verdict. We've supported Alberto 100 per cent up until now, and today I'd like to say that we as a team, supported by all our sponsors, will continue to fully support him, based on the ruling from CAS. The ruling states that it is very unlikely that this has anything to do with conscious cheating, so our trust in Alberto is still 100 per cent intact."

Then it was Alberto's turn – an emotional moment for him.

"To be honest, I feel very much under pressure right now," he said. "It's been very difficult, and there's not been a single morning when I haven't thought about how I've ended up in this situation. It's been a painful process, but it's been even more painful for my family who have suffered so much because of this."

He looked out across the forest of microphones that had been set up on the table in front of us.

"I've tried to understand the verdict, but I can't," he continued. "I've tried everything to prove my innocence. I know myself that I haven't doped. All my victories are not mine, but instead belong to the people, and they are the ones who need to decide what this verdict means."

I felt extremely concentrated and focused. My experience from other press conferences, when we had had our backs against the wall, served me well: press conferences like Ivan Basso's when he got thrown off the Tour before it had even started, and my own in 2007 when I admitted to having doped. On those occasions, there had been plenty of questions from the press, and this time we were fully prepared for that. Alberto dealt with the questions very well and, with the press conference winding up, Anders had planned what would happen next. It was all about getting Alberto away from the hotel as quickly as possible to take the intensity out of the situation.

We thanked everyone for coming and then, with the help of his assistant, Jacinto, we escorted Alberto down to his car in the underground car park and away from the hotel. Almost immediately, a calmness descended on the hotel.

I stayed behind to answer questions from journalists from the various TV stations and the newspapers, which were mostly about what I was going to do next. I had a plan, of course, as to what we'd do until Alberto was able to come back and hopefully ride the Tour of Spain. But what really occupied my thoughts was whether Alberto's ban was going to become a collective punishment for the team.

If cycling's governing body, the UCI, decided to ask for a re-evaluation of our ProTeam licence based on Alberto's case, it could have serious repercussions for us, with the possibility that we could lose the licence. In the worst-case scenario, I might have to close the team, although I didn't think, nor hope, that it would come to that.

Later that evening, we met up with Alberto and his brother at a little local restaurant that had opened up especially for us. We talked in English, and a little in French, as Alberto's brother spoke it very well, and acted as translator. We went through both the legal and more technical consequences of the verdict, which among other things meant that Alberto's contract with us was officially terminated. All images of him in our team kit needed to be taken off our website, and he could no longer wear our kit in training or any public appearances. However, we very much intended to continue working together once his ban had come to an end.

We were all very tired after the press conference, but were at the same time relieved that it had actually gone pretty well. Alberto asked how the other riders on the team were, and we told him that everything was okay, which made him even more keen to come back again.

"I'm going to go out training tomorrow," he said, with that same look in his eyes that we'd learned to recognise in the time he'd ridden for us. It was a look that said he wanted to show everyone what he was really made of.

While Alberto continued talking to Anders and Trey, I leaned back in my chair and thought back to the months I'd had the world's best rider riding for my team. I remembered Alberto meeting the team for the first time at our training camp in December 2010. We knew we had a real star in our midst; there was a special aura surrounding Alberto.

I quickly realised then that the most important thing to do was to establish a trusting relationship between the two of us – to show him that we were on his side during what was a difficult time. His experiences with some of the teams he'd ridden for in the past had scarred him, but our team-building trip was a new beginning for everyone on the team. A number of our big-name riders had left to join the new Leopard-Trek team, and quite a few of the team staff had gone there, too.

We needed to rebuild the team's culture, and people needed to rediscover where they stood in the hierarchy. At the same time, the riders who were new to the team needed to find their place and get used to our way of doing things.

One of the activities on the trip was a day of windsurfing and kite-surfing. We had some professional surfers – who looked like they'd stepped straight off the set a surf film – helping to show us what to do. There were big smiles all round, and it wasn't long before the nervousness gave way to complete enjoyment of the challenge at hand. Professional sports people always approach other sports with the same level of seriousness and will to win as they do their "own" sports, and Alberto certainly didn't hold back in the waves. I watched how all the new members of the team reacted to the challenge, and how the more established members of the team in turn reacted towards them. The outcome was important, as the way people react when they're taken out of their comfort zone with new activities like this is often the same way that they react "when the shit hits the fan" during races. Who was still able to help the others, and who was still able to make quick decisions?

One of the riders who had unfortunately left the team was Jens Voigt. He was a good example of someone who had always been a real leader on these survival camps that we'd often done as a team. When the others got tired, Jens would often take their rucksacks, and was sometimes powering along with three or four rucksacks at once, still motivating and encouraging his team-mates as he went.

That's exactly how Jens was at races, too. He was constantly on the radio to us, keeping us updated on what was happening in the race – who had got in a breakaway, and whether he thought it was an important one, always aware of what was best for the team. And one of the goals on this training camp was to get individuals to work together as a team to reach a common goal.

Since the Schleck brothers, Fabian Cancellara and the others had left the team, I'd gone through a period of introspection. I'd asked myself whether there was anything I could have done differently, and whether them leaving the team was in actual fact my fault. But I'd come to the conclusion that it's often a case of the grass being greener on the other side, and that it wasn't the first time that people had left a company to create their own new one. Perhaps my way of running things had been used by them as an excuse to try something different, but I decided that I was going to stick with my values and philosophies when it came to running my team.

As the owner of the team, I was known for being very involved with my riders' careers, and forming strong bonds with them. It meant that it made things that much more difficult if and when they came to leave the team, and so I thought long and hard about whether I should continue to invest so much of myself in the riders.

Eventually I decided that it was worth it, else I wasn't really being true to my own character. I just had to do what I thought was best for myself, the team and the riders – even if that meant risking disappointment if things didn't go they way I wanted them to.

With Alberto, I initially spent time getting to know him as a person. Little by little, I began to discover the best way to support him and help him to continue to develop as a rider. Even the best rider in the world could improve.

He already had a lot of the attributes I always tried to instil in my riders: as top sportsmen they needed to be able to make the best decisions irrespective of how they felt, and to take responsibility for their own actions. Sports people in that mould know that there are consequences if they don't take responsibility and are not capable of making the decisions that are best for their team. My relationship was different to the ones I'd had with, for example, the Schleck brothers, Basso or Carlos Sastre. Alberto had won a lot more races, and was a dedicated, top professional. I didn't need to grab him by the collar in order to make him train in a particular way. Instead, my work required patience and persistence because confidence is built up over time with gentle, well-timed coaching. The very essence of coaching is being able to change people without any detrimental effects.

Even before I'd signed Alberto to the team, I'd already noted where there was room for improvement in him. As a rival to my team's riders, I'd naturally studied his strengths and weaknesses. That knowledge stood me in good stead once we did sign a contract with him, and it became a case of then trying to push the right buttons to get him to see things my way. One of my goals, for example, was to tweak Alberto's time-trial position on the bike, which I had analysed and identified ways it could be improved. And so it proved when, having worked on it with him, we were able to shave 30 seconds off his time over a 30km time trial.

Unfortunately, Alberto's doping case from when he was with the Astana team loomed large over everything we did, and that brought with it a kind of uncertainty. A long ban would have serious consequences for Alberto's career, our team and my business.

No sooner had we signed Alberto's formal contract, tying him to our team from 1 January 2011, than the media was quoting UCI president Pat McQuaid saying that it was unlikely that Alberto would be riding that year's Tour de France. We knew that there was a risk that that could be the case, but it still surprised us that the head of the International Cycling Union was so busy speculating on the outcome of the case that the Spanish cycling federation hadn't even made a decision on yet.

But not long afterwards, while we were on a training camp in Mallorca, news came through about Alberto's case. The Spanish media wrote that the Spanish cycling federation had suggested a one-year suspension – although that really was just a suggestion rather than a ruling. The chaos that followed – not least various misunderstandings – meant that we were obliged to call a press conference at our hotel to clear things up, even though a definitive decision still hadn't been made.

A few weeks later, the actual verdict came in. The Spanish federation acquitted Alberto, which meant he wouldn't be suspended. As a team, it was back to plan A.

But that wasn't the end of it by a long shot. In March 2011, the UCI announced that they were appealing the decision and taking the case to the international sports arbitration body, CAS. The court told us that it hoped to reach a verdict ahead of the Tour de France, but that until then Alberto was free to race. Really, we needed to know as soon as possible whether we'd be able to race at the Tour with Alberto, both from a sporting point of view and in terms of our sponsors, who in turn needed to know what kind of exposure they were likely to get during the three weeks in France in July.

Despite Alberto's professionalism, and his continued willingness to train, he risked it all being for nothing if he was going to be prevented from riding the Tour. I tried to support him as best I could, and tried to show him that I was there for him no matter what.

But while he continued to train under a cloud of uncertainty, I turned some of my attention to the spring Classics, where I had another ace up my sleeve. Belgian Nick Nuyens was another new signing, coming to us from the Dutch Rabobank squad. Having in the past won Het Volk, Kuurne-Brussels-Kuurne and Paris-Brussels, he was our man for the Classics. A number of people had written him off as being past his best, but I could still see a lot of potential in him. At the prestigious cobbled "semi-Classic" on 23 March, Dwars door Vlaanderen, Nick won the race and proved the so-called experts wrong.

A week later, on 3 April, it was the Tour of Flanders. It was arguably the most important one-day Classic, and a race that Fabian

Cancellera had won for us in imperious fashion the year before. And he was the big favourite again.

But in my eyes, Nick was a serious outside contender, if he could do everything just right. Changing teams was like a breath of fresh air for him. He had a new training plan and we had helped him to make some adjustments to his riding position. Before the start of the season, I'd looked at his riding style, and we'd decided to try him with some shorter crank arms, which gave him a lighter pedal stroke.

The Tour of Flanders played out almost exactly as had been expected. It was a real demonstration of power from Fabian, while Nick played the waiting game. If he could ride smartly, and patiently, and if he could hang on until the closing stages of the race, then anything could happen.

With 40km to go, Fabian burst off the front with one of his trademark attacks. But on one of the following cobbled sections he seemed to lose some of his power, and the chasing group was able to get back up to him. Heading towards the finish, the pace was high, but Fabian again had the strength to attack with 5km to go, except that this time Sylvain Chavanel and Nick were able to go with him.

Nick had ridden a clever race, and was full of confidence having saved his energy as best he could. And in the final sprint to the line, he proved to be the strongest and beat Chavanel and Fabian. In the team car behind, we exploded in celebration. Winning the Tour of Flanders was not only a win in itself, but it was also a win for the team, for the team's philosophy and values and for our new beginning after everything that had happened in 2010.

There was a TV camera installed in our car, and the pictures of our celebrations would prove to those watching that there was little doubt just how much the victory meant to us and our sponsors.

Winning Flanders proved that we could still mix it with the sport's absolute best, despite having lost the riders who had moved on. It proved that our team structure, our values and our philosophy really worked, even after the huge turnover of riders and staff.

But we were no nearer to a resolution in Alberto's case, and no one knew when CAS might call the hearing and therefore give a verdict. It meant that in May Alberto was able to take part in the Tour of Italy.

Unfortunately, the Giro was hit by tragedy on stage three. On the descent of the Passo del Bocco, Leopard-Trek's Belgian rider Wouter Weylandt crashed heavily. Just a few minutes after the accident, we drove past where he was lying on the asphalt. "That doesn't look good," I remember saying. Doctors were fighting to save Wouter's life while he lay lifeless in a pool of blood. He was airlifted to hospital, but when we arrived at the stage finish we were given the sad news that he had died as a result of his injuries. He left behind his pregnant wife. It couldn't have been any more tragic. At that moment, everything else didn't seem to matter.

We informed our riders about what had happened, and many of them took it very badly – especially Matteo Tosatto, who had been team-mates with Weylandt at the Quick Step team. The Leopard-Trek squad were staying at a hotel not far from where our team bus was parked, and we could see the media descending on the hotel. I could only imagine what my former press officer, Brian Nygaard, who had become the manager of Leopard-Trek, was feeling. He now had the unenviable task of informing the rider's family that Wouter was dead.

"Do you want to take a walk?" I asked Anders, my new press officer. We walked and talked about the terrible tragedy, and found somewhere to have a glass of wine.

My relationship with Brian Nygaard hadn't been the same since he'd left our team, but I wanted to show my support during what was a terrible time. I wrote him a text message, saying, "I want you to know that we're thinking of you at this time when you need to try to be strong."

Shortly afterwards, my phone beeped with his reply: "Thank you, Bjarne."

The next day's stage was neutralised out of respect for Wouter, as anything else would have just been meaningless.

Prior to the race, we'd already decided that we didn't want Alberto to try to take the pink leader's jersey too early on, as it would take up too much energy trying to defend it. The race's ninth stage, on Sunday 15 May, was a mountainous 169km to the finish at Mount Etna – the famous volcano on the island of Sicily.

It was a stage we'd already identified as being crucial to the race's final classification.

Our tactic was to let the other teams do all the work until we got to Mount Etna, and that just before the start of the final climb Alberto would change bikes. I ran over to him with the new bike, which had special tyres with a particularly high tyre pressure, which would give Alberto the feeling that he was riding a lighter bike. It was to give him a psychological boost just before the climb started.

Alberto and I were very similar in that we were always looking for the latest piece of equipment to give us an advantage. Sure enough, he flew up the climb with the lead group of favourites, which included Vincenzo Nibali and Michele Scarponi. Then, Alberto put in one of his explosive accelerations, and went up the road alone. He soon caught Jose Rujano, who had attacked earlier, and together the two of them built up a solid advantage over the others, although I wanted Alberto to rid himself of Rujano before the finish.

During the stage, Alberto and I worked perfectly together. It felt almost as though I was sitting on the bike myself. Rujano had been able to follow Alberto's wheel because there had been a headwind on part of the climb. But with a kilometre and a half to go, I asked Alberto to take his foot off the accelerator in order to save energy and prepare himself for the crucial blow around the next hairpin bend when the wind would be behind them. "As soon as you come out of the corner, attack," I told him over the radio. It's much easier for another rider to sit on your wheel when you're going into a headwind than it is to follow when you've got a tailwind.

Alberto did as he was asked, attacking like only he can, dropping Rujano. He rode across the finish line alone as the winner of the stage, and took over the leader's jersey with a hefty advantage over his competitors. From that point on, he dominated the Giro, taking another stage win along the way before standing atop the podium at the end of the race having beaten Scarponi by nearly six minutes.

A few days before we celebrated Alberto's win at the Giro, CAS informed us that Alberto's case wouldn't be heard in the first week of June, as planned, and would instead take place after the Tour de France. It meant that Alberto could now prepare properly for the Tour. A week before it started, I got a call from him. "I feel ready," he told me. "And if I win the Tour, I want to ride the Vuelta, too."

"Of course," I said. All along it had remained unsaid between us that if he won the Giro, and was able to go to the Tour, then he'd try to win all three grand tours.

At the end of June, we arrived at the Tour de France to be met by a media ready for confrontation.

Before that, though, there was a close encounter with Leopard-Trek. There was a real rivalry between Andy Schleck, Brian Nygaard and Kim Andersen, one of my former directeurs sportifs, on one side, and Alberto and me on the other. But the enmity between us was nothing like as bad as some in the press had made it out to be. Our relationship was professional, and at the end of the day they were our rivals like everyone else.

It turned out that we were staying at the same hotel as them for the first few days of the race. One evening, Brian Nygaard turned up in the dining room and went round shaking hands with all my riders and team staff, as did Jens Voigt, smiling at everyone and hugging his former team-mates. We respected each other, and that's how we conducted ourselves at the hotel. The moment we stepped outside the hotel, however, it was like walking into another dimension. Suddenly the people around us were trying to make trouble and really stir up the rivalry between us.

On Thursday 30 June, two days before the start of the Tour, we held our pre-race press conference, where we knew we were going to get bombarded with questions from the press about the doping case. Anders was clear about what we should do: face it head on and talk about it now in an effort to stop it becoming a theme that would be revisited each day after every stage of the race. And sure enough, the journalists didn't hold back during the press conference, firing critical and aggressive questions at us.

In my opening statement, I had tried my best to call for fairness when dealing with Alberto, as the decision that he could take part in the race was down to the UCI and Tour organisers ASO.

"I beg you all to understand, but if you don't agree with the decision then you need to question the system, and not us. We are just going by the rules," I said.

One of the journalists asking a question was former pro rider Paul Kimmage, who had written a number of articles and books on doping in the sport. His question was more of a comment, as it seemed to me that he was determined to attack me.

Kimmage couldn't understand how I could talk about fairness "without blinking". He then went after Alberto, accusing him of never having spoken out against doping, to which Alberto calmly replied that that was nonsense.

For us, it was a case of not letting our feelings bubble over and turning the press conference into something bigger than it was. Even though we sat there and took the confrontational questions, it didn't mean that we should have to take it when they became aggressive and intimidating.

The tense and negative treatment Alberto had received was even more apparent later in the day when we attended the teams presentation at the Puy du Fou theme park. The arena it took place in was full with people cheering and applauding as the teams were presented, with Thor Hushovd, for example, appearing holding a "god of thunder's" hammer.

But when it was our turn, the mood in the arena changed. Most people clapped, but some whistled and others booed as the riders appeared. When Alberto was presented over the loudspeakers, he was greeted with a number of boos from the crowd. Things got worse after the presentation when he was trying to find his way back to the team bus. In all the chaos, he was left on his bike circling the arena among the hostile crowds looking for the bus, while we ran around looking for him. When he finally made it back to the safety of the bus, he was truly pumped up.

"If I wasn't feeling entirely motivated before, I certainly am now!" he said.

On the first stage of the race, which started in the Vendée, the crowd's behaviour continued out on the roads. I was in the team car, and in the last few kilometres of the stage there was a loud slap on the windscreen. It was the sound of a raw steak that someone had thrown at us. Even though I'd registered what had happened, I was busy concentrating as Alberto had been involved in a crash, and I was more worried about him getting to the finish than I was about reacting to immature grown men. The spectator had thrown the steak to demonstrate his disgust at Alberto taking part in the race. A number of journalists had heard about what had happened, but we tried to play down its importance.

That evening, Anders asked how I felt about what had happened.

"I did at least manage to see that it wasn't a very good cut of beef," I told him. We couldn't let such disappointing actions from the spectators bother us.

"You'll just have to drive with the window wound up," someone suggested, and after that we talked no more about it. In fact, once we left the Vendée, it was as though everyone's mood suddenly changed.

But it never became the Tour de France that we'd dreamed of. Alberto was unlucky, and was involved in a number of crashes in the first few days. Four crashes in the first nine days of the race took their toll, as well as losing him time to his rivals. In one of the crashes he injured his knee, and the pain was such that he considered pulling out of the race. The Giro had taken more out of him than we had at first thought. We knew all along that it was going to be extremely challenging to attempt victory at both the Giro and the Tour, but we'd agreed that it was worth a go.

It was as though Alberto never really got going at the Tour, and had begun to doubt whether his form was good enough. The doping case also affected him more than he was prepared to let on, and it would be tough to see him or anyone else perform at their best with the kind of pressure he had on his shoulders.

But Alberto wasn't prepared to leave the race without a fight. Stage 16 was a day when it was expected that the favourites would save their energy for the stages still to come. Alberto, though, attacked on the last climb of the day, dropping the Schleck brothers, and only Cadel Evans and Samuel Sanchez could follow him. The brothers lost even more time on the wet and technical descent before the finish. Alberto is an extremely good descender, and really pushed the pace. By the finish he'd taken a minute back on Andy Schleck in the general classification, and gave us new hope that he might be able to be in the mix for a podium finish after all.

But on the road to the Galibier was where I believe Alberto

lost the Tour. He didn't eat enough, which meant that later on in the stage he had problems and lost time to his rivals. That evening after the stage, I went to see him in his room. I'd decided that I was going to tell him that we could attack on the Alpe d'Huez stage the next day instead, but as I came into the room Alberto beat me to it: "I'm going to attack tomorrow."

We both agreed that we had nothing to lose so we planned for, and put everything into, a big attack from Alberto the next day.

As early as the first climb, he went on the offensive, with only very few riders being able to follow him, including Andy Schleck. They were caught at the bottom of Alpe d'Huez, but Alberto then attacked again. Later, he was caught again, too, but he'd finished the race with a real flourish. Even though the race didn't go the way he or we wanted, Alberto always maintained his position as team leader. Whenever he got back to the bus after a stage that hadn't gone well for him, he would be angry with himself and at what had happened. But whenever he met the press or public, he was always super-professional and calm and collected. He never lost his temper, even when the media or fans surrounded him and everyone wanted a piece of him. He also always had time for his team-mates, trying to ensure that they were happy. But whereas Andy Schleck had been very open and easy-going in his role as my team's leader, Alberto was a lot more serious and composed, even when things had gone badly.

A huge star like Alberto is used to being the centre of attention, but it also means that he is wary of people and their intentions before he can trust them. I like to think that I have made it through that filter – and not everyone does, which is only natural. There has to be a degree of distance with some people and, having been in a similar position to his before, I know that you can't possibly be best pals with everyone.

Alberto finished the 2011 Tour de France in fifth place overall, almost four minutes behind winner Cadel Evans. But the farce that was Alberto's doping case continued in the same vein two days after the Tour, when CAS once again announced that the hearing was to be delayed. Our patience was beginning to run out, and we were fed up with not being able to do anything about it. We felt that the way we were being treated was unreasonable, with the hearing being put back indefinitely. It had gone on for almost a year, which was no way to treat anybody, letting them dangle in uncertainty for so long.

Alberto didn't ride the world championship road race, which took place in Denmark at the end of September, as the course was too flat for him, and more suited to the big sprinters. The race was the perfect opportunity to showcase the best of what Denmark has to offer to the world's cycling fans watching at home. Pictures of the peloton leaving central Copenhagen bathed in sunshine for a 260km route lined with a quarter of a million people made us Danes proud. Favourites for the race included defending champion Thor Hushovd, Philippe Gilbert and Mark Cavendish.

Cavendish, in particular, was unlikely to get a better opportunity any time soon to win the Worlds than on the roads of Denmark. It was a flat route with a 14km finishing circuit and the finish on the climb of Geels Bakke. Cavendish had won 20 stages of the Tour de France in four years, as well as winning the green points jersey at the 2011 Tour, which gave him a lot of confidence going into the Worlds in Denmark.

"I'm in the best form I've ever been in, plus I've got the strongest team there's ever been," he told the British media ahead of the race.

Also on the British squad were Bradley Wiggins, who'd won silver in the time trial a few days before, and the experienced David Millar.

Cavendish is cool because he's very much his own man, and isn't scared to tell his team-mates, "I'm going to win today", which makes them want to work even harder for him. He possesses an extraordinary winner's instinct – an instinct that my friend, Brian Holm, who was Cavendish's directeur sportif on the HTC team, says he's only seen before in our former Telekom team-mate Erik Zabel.

Brian told me a story about when Cavendish was only 19 or 20 and was on his first training camp with the team. The team had hired Bayern Munich football club's psychologist, and each rider was due to have a half-hour session with him. It had cost a small fortune to hire the psychologist, but when it was Cavendish's turn, there was no sign of him. Brian went to the British rider's room for an explanation, and Cavendish simply told him that he didn't need a psychologist, adding: "Don't worry – I'll win races anyway."

Brian says that he told him: "Either you'll become the world's best rider or you're going to have a very short career."

Cavendish's strong points have become his acceleration, his ability to maintain a high top speed on flat roads and his aerodynamic position when sprinting, and he was able to put these skills to good use at the Worlds.

The men's road race climaxed with a bunch sprint, where Cavendish's strong GB team delivered him perfectly to the final rush to the line, and he gave it absolutely everything on the uphill finish to narrowly beat Australian Matt Goss by half a wheel length. German rider Andre Greipel was third, while Fabian was fourth. It was the first British gold medal since 1965 when Tom Simpson won the Worlds. Our Saxo Bank rider, Michael Mørkøv, was the best-placed Dane, in 18th place.

With the world champion's rainbow jersey comes great responsibility, but no doubt that will help Cavendish mature as a rider. On the occasions I've spoken to him, he's always been grateful for the way Saxo Bank treated his friend, Jonathan Bellis, who in 2009 had an accident on his scooter in Italy and was left in a coma for five weeks. Bellis had been one of our big talents, having won a bronze medal at the under-23 world championships in 2007. When he was transferred to London after what had been a very long stay in hospital in Italy, Trey and I visited him – not to talk about cycling, but to see how he was and to show our support for him. Bellis told us that he wanted to try to make a comeback to the sport, despite his terrible injuries as a result of the accident. Even though Bellis's contract ran out at the end of 2010, we extended it by another year, despite the fact that it was uncertain whether he'd be able to make a comeback at all. It was that helping hand that had pleased Cavendish. Both he and Bellis had at one time been on British Cycling's Academy programme together, directed by former pro Max Sciandri.

Cavendish now rides for Team Sky, together with Wiggins, Chris Froome and Edvald Boasson Hagen, and it seems to be a very strong team. It's going to be exciting to see how they deal with having so many stars and leaders on the squad, though – especially at the Tour de France.

But Team Sky's Tour plans were the least of my worries on that February evening in Pinto, sitting with Alberto and the others going over what had happened during the press conference a few hours before.

I was thinking more about how we were now going to rearrange our race programme until Alberto's likely return to the team in August. Just days later, the UCI added to our situation by bringing our ProTeam licence into question.

We'd started 2012 riding into a metaphorical headwind, and although it was said that I was at my best when up against it, it had all become a bit much. In the days and weeks following the press conference in Pinto, I wasn't in the greatest of moods, angry as I was at receiving what I perceived to be pretty shoddy treatment and being left in a very difficult position. I tried to counteract it by going out on more bike rides, during which I could both let off a bit of steam and try to give myself a new energy boost.

At the end of February, we had a training camp in Spain. The new season, however, wasn't the only thing on our mind; there was also the whole situation regarding our WorldTour licence to think about, too. The team's whole existence was on the line.

The UCI licence committee had told us to attend a hearing, as the UCI themselves were calling for us to have our licence taken away. Alberto's UCI points accounted for a huge percentage of our team's points for 2012, having won them during the previous season. With those 2011 points having been docked, and Alberto banned until August, the UCI was of the opinion that we no longer deserved to ride at WorldTour level.

Losing the licence could mean losing our invitations to all the big races, such as the Classics, the Tour, the Giro and the Vuelta.

On the first evening of the training camp in Spain, I took the opportunity to inform the riders and staff about the forthcoming hearing and the seriousness of the situation. During the whole process, I'd tried to keep them as updated as I could over email, but now that we were all together in one place, it was good to be able to talk to them face-to-face and be in a position to answer their questions.

Unsurprisingly, everyone was worried about what it could mean for them if we had our licence taken away, so I'd decided to be completely open about it and not to try to paint things in a positive light when it came to the possible consequences.

"The worst-case scenario is that the team could have to close down," I told them, but underlined that that really was the absolute worst-case scenario.

On Sunday 26th February, I travelled with our press officer, Anders, to Geneva for the hearing that was to take place the next day. On the Monday morning, we met with our director, Trey Greenwood, our lawyer, Henrik Schlüter, and Lars Seier from our main sponsor, Saxo Bank.

I felt that we were well prepared, and that we had a good case due to the extraordinary circumstances that had led to the unfortunate situation we found ourselves in after a year and a half of waiting.

The hearing took place at the Crowne Plaza in Geneva at 2pm. The licence committee was made up of three people, plus a secretary, the UCI had two representatives, while there were five of us – and we were all crammed into a small, overheated room, where the hearing took place over a number of hours.

It was a closed hearing, so unfortunately I'm not able to divulge exactly what was said, but we left afterwards safe in the knowledge that the committee now knew our side of the story.

However, we were soon plunged back into uncertainty again, left waiting for a decision and completely powerless to do anything about it. It had been bad enough having had to have waited for a decision about a single rider, but this time it was about the whole team. It was like having been put on 'pause'; the handbrake was on, and there was very little we could say when approached by the media.

"How are you going to approach the Tour of Flanders?" we'd be asked, yet we didn't even know if we were going to get to take part. We didn't know whether we'd be riding the Tour de France, or even the Giro, which was starting in Denmark in the town I was born in, Herning.

Then, on top of everything else, our Classics captain and 2011 Tour of Flanders winner Nick Nuyens crashed at Paris-Nice, breaking his hip, and was going to be unable to defend his Flanders title, whether we were invited or not.

It was a lot to take in, and playing the waiting game again affected me and the whole of the team. I felt as though I was being watched for signs as to my mood and humour. Was I happy? Or was I resigned to our fate? I tried to give the impression that I was feeling optimistic, and that everything would be okay, but inside the doubt had started to creep in.

I found it hard to understand why the UCI were so set on fighting against my team and me. Or that's what it felt like anyway.

Having contributed so much to the sport over the years, I was hoping that we'd be on the receiving end of some goodwill due to the circumstances.

The decision finally came after more than a month of waiting – on the evening of 2nd April, to be precise. Anders explained to me over the phone that the committee had rejected the UCI's reasons to take away our licence, and it felt as though time stood still for a few seconds. I immediately felt a wave of happiness and relief. For the first time in almost a year and a half, it felt as though we were finally back in business, and no longer in anyone else's thrall. Now we could look forward and concentrate on what it was all about: bike racing. I couldn't help breaking out into a huge roar: "Yes!"